STEP-BY-STEP

Barbecue
COOKBOOK

STEP-BY-STEP

Barbecue COOKBOOK

RECIPES COMPILED BY HILAIRE WALDEN

THUNDER BAY
P·R·E·S·S

San Diego, California

THUNDER BAY
P · R · E · S · S

Thunder Bay Press
An imprint of the Advantage Publishers Group
5880 Oberlin Drive, San Diego, CA 92121-4794
www.thunderbaybooks.com

Copyright © Salamander Books Ltd, 2002
A member of **Chrysalis** Books plc

All notations of errors or omissions should be addressed to
Thunder Bay Press, editorial department, at the above address. All
other correspondence (author inquiries, permissions) concerning the
content of this book should be addressed to Salamander Books Ltd,
8 Blenheim Court, Brewery Road, London, N7 9NY, U.K.

Library of Congress Cataloging-in-Publication Data

Walden, Hilaire.
   Step-by-Step Barbecue Cookbook / recipes compiled by Hilaire Walden.
      p. cm.
   Includes index.
   ISBN 1-57145-805-0
   1. Barbecue cookery. I. Title.

TX840.B3 W32 2002
641.5'784--dc21   2002069966

Printed in Taiwan

2 3 4 5 06 05 04 03 02

CONTENTS

INTRODUCTION

There can be few more relaxing pastimes than sitting on the patio or in the garden, a glass of wine or a long cool drink in your hand, and the scent of grilled food wafting through the air. Not only is food cooked on the barbecue at its best and most flavorsome, it is also very healthy—grilling avoids the need for extra fat and allows the food to retain all its nutrients.

Step-by-Step Barbecue Cookbook contains over 480 recipes and is divided into two sections to cover barbecue meals and accompanying dishes. The first section focuses on dishes to be cooked on the barbecue based around fish, poultry, meat, vegetables, and desserts. The second section covers side dishes, salads, relishes, sauces, and desserts to be prepared in the kitchen in

advance. Contrary to the popular belief that barbecues cater primarily for meat eaters, grilling is evolving fast to suit all contemporary tastes. A substantial portion of the book devoted to imaginative vegetarian recipes demonstrates the versatility of the barbecue.

With a few barbecue basics—a simple barbecue, some fuel, and basic tools—plus a grasp of simple grilling techniques, you'll be set to enjoy not only good food, but also the pleasure of cooking and eating outdoors. Once you have mastered a few of the many delicious recipes here, you will feel confident to try some ideas of your own. Remember that cooking over coals isn't an exact science—there is plenty of room for experimentation and indeed this is part of the appeal.

hood on the barbecue; if the weather turns bad, it helps to protect food while it's cooking, and it also prevents spattering and billowing of smoke.

If you like regular barbecues, you might want to consider building your own—you can use your own materials, or buy a ready-to-assemble pack. Either way, the barbecue should have three walls with bars built into the brickwork. Make sure there is enough space for it as a permanent structure in the garden, and think carefully about where you site it. It should be far enough away from the house not to be a fire hazard, in a convenient position for people to gather around, and shielded from strong breezes if possible.

Gas barbecues contain either vaporizer bars or lava bricks, which heat in the gas flame and absorb juices dripping from the food as it cooks, thus creating flavor. These barbecues ignite almost instantaneously and require no starter fuel. They retain an even heat and it is possible to have hot coals on one side and moderate on the other if the model has twin switches. Some are very sophisticated wagon models, but all have a gas bottle, which is cumbersome. However, the advantage of this type of barbecue is that you can use it at any time of the year.

Electric barbecues are more popular in some countries than in others. As with gas barbecues, they depend on lava bricks to produce an even heat—they take about 10 minutes to heat—and are usually uncovered. Electric barbecues must not be used in the rain, but the more sophisticated models can be used indoors with suitable ducting.

Fuel

Unless you are using a gas or electric barbecue, you will also need to buy suitable fuel. There are two types of coal fuel that can be used: lumpwood charcoal is cheaper, easier to light, and burns more hotly than its alternative, pressed briquettes. However, once lit, briquettes last longer. Wood can also be used as a fuel, but it is more difficult to start. If you do want to use wood, choose hardwoods, which burn longer. Allow the flames to die right down before cooking.

Aromatic wood chips are available for use on barbecues to impart flavors to the food. Oak and hickory wood chips are especially popular, but you may also wish to try more unusual ones, such as mesquite and cherry. You will need to soak the woodchips for about 30 minutes in cold water, then drain them before you place them on the ashen coals.

Firelighters, jelly starters, or lighting ignition fluid are also essential to start the barbecue. Make sure you follow the manufacturer's instructions carefully if you are using ignition fluid, and never use petrol, paraffin, or other similar flammable liquids for this purpose—apart from affecting the taste of the food, they are highly dangerous.

Barbecues

There are many different types of barbecues on the market, from simple disposable ones to highly sophisticated gas and electric types, and it is quite possible to make your own. If you are new to grilling, or about to invest in a new barbecue, it's worth taking a few minutes to consider the different options to decide which would suit you best.

Assuming you would want to use something more than once, the cheapest and simplest option is a shallow metal bowl on frame. There is no venting or cover but it is easy to light and simple to control. The kettle barbecue has its own hood, often with adjustable ducts, and is suitable for all types of grilling. There are several advantages to having a

Fish-shaped baskets enable whole fish to be turned half way through cooking without damaging them.

Rectangular or square hinged wire baskets are perfect for barbecuing cuts of meat or sliced vegetables.

For barbecuing chunks of meat, fish, vegetable or fruit, use long skewers with either square edges or ridges.

Accessories

The right equipment is a great help for straightforward grilling, and there are a few tools which are worth investing in:

- Wooden block or table—for keeping implements and food to hand.
- Long tools, including tongs and forks—ordinary kitchen tools are not long enough to keep the hands away from the heat source.
- Wire baskets, such as rectangular, hinged ones, to support the food.
- Skewers—square, metal, long wooden or bamboo ones are best.
- Brushes—for basting food with oil or marinade.
- Heavy-duty aluminum foil—for wrapping food to cook in the coals or on the grill rack.
- Tapers—better than short matches for lighting the barbecue.
- Oven gloves—but not the double-handed kind.
- Apron—a thick one with pockets is ideal.
- Metal griddle plates—for cooking certain fragile foods.
- Water sprayer—for dousing the flames if they become too unruly.
- Stiff wire brush and metal scrapers—important for cleaning the barbecue.

Lighting the barbecue

Before you light the barbecue, ensure that it is in the right position (a hot barbecue is obviously difficult to shift). There is no particular mystery to starting a charcoal fire. Simply spread a single layer of coals over the barbecue base, pile up the coals a little and push in firelighters or jelly starters. (Don't worry about instructions to make a pyramid, as it really is not necessary.) Light the fire with a taper rather than matches, and as soon as the fire has caught, spread the coals out a little and add further pieces as necessary.

The coals will probably take 30-40 minutes to become hot enough to start cooking over; when the flames have died down and the charcoal is covered with a white ash, it's time to commence cooking. (Lava bricks, on the other hand, only take a few moments to heat up sufficiently.) Charcoal will burn up to 1½ hours and occasionally pieces can be added around the edges. Use smaller pieces to poke through spaces in the grid, if necessary.

Checking and adjusting the temperature

Grilling can be done over high, medium, or low heat, depending on the type of food you are cooking. It is easy to adjust the heat on gas and electric barbecues, but more difficult with the open grid types unless you have a kettle barbecue with adjustable vents. To test the temperature of the barbecue, place your open hand over the coals. If you can keep your hand a few inches above the coals for as long as 5 seconds, the temperature is too low; for 3-4 seconds it is medium hot, and for only 2 seconds it is hot.

The right height for cooking is about 2–3 inches above the grid. On a lidded barbecue the heat will be greater when the lid is lowered. If you want to cook over medium heat and the coals have become too hot, either place the food away from the center of the barbecue and when cooking is completed, push it right to the edges to keep it warm, or push the coals aside to distribute the heat. To make the fire hotter, poke away the ash, push the coals together, and gently blow (you can use a battery-operated fan for this—it is invaluable and inexpensive).

Using marinades

Marinating plays a vital part in grilling, as it adds depth of flavor. If food has been marinated in the refrigerator, allow it to come back to room temperature before cooking. Marinades that contain acidic elements, such as vinegar or citrus juice, will tenderize the food. Oils in marinades help prevent food from sticking, while herbs and spices create mouthwatering flavors. Marinating can turn the simplest vegetable into something special.

Cooking in foil

Wrapping food in heavy-duty or double-thickness aluminum foil prevents the outside of the food from burning before the inside is cooked and keeps the juices trapped inside. For foods that require some browning, leave some space between the covering and the food, otherwise wrap into tight packets. Make sure the edges of the foil are firmly sealed.

Cooking in the coals

This is also known as "cooking in the embers," and the food can be either wrapped in foil and dropped into the coals, or, in some cases, even placed directly in the coals without any wrapping.

Using skewers

Most skewered food is marinated first. While cooking, the food should be brushed either with oil, or with a marinade or baste, and the skewers will need to be turned frequently. Wooden handles on skewers are preferable as they obviously don't get as hot as metal ones. Look for long skewers, which go fully across the grid and hold enough for 2–3 servings. Make sure wooden handles protrude from the edge of the grid to prevent scorching. Bamboo skewers are good for smaller portions, but you will need to soak them for at least an hour before using them, or they are likely to burn. It is generally best to oil metal skewers before use. Serve food on the skewers or transfer onto the plates with a fork.

Grilling

All barbecues can be used for grilling on top of the flame—indeed this is the cooking method generally associated with barbecues. Most of the recipes in this book could also be cooked under a conventional broiler if the weather drives you indoors, although the true barbecue flavor will be lacking.

Frying

A heavy-based skillet or griddle can be used over a barbecue in the same way as on the ordinary cooker hob. Merely grease the surface and the cooking becomes a cross between baking over the barbecue and shallow frying. Should the food start cooking too quickly, just move the pan to the side of the barbecue. Coals need to be very hot for successful barbecue frying.

Cooking times

Although times are given in the recipes, they must be regarded as a guide only. There are so many variables—cooking times will be affected by the thickness of the food, the type and heat of the coals, the position of the rack, the weather, and many other factors. One of the great pleasures of grilling is that it is a chance for you to experiment and try out different options.

Cleaning up

When you have finally finished with the barbecue, push the coals away from the center and they will die down. Cleaning the grill rack is best done while it is still hot. Use a metal scraper or stiff wire brush to dislodge food residues into the fire. If bits of food remain, remove it when cold and wash in soapy water. When the embers are completely cold, sift away surplus ash and cover the barbecue with the lid.

Safety Tips

- Always place the barbecue on even ground and away from trees, buildings, and fences.
- Never use petrol or similar flammable liquid to light the barbecue, and keep boxes of matches away from the flames.
- Have a bottle of water handy to douse the flames if necessary.
- Once the barbecue is alight, do not leave it unattended and keep children away from it.
- Always use long-handled tongs when handling food on the barbecue.
- Keep food to be barbecued in the refrigerator until you are ready to cook it, then keep it covered and out of the sun.
- Allow embers to cool completely (for several hours) before disposing of them.
- Allow transportable barbecues to cool completely before packing them away.

BARBECUE DISHES

WHOLE LAURIER FLOUNDER

4 1-lb. flounders
STUFFING:
1½ cups soft bread crumbs
¼ cup butter, melted
2 teaspoons lemon juice
1 teaspoon grated lemon rind
2 teaspoons chopped fresh parsley
salt and freshly ground black pepper
1 oz. cooked peeled shrimp, thawed if frozen, finely
  chopped
1 egg, beaten
20 bay leaves
olive oil, for brushing and basting
16–20 vine leaves (from a package), soaked and
  drained
2 lemons and parsley sprigs, to garnish

Remove heads and clean fish. Make an incision to the bone through white skin to form a pocket and lift flesh away from bone. Mix together bread crumbs, butter, lemon juice and peel, parsley, salt and pepper, shrimp, and egg. Spoon into pockets. Insert 3–4 bay leaves over stuffing to hold in place. Brush fish all over with olive oil.

Line rectangular hinged grill baskets with oiled vine leaves. Arrange remaining bay leaves over vine leaves and place fish between. Grill on a rack over medium coals for 10–15 minutes on each side, basting occasionally with oil, until fish is cooked. Remove fish from baskets and discard charred leaves. Serve garnished with halved crescent lemons, vandyked around edges, and sprigs of parsley.

Serves 4.

RED MULLET WITH FENNEL

4 8-oz. red mullets
fennel leaves, to garnish
MARINADE:
¼ cup vegetable oil
1 teaspoon lemon juice
1 teaspoon fennel seeds
¼ teaspoon sea salt
¼ teaspoon freshly ground black pepper

Mix marinade ingredients together in a large shallow dish.

Scrape away hard scales, remove gills and fins, and clean inside of fish but do not remove liver. Rinse, drain, and wipe dry with paper towels. Score through the skin twice on each side. Put fish in marinade and leave for 1 hour in a cool place, basting occasionally.

Drain fish and lay on a wire rack. Grill over hot coals for 6–8 minutes on each side, basting occasionally with marinade to prevent sticking and encourage browning. Garnish with fennel leaves.

Serves 4.

Note: To speed up cooking, an oiled baking tray may be inverted over fish.

JOHN DORY WITH ORANGE

4 John Dory fillets, about 5½ oz. each
4 mint sprigs
4 teaspoons dry white vermouth
finely grated rind and juice of 1 orange
1–2 teaspoons virgin olive oil
salt and freshly ground black pepper
orange slices, to garnish

MULLET WITH ANCHOVY SAUCE

4 red mullets, about 8 oz. each, scaled and cleaned
8 canned anchovy fillets, drained and rinsed
flour, for coating
salt and freshly ground black pepper
olive oil, for brushing
½ cup freshly squeezed orange juice
4 teaspoons tomato, peeled, seeded, and chopped
chopped fresh parsley, capers, and orange sections,
    to garnish

Cut 4 pieces of foil, each large enough to enclose one piece of fish. Oil top side of each piece. Place a fish in center of each piece of foil.

Pinch out center of each mint sprig and set aside for garnish. Finely chop remaining mint, then mix with vermouth, orange rind and juice, olive oil, and salt and pepper.

Using the point of a sharp knife, cut 2 diagonal slashes in both sides of each fish. Cut 4 anchovy fillets into 4 pieces and insert one piece in each slash. Roughly chop remaining anchovy fillets. Season flour with salt and pepper, then coat fish lightly and evenly.

Fold up sides of foil, spoon one quarter of orange mixture over each fish, then seal edges of foil tightly. Place foil parcels on a barbecue rack and grill over hot coals for 12–15 minutes. Serve garnished with orange slices and mint sprigs.

Serves 4.

Brush fish with oil, then grill on a rack over very hot coals until crisp and fish just begins to flake when pierced with a knife, about 5 minutes each side. Transfer to a warm serving plate and keep warm. Add orange juice, tomato, and chopped anchovies to a saucepan. Place over direct heat and boil until thickened to a light sauce. Season with pepper. Pour sauce around fish and garnish with parsley, capers, and orange sections.

Serves 4.

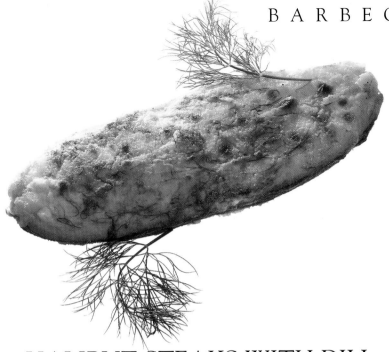

HALIBUT STEAKS WITH DILL

4–6 dill sprigs
8 teaspoons thick mayonnaise
salt and freshly ground black pepper
4 halibut steaks, 1 in. thick
4–6 teaspoons yellow cornmeal
fresh dill, to garnish

Strip the feathery leaves of dill away from stalk. Mix leaves with mayonnaise and season with salt and pepper.

Spread both sides of each fish steak with mayonnaise, then dip in cornmeal to lightly coat.

Grill halibut steaks on a rack over hot coals for 10–15 minutes, turning once, until fish is opaque and flaky when tested with tip of sharp knife. The surface of cooked steaks should be golden brown. If browning occurs before fish is cooked through, reduce heat or move to edge of barbecue to finish cooking. Garnish with fresh dill.

Serves 4–6.

LIME FISH SKEWERS

12 oz. monkfish tails, skinned and cut into ¾-in. cubes
12 oz. trout fillets, skinned and cut into ¾-in. pieces
2 limes
1 teaspoon sesame oil
generous pinch five-spice powder
freshly ground black pepper
strips of lime rind and lime wedges, to garnish

Place monkfish and trout in a shallow dish. Juice one of the limes and grate the rind. Mix juice and rind with sesame oil and five-spice powder, pour over fish, cover, and chill 30 minutes.

Soak 4 bamboo skewers in cold water for 30 minutes. Halve and quarter remaining lime lengthwise, and then halve each quarter to make 8 wedges. Slice each piece of lime in half crosswise to make 16 small pieces.

Thread monkfish, trout, and lime pieces on to skewers. Brush with marinade and season with pepper. Grill on a rack over hot coals for 2 minutes on each side, brushing occasionally with marinade to prevent drying out. Drain on paper towels, garnish with lime rind and lime wedges.

Serves 4.

BREAM WITH TARRAGON

2 tablespoons white wine vinegar
1½–2 teaspoons Dijon mustard
1 small shallot, finely chopped
1 clove garlic, finely crushed
½ cup olive oil, plus extra for brushing
14 oz. tomatoes, peeled, seeded, and diced
1½ tablespoons chopped fresh tarragon
2 tablespoons finely chopped fresh chives
salt and freshly ground black pepper
pinch superfine sugar (optional)
4 red bream or red mullet, about 10 oz. each, scaled
4 tarragon sprigs
tarragon sprigs and lime wedges, to garnish

SMOKED BREAM

2 x 1–1½ lb. bream
½ cup sea salt
2 handfuls hickory chips, for barbecuing
olive oil, for brushing

Clean and gut fish and put in a large shallow glass or plastic dish. Dissolve salt in 4 cups cold water. Pour over fish and leave to soak for at least 30 minutes.

Whisk together vinegar, mustard, shallot, and garlic until mixture is emulsified, then gradually whisk in oil. Add tomatoes, tarragon, and chives, and season with salt and pepper. Add a pinch of sugar, if desired, then leave to stand for 30–60 minutes.

Drain fish thoroughly. Put on wire rack and leave in an airy room for about 2½ hours until dry. Fish must be dry to the touch before starting to smoke. Meanwhile, soak hickory chips in water for 30 minutes. Using a covered barbecue, light coals and push to one side (fish must not be placed directly over coals). Wait until burned down to white ash stage, then add drained hickory chips.

With the point of a sharp knife, cut 2 slashes on each side of the fish. Season fish, put a tarragon sprig in each cavity, and brush with oil. Grill on a rack over hot coals for 10–11 minutes, turning and brushing with oil once. Transfer to serving plates. Stir tomato mixture, spoon some on to fish, and serve remainder separately. Garnish with sprigs of tarragon and lime wedges.

Serves 4.

Thoroughly brush each fish with oil and place on barbecue rack away from coals. Close lid and grill fish for 30–45 minutes, turning once, or until the flesh flakes when tested with a knife.

Serves 4–6.

Variation: Use red snapper instead of bream, if preferred.

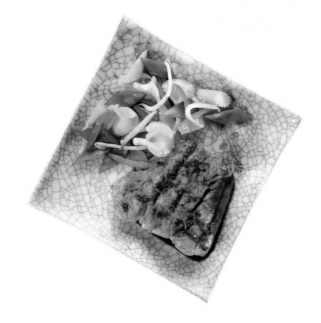

COD WITH TERIYAKI GLAZE

2 tablespoons soy sauce
1 tablespoon rice wine or medium sherry
1 tablespoon light brown soft sugar
1 teaspoon grated fresh ginger
4 pieces cod fillet, with skin
chervil sprigs, to garnish

In a small saucepan, gently heat together soy sauce, rice wine or sherry, sugar, and ginger for 2–3 minutes until lightly syrupy. Leave to cool.

Grill fish on a rack over hot coals, skin-side down, for 3 minutes, then turn fish over and grill for 3–4 minutes, until skin is crisp and flesh almost cooked.

Turn fish over, brush top liberally with sauce and return to grill for 1 minute. Transfer fish to warm serving plates and pour any remaining sauce over. Garnish with sprigs of chervil.

Serves 4.

COD WITH VINEGAR SAUCE

1 tablespoon sunflower oil
6 shallots, sliced
2 tablespoons white rice vinegar
2 teaspoons sugar
1 tablespoon light soy sauce
1¼ cups vegetable stock
1 teaspoon cornstarch mixed with 2 teaspoons water
4 cod steaks, about 6 oz. each
salt and freshly ground black pepper
2 tablespoons chopped fresh chives

Heat half the oil in a nonstick or well-seasoned wok and stir-fry shallots for 2 or 3 minutes.

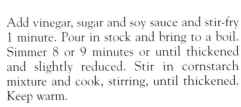

Add vinegar, sugar and soy sauce and stir-fry 1 minute. Pour in stock and bring to a boil. Simmer 8 or 9 minutes or until thickened and slightly reduced. Stir in cornstarch mixture and cook, stirring, until thickened. Keep warm.

Season cod steaks on both sides and place on barbecue rack over hot coals. Brush with remaining oil and cook 4 minutes on each side or until cooked through. Drain on paper towels. Remove skin. Stir chives into vinegar sauce and spoon over cod steaks.

Serves 4.

MARINATED FISH

4 flat fish such as flounder or dab, about 12 oz. each
4 large cloves garlic, cut into fine slivers
1-in. piece fresh ginger, cut into fine slivers
¼ cup peanut oil
¼ cup light soy sauce
1 tablespoon sesame oil
1 tablespoon rice wine
4 scallions, thinly sliced

With the point of sharp knife, cut 5 diagonal slashes, herringbone style, in both sides of each fish. Place in a shallow dish.

Put garlic, ginger, peanut oil, soy sauce, sesame oil, and rice wine in a small saucepan. Heat to simmering point and pour over fish, spooning marinade into slashes. Refrigerate for at least 1 hour, turning fish every 30 minutes.

Lift fish from marinade and grill on a rack over hot coals, pale skin-side down, for 3 minutes. Turn carefully and cook for an additional 1–2 minutes depending on thickness of fish. Grill in batches if necessary, keeping cooked fish warm. Reheat any remaining marinade and pour over fish. Sprinkle with scallions and serve.

Serves 4.

GRILLED FLAT FISH

1¼ lb. flat fish, such as flounder, cleaned
salt and freshly ground black pepper
1 tablespoon vegetable oil, plus extra for brushing
½ teaspoon very finely chopped garlic
½ teaspoon chopped fresh ginger
2 shallots, finely chopped
2–3 small fresh red chilies, cored, seeded, and chopped
1 tablespoon chopped scallions
2 tablespoons fish sauce and 1 teaspoon sugar
1 tablespoon tamarind water or lime juice
2–3 tablespoons chicken stock or water
2 teaspoons cornstarch

Score both sides of the fish at 1-in. intervals

and rub with salt and pepper.
Let fish stand 25 minutes. Brush both sides of fish with oil and grill on a rack over medium-hot coals about 4 minutes each side until lightly brown but not burned. Place on a warmed serving dish.

Heat 1 tablespoon oil in a small pan and stir-fry garlic, ginger, shallots, chilies, and scallion 1 minute, then add fish sauce, sugar, tamarind water or lime juice, and broth or water, bring to a boil and simmer 30 seconds. Mix cornstarch with 1 tablespoon water and stir into sauce to thicken. Pour sauce over fish.

Serves 2 on its own, or 4–6 with other dishes as part of a meal.

CORIANDER FISH KABOBS

1½-lb. monkfish fillet
⅔ cup plain yogurt
3 cloves garlic, crushed
2 teaspoons garam masala
1 tablespoon ground coriander
salt and freshly ground black pepper
1 fresh green chili, cored, seeded, and cut into thin
   rings
1 scallion, finely sliced
1 lime, cut into quarters and finely sliced

Remove any bones from fish, rinse and pat dry with paper towels. Cut into 1-in. cubes and thread on to skewers.

Mix together yogurt, garlic, garam masala, coriander, salt, and pepper. Put kabobs in a nonmetal dish; add yogurt marinade. Cover and refrigerate 2–3 hours to allow fish to absorb flavors.

Place kabobs on a rack and grill over hot coals for 3–4 minutes. Turn kabobs over, sprinkle with chili, onion, and lime slices; baste with any remaining marinade. Grill an additional 3–4 minutes, until fish just begins to flake. Serve hot.

Serves 4.

Note: If using bamboo or wooden skewers, soak in water 30 minutes before using.

SPICED FISH

4 fillets sole, about 8 oz. each
salt and freshly ground black pepper
⅔ cup plain yogurt
2 cloves garlic, crushed
2 teaspoons garam masala
1 teaspoon ground coriander
½ teaspoon chili powder
1 tablespoon lemon juice
lemon wedges, to garnish

Rinse fish, pat dry with paper towels, and place in a shallow nonmetal dish. Sprinkle with salt and pepper.

Mix together yogurt, garlic, garam masala, coriander, chili powder, and lemon juice. Pour over fish. Cover and refrigerate 2–3 hours to allow fish to absorb flavors.

Grill fish on a rack over hot coals for about 8 minutes, basting with any remaining marinade, and turning halfway through cooking, until fish just begins to flake. Serve hot, garnished with lemon wedges.

Serves 4.

FISH WITH MUSHROOM CRUST

RED MULLET IN VINE LEAVES

6 oz. chestnut mushrooms, finely chopped
2 tablespoons lemon juice
2 tablespoons whole-grain mustard
2 firmly packed tablespoons fresh bread crumbs
3 scallions, finely chopped
1¼ tablespoons finely chopped fresh parsley
salt and freshly ground black pepper
4 turbot escalopes or fillets, about 5 oz. each
lemon slices and parsley sprigs, to garnish

In a bowl, firmly mix together mushrooms, lemon juice, mustard, bread crumbs, scallions, 1 tablespoon parsley, and salt and pepper.

Grill turbot on a rack over hot coals, skin-side up, for 2 minutes. Turn fish over, spread with mushroom mixture and pat it in.

Grill fish until mushroom mixture has set and fish flakes. Sprinkle with remaining chopped parsley. Garnish with lemon slices and sprigs of parsley.

Serves 4.

juice ½ lemon
¼ cup olive oil
4 red mullet, cleaned and scaled
4 fennel sprigs
8 vacuum-packed vine leaves, rinsed and dried
lemon twists, to garnish
ROMESCO SAUCE:
scant ½ cup olive oil
1 large red bell pepper, peeled, seeded, and chopped
2 large ripe tomatoes, peeled and chopped
4 cloves garlic, chopped
1 fresh red chili, cored, seeded, and chopped
1 slice day-old bread
¼ cup ground almonds
2 tablespoons red wine vinegar
salt and freshly ground black pepper

To make the sauce, heat 3 tablespoons of the oil in a skillet. Add bell pepper, tomatoes, garlic, and chili and cook gently for 5 minutes. Break up bread and add to pan, turning in oil until lightly browned. Put mixture in a food processor or blender and process for a few seconds. Add almonds, vinegar, and salt and pepper. Process to a rough purée. With motor running, pour in remaining oil to form a thick sauce.

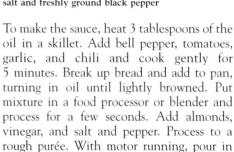

Mix together lemon juice and olive oil in a shallow dish. Add fish and turn in oil mixture. Put a fennel sprig inside each fish. Put 2 vines leaves side by side on counter. Put a fish on top and roll up, pressing leaves together to seal. Brush with oil mixture. Grill on a rack over hot coals for 5–8 minutes on each side, until vine leaves are crisp and fish flakes easily. Garnish with lemon twists and serve with romesco sauce.

Serves 4.

MACKEREL & RHUBARB SAUCE

6 fresh mackerel
salt and freshly ground black pepper
vegetable oil, for brushing
SAUCE:
8 oz. trimmed rhubarb
1 teaspoon lemon juice
¼ cup sweet cider
3 tablespoons soft brown sugar
¼ teaspoon grated nutmeg

Clean and gut mackerel, remove and discard heads. Season insides with salt and pepper. Brush all over with oil.

Make long folded, double thickness foil strips about ½ in. wide. Wrap around fish, placing one near the top and the other in the center. Folding open ends twice to achieve a tight fit, at the same time form a flat loop to enable the fish to be handled easily.

Combine sauce ingredients in a heavy-based saucepan. Cover and cook gently, shaking pan occasionally until rhubarb is very soft. Purée in a blender and return to pan. Cover and keep hot. Brushing frequently with oil, grill the mackerel on a rack over medium-hot coals for 7–10 minutes on each side until juices run clear when pricked with the point of a sharp knife. Use foil loops to help turn fish carefully. Serve with hot rhubarb sauce.

Serves 6.

SPICED FISH IN BANANA LEAVES

1¼ lb. white fish fillets
banana leaves or aluminum foil
oil, for brushing
SPICE PASTE:
6 shallots, chopped
2 cloves garlic, smashed
2 fresh red chilies, cored, seeded, and chopped
1-in. piece fresh ginger, chopped
4 candlenuts or cashew nuts
½ teaspoon tamarind paste
2 teaspoons each ground coriander and ground cumin
¼ teaspoon ground turmeric
salt

For spice paste, put all ingredients in a blender and mix to a paste.

Cut fish into 4 x 2-in. pieces ½ in. thick. Coat top of each piece thickly with spice paste. If using banana leaves, hold them over a flame to soften. Oil leaves thoroughly and cut into pieces to wrap around pieces of fish (or do this with foil). Secure with wooden toothpicks.

Grill fish pockets on a rack over hot coals for 8–10 minutes, turning halfway through. Partially tear away banana leaf or foil to reveal fish. Serve with lime wedges.

Serves 4.

MACKEREL & GOOSEBERRIES

1 lb. gooseberries
1 teaspoon fennel seeds
2 mackerel, 1 lb. each, cut into 4 fillets
1 tablespoon olive oil
salt and freshly ground black pepper
1 tablespoon pastis
1 teaspoon sugar
2 tablespoons butter, diced
parsley sprigs, to garnish

Put gooseberries and fennel seeds in a saucepan with just enough water to cover. Bring to a boil then simmer for 7–10 minutes, until very soft.

With the point of a knife, make three slashes in each mackerel fillet. Season fish, brush with oil on each side and grill on a rack over hot coals for 10 minutes, turning once.

Set aside a few gooseberries for garnish. Press remainder through a nylon sieve into a saucepan, pressing hard to extract all the juice. Add pastis, sugar, and salt and pepper, and heat gently, gradually beating in butter. Pour sauce over fish and garnish with reserved gooseberries and parsley.

Serves 4.

Note: Pastis is an aniseed-flavored liqueur.

SESAME-COATED WHITING

1 tablespoon Dijon mustard
1 tablespoon tomato paste
1½ teaspoons finely chopped fresh tarragon
squeeze lemon juice
freshly ground black pepper
9 tablespoons sesame seeds
2 tablespoons all-purpose flour
1 egg, lightly beaten
4 whiting fillets, about 5 oz. each, skinned
olive oil, for brushing
tarragon sprigs and lemon wedges, to garnish

In a bowl, mix mustard, tomato paste, tarragon, lemon juice, and pepper.

Combine sesame seeds and flour, and spread evenly on a large plate. Pour egg on to another plate. Spread mustard mixture over both sides of each fish fillet, then dip in egg. Coat fish evenly in sesame seed and flour mixture, then refrigerate for 30 minutes.

Brush one side of each fillet lightly with oil, then grill on a rack over hot coals for 2 minutes. Turn fish over, lightly brush top side with oil, and grill for an additional 2 minutes. Using a fish slice, transfer fish to a warm serving plate. Garnish with sprigs of tarragon and lemon wedges.

Serves 4.

SALMON WITH GINGER DIP

4 salmon fillets, about 6 oz. each, skinned
2 tablespoons light soy sauce
1 tablespoon dry sherry
1-in. piece fresh ginger, peeled and cut into thin
  strips
1 teaspoon sunflower oil
freshly ground black pepper
4 scallions, shredded, to garnish
DIP:
2 tablespoons sweet sherry
1 tablespoon light soy sauce

Using a sharp knife, lightly score the top of salmon fillets in diagonal lines, taking care not to slice all the way through.

Place salmon in a shallow dish. Mix together soy sauce, sherry, and ginger strips, and spoon over salmon. Cover and chill 1 hour.

Brush barbecue rack lightly with oil. Remove salmon from marinade and place on rack. Season with pepper, and grill over hot coals 2 or 3 minutes on each side. Meanwhile, mix together ingredients for dip and set aside. Drain salmon on paper towels. Garnish with scallions and serve with dip.

Serves 4.

MACKEREL WITH YOGURT

½ cucumber, peeled
salt and freshly ground black pepper
¾ cup thick plain yogurt, preferably Greek style
1¼ tablespoons chopped fresh mint
1 clove garlic, finely crushed
½ teaspoon harissa or pinch chili powder
2 teaspoons ground cumin
2 tablespoons light olive oil
squeeze lemon juice
4 mackerel, cleaned

Halve cucumber lengthwise, scoop out seeds, and thinly slice flesh.

Spread flesh in a colander, sprinkle with salt, and leave to drain for 30 minutes. Rinse cucumber, dry with paper towels, then mix with yogurt and mint. Cover and chill for 2 hours. Put garlic in a mortar, or small bowl, then pound in harissa or chili powder, cumin, and oil, using a pestle or end of a rolling pin. Add lemon juice and season with salt and pepper.

With the point of a sharp knife, cut 2 slashes in each side of the fish. Spread spice mixture over fish and leave for 15–30 minutes. Grill fish on a rack over hot coals for 7–8 minutes on each side. Serve with cucumber mixture.

Serves 4.

TROUT IN SAFFRON FUMET

6 small rainbow trout
6 peppercorns
½ stick celery, coarsely chopped
1 parsley sprig
1 bay leaf
1 thyme sprig
3 thick slices carrot
1 shallot, coarsely chopped
¼ teaspoon salt
2 teaspoons white wine vinegar
½ cup dry white wine
½ teaspoon powdered saffron
¼–⅓ cup butter
celery leaves, to garnish

Remove heads and tails from fish; set aside.

Taking each fish in turn, slit along belly. Open flaps and place, open-edges down, on a counter or board. Press with thumbs along backbone to flatten. Reverse fish and lift out backbone and set aside. Put fish heads, tails and backbones in a large saucepan, add 1¼ cups water and remaining ingredients except butterflied fish, saffron, butter, and celery leaves. Bring to a boil, then remove scum. Reduce heat, cover and simmer for 30 minutes.

Strain liquor into bowl through a fine nylon sieve. Return to saucepan, add saffron and boil vigorously, uncovered, until reduced to ¼ cup. Leave to cool. Place trout, flesh-side down, in large shallow dishes. Pour saffron fumet over fish and leave to marinate for 30 minutes. Remove from marinade. Melt butter and brush over fish. Grill fish in rectangular hinged baskets over hot coals for 2–3 minutes on each side. Garnish with celery leaves.

Serves 6.

AROMATIC SALMON

6 middle-cut salmon cutlets, ¾ in. thick, 6 oz. each
salt and freshly ground black pepper
flour, for coating
½ cup butter
handful of winter savory or 1–2 tablespoons dried winter savory, moistened
2 tablespoons lumpfish caviar
winter savory or tarragon, to garnish

Rinse salmon and pat dry on paper towels. Season with salt and pepper; dip in flour and shake off surplus.

Melt butter and brush over salmon steaks. Place in a rectangular hinged basket. Sprinkle the winter savory over the coals when they are hot.

Grill fish on a rack over hot coals for 4–5 minutes on each side, basting occasionally with melted butter. If the cutlets start to brown too quickly, reduce heat or move basket to side of barbecue. The cutlets are cooked when it is easy to move center bone. Serve sprinkled with lumpfish caviar and garnish with winter savory or tarragon.

Serves 6.

TANDOORI TROUT

seeds from 6 cardamom pods
2 teaspoons cumin seeds
4 tablespoons plain yogurt, preferably Greek style
1 large clove garlic, chopped
2 tablespoons lime juice
1-in. piece fresh ginger, chopped
1 teaspoon garam masala
pinch ground turmeric
¼ teaspoon red bell pepper
salt
1 teaspoon red food coloring (optional)
2 trout, about 10 oz. each
oil, for brushing
lemon and lime wedges and cilantro sprigs, to garnish

Heat a small heavy pan, add cardamom and cumin seeds, and heat until fragrant. Tip into a mortar or small bowl and crush with a pestle or end of a rolling pin. Put yogurt, garlic, lime juice, all the spices, red bell pepper, and salt into a blender, and mix to a paste. Add food coloring, if desired.

With the point of a sharp knife, make 3 deep slashes in each side of the trout. Spread spice mixture over trout, working it into the slashes. Place in a shallow, nonmetallic dish, cover, and leave to marinate in refrigerator for 4 hours. Brush barbecue rack with oil. Sprinkle a little oil over fish and grill over hot coals for about 7 minutes on each side. Serve garnished with lemon and lime wedges, and sprigs of cilantro.

Serves 2.

PINK GRAPEFRUIT TROUT

6 small brown trout
4 pink grapefruit
¼ cup dry white wine
4 scallions, trimmed and finely sliced
16 black peppercorns, lightly crushed
2 tablespoons heavy cream
⅓ cup butter
salt

Clean and gut fish, removing heads, if desired. Place each fish on oiled, double thickness foil, large enough for loose wrapping.

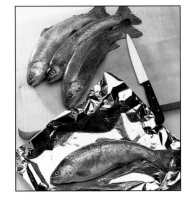

Thinly pare peel from 1 grapefruit and shred finely. Place shredded peel in a small saucepan. Cover with cold water, bring to a boil, then continue cooking for 3–4 minutes to soften. Drain and set aside. Remove pith, membranes, and any pips from pared grapefruit, and segment flesh. Set aside for garnish. Grate peel and squeeze juice from remaining 3 grapefruit and put in a medium saucepan. Add wine, scallions, and peppercorns. Simmer for 10–15 minutes until about ⅔ cup of liquid remains.

Remove from heat, stir in cream and butter; stir until butter melts, then strain into a jug. Season with salt and mix in softened peel. Pour a little sauce over each fish and fold up foil, leaving a 1-in. space over fish for steam to circulate. Grill on a rack over hot coals for 20 minutes, but do not turn fish pockets over. To serve, open foil, pour extra sauce over trout, and garnish with reserved grapefruit segments.

Serves 4.

GRILLED SARDINES

2¼ lb. fresh sardines, cleaned and scaled
2 tablespoons coarse sea salt
1 tablespoon chopped fresh oregano
1 tablespoon chopped fresh parsley
1 tablespoon chopped fresh fennel
lemon slices, to garnish
AVGOLEMONO SAUCE:
1¼ cups fish stock
salt and freshly ground black pepper
1 tablespoon cornstarch
2 extra large egg yolks
juice 1 lemon

Slash each sardine twice on each side. Sprinkle with sea salt; put herbs inside cavities. Leave for 30 minutes. To make the sauce, put fish stock in a saucepan, season, and heat. In a bowl, mix cornstarch with a little water. Whisk a little hot stock into cornstarch mixture. Return to pan. Cook gently for 10–15 minutes, stirring, until sauce thickens. In a bowl, beat egg yolks. Stir in lemon juice. Add a little of hot sauce; return sauce to pan. Cook gently, without boiling, until thickened.

Grill sardines in rectangular hinged baskets over hot coals for 1½–2 minutes on each side, until skins are brown and crisp. Garnish fish with lemon slices and serve with the sauce.

Serves 4.

SARDINES WITH HERBS

2¼ lb. fresh sardines, cleaned
6 tablespoons olive oil
3 tablespoons lemon juice
3 tablespoons mixed chopped fresh parsley, basil, and tarragon
salt and freshly ground black pepper
basil sprigs, to garnish

Put sardines in a shallow nonmetallic dish. Mix together oil, lemon juice, herbs, and salt and pepper, and pour over sardines. Cover and leave in a cool place for 2 hours, turning sardines occasionally.

Remove sardines from marinade, Grill in rectangular hinged baskets over hot coals for 2–3 minutes. Turn over, brush with marinade, and cook for an additional 3 minutes. Garnish with basil sprigs and serve.

Serves 4.

SARDINES IN CILANTRO SAUCE

2¼ lb. fresh sardines (at least 12)
¼ cup olive oil
grated rind 1½ limes
1½ tablespoons lime juice
¾ teaspoon finely crushed, toasted coriander seeds
3 tablespoons chopped fresh cilantro
salt and freshly ground black pepper
cilantro sprigs, to garnish
lime wedges, to serve

Put sardines in a shallow, nonmetallic dish. Thoroughly whisk together oil, lime rind and juice, coriander seeds, chopped cilantro, and salt and pepper.

Spoon cilantro mixture over sardines and leave for 1 hour, turning sardines over once.

Remove sardines from dish and grill in rectangular hinged baskets over hot coals for 4–5 minutes on each side, basting with cilantro mixture. Serve sardines garnished with sprigs of cilantro and accompanied by lime wedges.

Serves 4.

TARAMA SARDINES

6 fresh sardines
2 tablespoons lemon juice
freshly ground black pepper
3–4 tablespoons taramasalata
parsley sprigs, to garnish

Cut off and discard sardine heads and, using a small skewer or teaspoon, carefully clean out inside of each fish. Rinse and pat dry on paper towels.

Brush inside sardines with lemon juice and season with black pepper. Carefully fill cavities with taramasalata.

Place sardines in a hinged fish basket and grill over hot coals for 3–4 minutes on each side. Arrange sardines in a spoke design on a round wooden platter. Garnish by inserting sprigs of parsley into the taramasalata.

Serves 6.

Variation: Use small trout if sardines are not available and double the quantity of taramasalata.

ROASTED GRAY MULLET

SARDINES IN VINE LEAVES

3¼–3½ lb. gray mullet, cleaned
salt and freshly ground black pepper
1 bay leaf
1 rosemary sprig
6 tablespoons olive oil
juice 2 small lemons
1 teaspoon dried oregano
1 tablespoon chopped fresh parsley
2 cloves garlic, finely chopped
bay leaves and lemon wedges, to serve

Season cavity of fish with salt and pepper.
Place one bay leaf and rosemary inside the
fish.

3 unwaxed thin-skinned lemons, cut into quarters
  lengthwise
3 tablespoons sea salt
2 tablespoons sugar
12 large vine leaves in brine
12 fresh sardines, scaled and gutted
salad leaves, to garnish
STUFFING:
4 tablespoons chopped fresh cilantro
4 tablespoons chopped fresh parsley
2 cloves garlic, crushed
salt and freshly ground black pepper
¼ cup olive oil

Grill mullet on a rack over medium-hot
coals for about 8 minutes on each side.

Preheat oven to 375°F. Place lemon quarters
in an ovenproof dish with salt and sugar and
mix well. Cover with foil. Bake for 1–1½
hours until soft. Leave to cool. Place vine
leaves in a bowl and cover with cold water.
Leave to soak for 1 hour, changing the water
twice. Drain and pat dry. Remove backbone
from sardines by pressing down along length
of backbone to flatten them. Pull out
backbone and wash and dry the fish.

Meanwhile, whisk together oil, lemon juice,
oregano, parsley, and garlic until thick. Lay
fish on a serving platter and garnish with bay
leaves and lemon wedges. Pour sauce over
fish and serve at once.

Serves 6.

To make the stuffing, in a bowl mix together
cilantro, parsley, garlic, salt, pepper, and
olive oil. Stuff fish with herb mixture. Roll
each fish up in a vine leaf. Place on a
barbecue rack over hot coals and cook for
3–5 minutes on each side until the vine
leaves are crisp and fish flakes easily when
tested with a knife. Garnish with salad
leaves, and serve with the roasted lemons.

Serves 4–6.

TUNA & GINGER VINAIGRETTE

1-in. piece fresh ginger, finely chopped
2 large scallions, white and some green parts, thinly
　　sliced
1 cup olive oil
juice 2 limes
2 tablespoons soy sauce
2 tablespoons sesame oil
1 bunch fresh cilantro, finely chopped
freshly ground black pepper
6 tuna steaks, about 5–6 oz. each
cilantro sprigs, to garnish

To make vinaigrette, stir together ginger, scallions, olive oil, lime juice, and soy sauce, then whisk in sesame oil. Add chopped cilantro and season with pepper; set aside.

Grill tuna on a rack over hot coals for 3½–4 minutes each side, or a little longer for well-done fish. Spoon some dressing on to 6 plates and add fish. Garnish with sprigs of cilantro. Serve any remaining dressing separately.

Serves 6.

BASS WITH GINGER & LIME

2 shallots, finely chopped
1½-in. piece fresh ginger, finely chopped
juice 2 limes
¼ cup rice wine vinegar
1 cup olive oil
2 tablespoons Chinese sesame oil
2 tablespoons soy sauce
salt and freshly ground black pepper
6–8 bass fillets, about 6 oz. and ½ in. thick each
leaves from 1 bunch cilantro
toasted sesame seeds, to garnish

In a bowl, mix together first 8 ingredients. Set aside.

Brush fish lightly with ginger mixture, then grill on a rack over hot coals for 2–3 minutes on each side.

Just before serving, set aside a few cilantro leaves for garnish, chop remainder, and mix into ginger mixture. Spoon some on to serving plates at room temperature and place fish on top. Sprinkle with sesame seeds and garnish with reserved cilantro.

Serves 6–8.

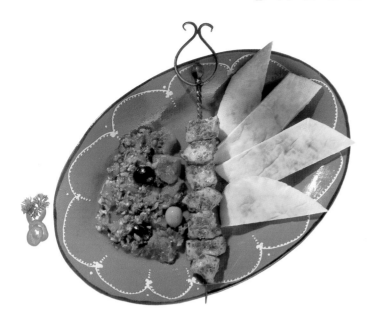

SWORDFISH KABOBS

1½ lb. skinless, boneless swordfish steaks
CHERMOULA:
4 cloves garlic
1 teaspoon salt
juice 2 lemons
1 tablespoon ground cumin
2 teaspoons paprika
1 fresh red chili, cored, seeded, and roughly chopped
½ oz. fresh cilantro
½ oz. fresh parsley
¼ cup olive oil

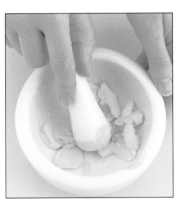

To make chermoula, in a mortar and pestle, crush garlic with salt. Place in a blender or food processor.

Add lemon juice to food processor with cumin, paprika, red chili, cilantro, and parsley. Process briefly then gradually add olive oil and reduce to a coarse purée. Transfer to a bowl. Cut swordfish into 1-in. cubes and add to chermoula mixture. Mix well to coat, cover, and leave in a cool place for 1 hour.

Thread fish on to skewers and spoon marinade over fish. Grill on a rack over hot coals for 3–4 minutes on each side, until the fish is lightly browned and flakes easily when tested with a knife.

Serves 4.

Note: If using bamboo or wooden skewers, soak in water 30 minutes before using.

HERBED SWORDFISH KABOBS

2¼ lb. swordfish, skinned and boned
juice 2 lemons
2 onions, peeled
18 cherry tomatoes
⅔ cup olive oil
½ teaspoon garlic salt
½ teaspoon freshly ground black pepper
6–8 tablespoons finely chopped fresh chives
6–8 tablespoons finely chopped fresh parsley
lemon slices and parsley sprigs, to garnish

Cut fish into 1½-in. cubes and marinate in half the lemon juice for 1 hour, turning once.

Halve onions and remove centers, leaving a three-layer wall. Separate layers, cutting each in half and curve to form a cone. Alternately thread fish cubes, onion cones, and whole tomatoes on to skewers. Beat together oil, garlic salt, pepper, and remaining lemon juice, and brush over kabobs.

Grill on a rack over medium-hot coals for 10–15 minutes, turning frequently and brushing with oil baste. Mix together chives and parsley, and spread on a chopping board. Roll hot kabobs in herb mixture before serving. Serve garnished with lemon slices and parsley.

Serves 6.

Note: If using bamboo or wooden skewers, soak in water 30 minutes before using.

BAKED BASQUE COD

3 tablespoons olive oil
1 small green bell pepper, seeded and diced
1 onion, finely chopped
2 tomatoes, peeled and diced
1 clove garlic, crushed
2 teaspoons chopped fresh basil
4 cod fillets, 6 oz. each, skinned
juice ½ lemon
salt and freshly ground black pepper
lemon slices, to garnish

Brush 4 large squares of foil with a little of the oil.

Mix together green bell pepper, onion, tomatoes, garlic, and basil. Put a cod fillet on each piece of foil. Top each fillet with bell pepper and onion mixture.

Drizzle with lemon juice and remaining oil. Season with salt and pepper then fold foil to make 4 pockets. Grill pockets on a rack over medium-hot coals 20–30 minutes until fish flakes easily when tested with a knife. Unwrap foil pockets and transfer fish, vegetables, and cooking juices to warmed serving plates. Garnish with lemon slices and serve.

Serves 4.

MONKFISH KABOBS

1 small red onion, finely chopped
1 clove garlic, crushed
2 tablespoons chopped fresh cilantro
4 tablespoons chopped fresh parsley
1 teaspoon ground cumin
1 teaspoon paprika
¼ teaspoon chili powder
pinch saffron strands
¼ cup olive oil
juice 1 lemon
½ teaspoon salt
1½ lb. monkfish fillets, skinned
flat-leaf parsley sprigs and chives, to garnish
CHERRY TOMATO SALSA:
8 oz. red and yellow cherry tomatoes, halved
1 small red onion, thinly sliced
½ cup vinaigrette
1 small fresh green chili, cored, seeded, and sliced
1 tablespoon chopped fresh chives

Mix together onion, garlic, cilantro, parsley, cumin, paprika, chili powder, saffron, olive oil, lemon juice, and salt. Cut monkfish into cubes and add to marinade. Mix well and leave in a cool place for 1 hour.

Make cherry tomato salsa. In a bowl, mix tomatoes, onion, vinaigrette, chili, and chives. Leave to stand for 30 minutes. Thread monkfish on to 4 metal skewers and brush with marinade. Grill monkfish on a rack over hot coals for 3 minutes on each side until cooked through and lightly browned. Garnish with parsley sprigs and chives, and serve with cherry tomato salsa.

Serves 4.

SHRIMP KABOBS

½ cup vegetable oil
6 tablespoons lime juice
½-in. piece fresh ginger, grated
2 large cloves garlic, finely crushed
1 fresh red chili, cored, seeded, and finely chopped
leaves from small bunch of cilantro, chopped
1 tablespoon light soy sauce
½ teaspoon light brown sugar
1½ lb. raw, unpeeled large shrimp

Soak 8 long wooden or bamboo skewers in water for 20–30 minutes. In a bowl, whisk together oil, lime juice, ginger, garlic, and chili. Stir in cilantro, soy sauce, and sugar.

Drain skewers. Thread shrimp on to skewers. Place them in a shallow nonreactive dish. Pour ginger mixture evenly over shrimp. Turn skewers, cover and refrigerate for 1–2 hours, turning occasionally. Return to room temperature for 30 minutes.

Transfer kabobs to barbecue rack, reserving marinade. Grill shrimp over hot coals for 4–6 minutes, turning halfway through cooking time, until they turn pink. Brush with reserved marinade occasionally.

Serves 4.

Note: Dipping Sauce (see page 128) makes the ideal accompaniment.

CRAB-STUFFED FISHCAKES

1½ lb. ground white fish
1 small onion, very finely chopped
4 tablespoons medium matzo meal
1 tablespoon ground almonds
salt and freshly ground black pepper
1 egg, beaten
4 oz. mixed white and brown crabmeat
TO COAT:
2 eggs, beaten
1 oz. medium matzo meal
sunflower oil, for brushing

In a bowl, combine fish, onion, matzo meal, almonds, and salt and pepper.

Bind mixture with egg, adding more matzo meal, if necessary, to form a mixture which holds together when shaped. Divide into 16 portions, shape into balls and flatten with the palm of a hand on a counter sprinkled with matzo meal. Place 1 teaspoon of crabmeat in centers and wrap ground fish around to re-form into balls. Press down lightly to make fishcakes.

To coat, dip fishcakes in beaten egg and then in matzo meal. Brush both sides of each fishcake with sunflower oil. Cook on barbecue rack over hot coals for 6–8 minutes on each side.

Serves 6–8.

Note: Cucumber Raita (see page 132) makes the ideal accompaniment.

GRILLED SHRIMP

LEMON SWORDFISH KABOBS

1 lb. large raw shrimp, shelled with tails left on
5 tablespoons extra-virgin olive oil
½ clove garlic, finely crushed
juice 1 lemon
salt and freshly ground black pepper
1 small beefsteak tomato, peeled, seeded, and finely
  chopped
½ small fresh red chili, cored, seeded, and finely
  chopped
1 tablespoon finely chopped fresh parsley
parsley sprigs and lemon slices and rind, to garnish

juice ½ lemon
12 teaspoons olive oil
1 tablespoon chopped fresh fennel
1 tablespoon chopped fresh chives
1 clove garlic, crushed
salt and freshly ground black pepper
1 lb. swordfish
1 small onion
16 cherry tomatoes
lemon slices and fresh herbs, to garnish

Using a small sharp knife, make a cut along back of each shrimp and remove black vein. Thread shrimp on to 4 skewers and place in a shallow dish. In a small bowl, stir together 2 tablespoons of the oil, the garlic, 1½ tablespoons lemon juice, salt, and pepper. Pour over shrimp and let stand 30 minutes.

In a bowl, mix together lemon juice, olive oil, fennel, chives, garlic, salt, and pepper. Cut swordfish into ¾-in. cubes. Place in bowl of marinade and leave for 1 hour. Cut onion into quarters and separate layers.

Transfer shrimp skewers from dish and place on barbecue rack. Brush with any remaining marinade and grill over hot coals for 3–4 minutes until bright pink. In another small bowl, stir together remaining oil and lemon juice, tomato, chili, parsley, salt, and pepper. Spoon over hot shrimp and serve garnished with parsley, and lemon slices and rind.

Serves 4.

Note: If using bamboo or wooden skewers, soak in water 30 minutes before using.

Thread swordfish, onion, and tomatoes on to 8 skewers. Grill on a rack over hot coals for 5–10 minutes, turning frequently and brushing with any remaining marinade. Serve garnished with lemon slices and herb sprigs.

Serves 8.

Note: If using bamboo or wooden skewers, soak in water 30 minutes before using.

SHRIMP WITH MAYONNAISE

3 tablespoons olive oil
juice ½ lemon
2 cloves garlic, crushed
1 tablespoon chopped fresh fennel
salt and freshly ground black pepper
20 raw large shrimp
radicchio leaves and fennel sprigs, to garnish
SAFFRON MAYONNAISE:
⅔ cup fish stock
generous pinch saffron strands
⅔ cup mayonnaise
1 teaspoon lemon juice

Mix together oil, lemon juice, garlic, fennel, and salt and pepper.

Put shrimp in a shallow dish and pour marinade over. Turn to coat in marinade. Leave in a cool place for 2 hours. To make saffron mayonnaise, put fish stock in a saucepan and boil until reduced to 1 tablespoon. Add saffron strands and leave to cool. Strain stock into a bowl and stir in mayonnaise. Add lemon juice and salt and pepper.

Remove shrimp from marinade and thread on to skewers. Grill on a rack over hot coals for 10 minutes, turning once. Remove from skewers and arrange on serving plates. Garnish with radicchio leaves and fennel, and serve with the saffron mayonnaise.

Serves 4.

Note: If using bamboo or wooden skewers, soak in water 30 minutes before using.

LUXURY GINGER SCAMPI

1½ lb. raw Dublin Bay shrimp tails or frozen, peeled
  raw shrimp tails, thawed
marjoram sprigs and lemons slices, to garnish
MARINADE:
⅔ cup vegetable oil
finely grated peel and juice 1 small lemon
6 tablespoons soy sauce
1 clove garlic, crushed
1 teaspoon finely grated fresh ginger
½ teaspoon dried marjoram

Mix together the marinade ingredients.

Wash shrimp but leave shells intact if using unpeeled shrimp tails. Mix with marinade and leave in a cool place for 2 hours. Baste occasionally.

Thread crosswise on to skewers and grill on a rack over hot coals for 7–10 minutes, turning frequently until shrimp are opaque. Remove from skewers and serve at once, garnished with marjoram sprigs and lemon slices.

Serves 6.

Note: If using bamboo or wooden skewers, soak in water 30 minutes before using.

MEDITERRANEAN SHRIMP

juice 1 large lemon
about ⅔ cup vegetable oil
18 raw jumbo shrimp, fresh or frozen, thawed if
  frozen
2 lemons and ¼ cucumber, to garnish

To prepare garnish, cut off each end of lemons and slice middle sections thinly. Using a canelle knife, remove equidistant strips of cucumber skin lengthwise. Thinly slice cucumber. Curve cucumber slices round lemon slices before threading on to wooden toothpicks.

Put lemon juice in one shallow dish and oil in another. Dip shrimp, 2 or 3 at a time, into lemon juice. Shake off surplus, then dip into the oil.

Grill shrimp on a rack over hot coals for 10–12 minutes, brushing frequently with remaining oil. Serve hot, garnished with lemon and cucumber sticks, and have finger-bowls nearby.

Serves 6.

Note: Buy whole, unpeeled jumbo shrimp. The gray-brown translucent appearance of these shrimp changes to orangey-pink when cooked.

BUTTERFLIED SHRIMP

1 lb. jumbo shrimp
juice 1 lemon
5 tablespoons extra-virgin olive oil
½ clove garlic, crushed
2 tablespoons sun-dried tomato paste
pinch red pepper
1 tablespoon chopped fresh basil
salt and freshly ground black pepper
fresh basil leaves to garnish

Remove heads and fine legs from shrimp. Using sharp scissors cut shrimp lengthwise almost in half, leaving tail end intact.

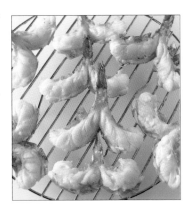

Place shrimp in a shallow dish and pour half of the lemon juice and 2 tablespoons of the olive oil over. Stir in garlic. Leave for at least 30 minutes. Arrange shrimp on barbecue rack and cook over hot coals for about 3 minutes until shrimp have curled or 'butterflied' and are bright pink.

In a small bowl, mix together remaining lemon juice and 3 tablespoons olive oil, the sun-dried tomato paste, red pepper, basil, salt, and pepper. Either spoon over shrimp or serve separately for dipping. Garnish shrimp with basil sprigs.

Serves 4.

SHRIMP BALLS

1½ lb. raw, unpeeled large shrimp
1 clove garlic, chopped
1½ tablespoons fish sauce
½ teaspoon light brown sugar
2 teaspoons peanut oil
1 tablespoon cornstarch
1 egg, beaten
salt and freshly ground black pepper
1½ oz. dried coconut
2 tablespoons dried bread crumbs
cilantro sprigs, to garnish
Dipping Sauce or Spicy Sauce (see page 128), to serve

Set aside 8 shrimp in their shells. Peel remaining shrimp.

With the point of a sharp knife, cut a slit along the back of each shrimp. Remove and discard black intestinal thread. Put peeled shrimp in a food processor. Add garlic, fish sauce, sugar, oil, cornstarch, egg, salt, and pepper. Mix to a smooth purée. Transfer to a bowl, cover, and chill for 1½ hours.

On a baking tray, combine coconut and bread crumbs. Wet the palms of your hands; roll the shrimp mixture into 1-in. balls. Coat balls in coconut mixture. Thread on oiled, long metal skewers, adding a reserved shrimp to each skewer. Grill on a rack over hot coals, turning occasionally, for about 6 minutes until balls are firm and whole shrimp are pink. Garnish and serve with the dipping sauce of your choice.

Serves 8.

SHRIMP & VERMICELLI

vegetable oil, for deep-frying
4 oz. rice vermicelli
1 lb. raw unpeeled shrimp
2 teaspoons vegetable oil
2–3 scallions, chopped
2–3 small fresh red chilies, cored, seeded, and chopped
1 tablespoon roasted peanuts, crushed
cilantro leaves, to garnish
Spicy Fish Sauce (see page 128), to serve

Heat oil for deep-frying to 300°F. Break the vermicelli into short strands and deep-fry, a handful at a time, 30–35 seconds, or until the strands puff up and turn white.

Remove vermicelli and drain, then place on a warm serving dish or plate. Grill shrimp on a rack over hot coals, turning once; large shrimp will take about 6–7 minutes, smaller ones 3–4 minutes to cook. When cooked, arrange them on the bed of crispy rice vermicelli.

Heat the 2 teaspoons oil in a small saucepan until hot, removing from the heat before it starts to smoke, add scallions and chilies and let stand a few minutes, then pour mixture over shrimp. Garnish with crushed peanuts and cilantro leaves and serve hot with the Spicy Fish Sauce as a dip.

Serves 4.

SHRIMP & MUSTARD SEEDS

1 lb. large unpeeled shrimp
1 tablespoon mixed black and yellow mustard seeds
½ teaspoon ground turmeric
½ teaspoon red pepper
salt
1 fresh green chili, cored, seeded, and finely chopped
2 tablespoons butter, melted
orange and lime peel, to garnish

Peel shrimp, leaving tail shells on. Make a small incision along the spines and remove black vein. Put 2 or 3 shrimp on each short wooden skewer. Set aside.

Set aside 1 teaspoon of mustard seeds. Grind remainder in a coffee grinder or with a mortar and pestle. Transfer to a medium bowl and mix in turmeric, red pepper, and salt. Add 6 tablespoons of water and chili; blend to a smooth paste. Add shrimp, turning to coat them in the paste; refrigerate 30 minutes.

Brush skewers with melted butter and sprinkle with reserved mustard seeds. Grill on a rack over hot coals for 3–5 minutes, until shrimp are pink, turning once, and basting occasionally with remaining marinade. Serve hot, garnished with orange and lime peel.

Serves 4.

Note: When using bamboo or wooden skewers, soak in water 30 minutes before using.

SHRIMP WITH ASIAN SAUCE

1½ lb. large raw shrimp
lime wedges and basil sprigs, to garnish
MARINADE:
handful Thai or ordinary fresh basil, finely chopped
2 tablespoons finely chopped garlic
2 tablespoons finely chopped fresh ginger
2 tablespoons finely chopped green chilies
2 teaspoons rice wine or medium dry sherry
2½ tablespoons peanut oil
1 teaspoon Chinese sesame oil
salt and freshly ground black pepper

To make marinade, pound ingredients together in a mortar and pestle or using the end of a rolling pin in a bowl.

Discard legs and heads from shrimp then, using strong scissors, cut shrimp lengthwise in half leaving tail end intact. Remove dark intestinal vein. Rub marinade over shrimp, spoon any remaining marinade over, cover and leave in a cool place for 1 hour.

Grill shrimp on a rack over hot coals for about 3 minutes until curled, or 'butterflied', and bright pink. Garnish with lime wedges and sprigs of basil. Serve any remaining marinade separately.

Serves 4–6.

SEAFOOD SKEWERS

12 scallops
12 large raw peeled shrimp
8 oz. firm white fish fillet, such as halibut, cod, or
   monkfish, cut into 12 cubes
1 onion, cut into 12 pieces
1 red or green bell pepper, cut into 12 cubes
½ cup dry white wine or sherry
1 tablespoon chopped dill
1 tablespoon chopped holy basil leaves
1 tablespoon lime juice or vinegar
salt and freshly ground black pepper
vegetable oil, for brushing
Spicy Fish Sauce (see page 128), to serve

SQUID & SHRIMP KABOBS

12 oz. cleaned squid
juice ½ lemon
2 teaspoons honey
2 tablespoons olive oil
8 large raw peeled shrimp
salt and freshly ground black pepper
lemon slices and chopped fresh parsley, to garnish
GARLIC MAYONNAISE:
4 cloves garlic
2 egg yolks
1¼ cups olive oil
juice ½ lemon

In a bowl, mix scallops, shrimp, fish, onion, and bell pepper with the wine, dill, basil, lime juice or vinegar, salt, and pepper. Marinate in the refrigerator 2–3 hours. Meanwhile, soak 6 bamboo skewers in hot water for 30 minutes.

Cut squid into ¼-in. rings. In a bowl, mix together lemon juice, honey, and 2 tablespoons oil. Add squid. Cover and marinate in the refrigerator for 6 hours. To make mayonnaise, crush garlic to a smooth pulp using a mortar and pestle. Put garlic in a blender or food processor with egg yolks and a little salt. With motor running, gradually pour in half the olive oil. When mixture begins to thicken, add lemon juice and pepper. Add remaining oil. Soak 4 bamboo skewers in hot water for 30 minutes.

Thread seafood and vegetables alternately on to the skewers so that each skewer has 2 pieces of every ingredient. Brush each filled skewer with a little oil and grill on a rack over medium-hot coals 5–6 minutes, turning frequently. Serve hot with Spicy Fish Sauce as a dip.

Serves 6.

Drain squid and pat dry with paper towels. Thread on to wooden skewers, alternating with shrimp. Season with salt and pepper. Grill on a rack over medium-hot coals for 4–5 minutes, turning frequently, until golden. Cut lemon slices in half and dip cut edges in chopped parsley. Garnish kabobs with lemon slices and serve with garlic mayonnaise.

Serves 4 as an appetizer.

SCALLOPS WITH TINDOORIS

2¼ lb. fresh or frozen scallops, thawed if frozen
12 tindooris (see Note)
⅔ cup olive oil
1 tablespoon lemon juice
1 tablespoon lime juice
¼ teaspoon lemon pepper
¼ teaspoon onion salt
lemon and lime slices, to garnish

Remove any dark veins, then rinse scallops and pat dry with paper towels. Rinse tindooris and halve lengthwise. Add to a saucepan of fast boiling water and cook for 1 minute. Drain and leave to cool.

Combine remaining ingredients, except garnish, in a large bowl. Put scallops into mixture and leave for 45 minutes to 1 hour, stirring occasionally. Add tindooris during the last 15 minutes.

Thread scallops and tindooris on to oiled metal skewers and grill on a rack over medium-hot coals for 5–10 minutes, basting frequently with marinade. Scallops are cooked when opaque. Garnish with lemon and lime slices.

Serves 6–8.

Note: Tindooris are a vegetable the size of a gherkin with smooth dark green skin and a texture similar to zucchini. They are obtainable from most Asian stores.

SHRIMP KABOBS & MANGO SALSA

1 fresh red chili, cored, seeded, and finely chopped
½ teaspoon paprika
½ teaspoon ground coriander
1 clove garlic, crushed
juice ½ lime
2 tablespoons oil
20 large, raw shrimp in shells, heads removed and deveined
MANGO SALSA:
1 mango, peeled and diced
½ small red onion, finely diced
1 fresh red chili, cored, seeded, and finely chopped
3 tablespoons chopped fresh cilantro
grated rind and juice 1 lime
salt and freshly ground black pepper

To make salsa, in a bowl mix together mango, red onion, chili, cilantro, lime rind and juice, and salt. Set aside. Meanwhile, soak 4 bamboo skewers in hot water for 30 minutes.

In a bowl, mix together chili, paprika, ground coriander, garlic, lime juice, oil, and salt and pepper. Place shrimp in a dish. Add spice mixture and mix to coat thoroughly. Cover and leave in a cool place for 30 minutes. Thread shrimp on to skewers and grill on a rack over medium-hot coals, basting and turning frequently, for 6–8 minutes until pink. Serve with mango salsa.

Serves 4.

GRILLED LOBSTER

2 freshly cooked lobsters, 2¼ lb. each
½ cup butter, softened
2 teaspoons lemon juice
salt and freshly ground black pepper
lemon wedges and parsley sprigs, to garnish

On a chopping board and using a heavy sharp knife, split lobsters in half by cutting lengthwise along line down the back and through the tail. Crack claws. Remove gills, grayish sac near head, and black vein which runs lengthwise along tail.

Remove the coral and beat into half the butter and set aside; melt remaining butter. Sprinkle lobster flesh with lemon juice and season lightly with salt and pepper. Spoon melted butter over.

Grill lobster, flesh side uppermost, on an oiled rack over medium-hot coals for about 5–10 minutes. Turn over and cook for 3–4 minutes until lobster meat is hot and browning slightly. Serve topped with coral butter. Garnish with lemon wedges and parsley sprigs.

Serves 4.

CHILI SHRIMP SKEWERS

12 raw large shrimp
2 tablespoons vegetable oil
2 tablespoons lime juice
2 cloves garlic, crushed
½ teaspoon paprika
½ teaspoon ground turmeric
2 fresh green chilies, cored, seeded, and finely
   chopped
1 tablespoon chopped fresh cilantro
lime slices, to garnish

Peel shrimp, leaving tail shells on. Make a small incision along the spines and remove black vein. Thread on to metal skewers and set aside.

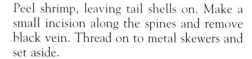

Whisk together vegetable oil, lime juice, garlic, paprika, and turmeric. Stir in chilies. Put skewered shrimp in a nonmetal dish; add marinade. Cover and refrigerate 30 minutes, basting occasionally.

Drain skewered shrimp and grill on a rack over medium-hot coals for 3–5 minutes, turning and basting occasionally with the marinade, until shrimp are pink. Sprinkle with chopped cilantro and serve hot, garnished with lime slices.

Serves 4.

LOUISIANA ANGELS

9 bacon slices
18 button mushrooms
½ cup butter
2 tablespoons lemon juice
3 tablespoons chopped fresh parsley
pinch red pepper
18 fresh oysters, shelled
cornstarch, for dusting
6 slices toast, crusts removed, cut into fingers

Stretch bacon slices slightly with back of a knife. Halve slices crosswise. Lightly fry until opaque and still limp. Drain; set aside.

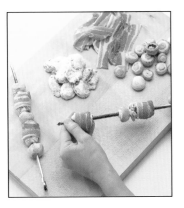

Cook mushrooms in saucepan of boiling water for 1 minute. Drain. To make maitre d'hôtel butter, melt butter in a pan. Remove from heat and stir in lemon juice, parsley, and red pepper. Keep warm. Dust oysters with cornstarch. Wrap bacon slices round oysters and, alternating with mushrooms, thread onto 4–6 metal skewers. (Try to spear through 'eyes' of oysters to keep them in position.)

Brush skewers generously with maitre d'hôtel butter. Grill on a rack over medium-hot coals for 3–5 minutes until oysters are just brown. Do not overcook or oysters will toughen. Remove from skewers and serve on toast, recrisped on barbecue (or in the oyster shells, if desired). Spoon remaining maitre d'hôtel butter on top.

Serves 6.

ANGELS ON HORSEBACK

4 bacon slices
8 fresh oysters, shelled
4 slices bread
unsalted butter, for spreading
freshly ground black pepper
corn salad and lemon twists, to garnish

Stretch bacon slices slightly with back of a knife. Halve slices crosswise. Wrap a piece of bacon around each oyster. Toast bread and keep warm.

Place oysters on barbecue rack with ends of bacon underneath. Grill oysters over hot coals until crisp, turn over and crisp the other side.

Meanwhile, cut 2 circles from each slice of toast and butter toast circles. Place an oyster on each circle, season with pepper, and serve garnished with corn salad and lemon twists.

Makes 8.

GRILLED CHICKEN

TIKKA KABOBS

¼ cup olive oil
juice ½ lemon
1 tablespoon chopped fresh marjoram
1 tablespoon chopped fresh thyme
6 boneless chicken breast halves
cooked rice, to serve
salt and freshly ground black pepper
thyme and marjoram sprigs, and lemon rind strips, to
  garnish

In a shallow dish, mix together oil, lemon juice, marjoram, and thyme.

⅔ cup plain yogurt
1 tablespoon grated fresh ginger
2 cloves garlic, crushed
1 teaspoon chili powder
1 teaspoon ground cumin
1 teaspoon turmeric
1 tablespoon coriander seeds
juice 1 lemon
½ teaspoon salt
2 tablespoons chopped fresh cilantro
12 oz. chicken meat, cubed
RAITA:
⅔ cup plain yogurt
2 teaspoons mint jelly
3 oz. finely chopped cucumber
2 scallions, finely chopped

Prick chicken with a fork. Turn chicken pieces in marinade, then cover the dish and marinate in the refrigerator for up to 8 hours.

Blend the first 10 ingredients in a blender or food processor until smooth. Pour into a bowl. Stir in cubed chicken, cover, and allow to marinate in the refrigerator overnight.

Remove chicken from marinade and place, skin side down, on barbecue rack. Brush with marinade mixture and grill over hot coals for 8–10 minutes, basting occasionally with marinade. Turn and cook for an additional 8–10 minutes until golden brown and cooked through. Heat any remaining marinade in a small pan and stir into rice with salt and pepper. Serve chicken with the rice, garnished with thyme and marjoram sprigs, and strips of lemon rind.

Serves 6.

Thread chicken on to skewers and grill on a rack over hot coals for 15–20 minutes, turning frequently and brushing with any remaining marinade. In a bowl, mix together raita ingredients. Serve kabobs on a bed of pilaf rice, garnished with sprigs of cilantro and lemon wedges. Hand the raita separately.

Serves 4.

Note: If using bamboo or wooden skewers, soak in water 30 minutes before using.

CHICKEN & MANGO YAKITORI

MANGO CHICKEN

3 skinless, boneless chicken breast halves, about
  6 oz. each
1 large ripe mango
⅓ cup chicken stock
⅓ cup sake or sweet white wine
⅓ cup dark soy sauce
1½ tablespoons soft brown sugar
2 tablespoons sweet sherry
1 clove garlic, crushed

Cut chicken into long, thin strips about
¼ in. wide. Peel and pit the mango and cut
flesh into ¾-in. pieces. Thread a strip of
chicken on to a skewer, followed by a piece
of mango.

Wrap the chicken over mango, thread
chicken on to skewer again, then add
another piece of mango, and thread chicken
again so that chicken weaves over and under
mango. Make all the kabobs in the same way.
Place all the remaining ingredients in a small
pan and heat gently until sugar has
dissolved, then bring to a boil for 1 minute.
Set aside to cool.

Put a small amount of sauce aside to use as a
dip. Brush a little of remaining sauce over
kabobs. Grill on a rack over hot coals for 2–3
minutes or until cooked, brushing with sauce
frequently. Serve hot with the reserved
sauce.

Makes 16–20.

Note: If using bamboo or wooden skewers,
soak in water 30 minutes before using.

2 ripe mangoes
juice ½ small lime
1 tablespoon mango chutney
½ cup salted butter
1 tablespoon lemon juice
pinch ground ginger
pinch red pepper
pinch ground cloves
pinch salt
6 skinless, boneless chicken breast halves, 4 oz. each
lime twists, to garnish

Prepare mangoes by cutting lengthwise, from
top to bottom of the fruit, as close to the pit
as possible.

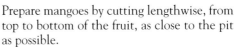

Cut flesh away from the pit. Peel, then thinly
slice flesh lengthwise. Finely chop 2 oz. of
less attractive slices for use in mango butter.
Sprinkle remaining slices with lime juice and
set aside for garnish. To prepare mango
butter, thoroughly blend together chutney,
chopped mango flesh, butter, lemon juice,
ground ginger, red pepper, cloves, and salt.

Make small horizontal slits in both sides of
chicken breast halves and insert mango
butter into each. Melt remaining mango
butter and use to brush over chicken during
cooking. Grill on a rack over hot coals for
7–8 minutes on each side, basting frequently
with melted mango butter. Serve chicken
garnished with reserved mango slices and
lime twists.

Serves 6.

TANDOORI CHICKEN

4 chicken leg quarters, skinned
juice 1 lemon
salt
2 teaspoons ground turmeric
2 teaspoons paprika
1 teaspoon garam masala
1 teaspoon ground cardamom
½ teaspoon chili powder
pinch saffron powder
2 cloves garlic, crushed
2 teaspoons chopped fresh ginger
1 tablespoon olive oil
¾ cup plain yogurt

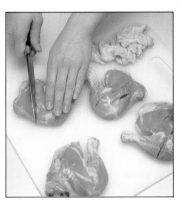

Cut deep diagonal cuts in the chicken flesh.

Pour lemon juice over and sprinkle with a little salt. Mix together all the remaining ingredients and use to coat chicken quarters; cover and marinate in the refrigerator for 4 hours or overnight.

Grill chicken on a rack over hot coals for 25 minutes, brushing with any excess marinade, and turning frequently until chicken is tender and juices run clear when chicken leg is pierced with a knife. A slight blackening of the chicken gives an authentic look.

Serves 4.

GRILLED CHICKEN SKEWERS

6 chicken thighs, total weight about 2¼ lb.
2 cloves garlic, finely chopped
⅔ cup coconut milk
2 teaspoons ground coriander
1 teaspoon each ground cumin and ground turmeric
juice 1 lime
leaves from 8 cilantro sprigs, chopped
3 tablespoons light soy sauce
2 tablespoons fish sauce
3 tablespoons light brown sugar
½ teaspoon crushed dried chilies

Using a sharp knife, slit along underside of each chicken thigh and remove bone, scraping flesh from bone.

Cut each boned thigh into 6 pieces. Put in a bowl. In a small bowl, mix together garlic, coconut milk, coriander, cumin, and turmeric. Pour over chicken. Stir to coat then cover and refrigerate for 2–12 hours. To make sauce, in a small serving bowl, mix together remaining ingredients. Set aside.

Soak 8 short wooden or bamboo skewers for 30 minutes. Thread chicken, skin side up, on skewers. Grill on a rack over hot coals for 4–5 minutes. Turn over and cook for an additional 2–3 minutes or until juice runs clear when chicken is pierced with a knife. Serve with the sauce.

Serves 4–6.

CHICKEN TERIYAKI

1½ lb. skinless, boneless chicken breast halves
1 lb. 8 oz. canned water chestnuts
¼ cup dry sherry
¼ cup medium-dry white wine
¼ cup shoyu sauce
2 cloves garlic, crushed
sunflower oil, for brushing
shredded lettuce, onion rings, parsley sprigs, and
  paprika, to garnish (optional)

Cut chicken into 1-in. cubes. Drain water chestnuts and mix with chicken in a dish.

In a small bowl, mix together sherry, wine, shoyu sauce, and garlic. Pour over chicken and water chestnuts, cover, and leave to marinate for 30–60 minutes, stirring occasionally. Using a slotted spoon, remove chicken and water chestnuts from marinade. Thread pieces of chicken and water chestnuts alternately on to 8 long skewers. Set aside any remaining marinade.

Brush chicken and chestnuts with oil and grill on a rack over hot coals for about 10 minutes, turning frequently and basting with reserved marinade and oil. Arrange shredded lettuce on a large platter and place skewers in a crisscross pattern on top. Garnish with raw onion rings, parsley, and a sprinkling of paprika, if desired.

Serves 8.

Note: If using bamboo or wooden skewers, soak in water 30 minutes before using.

CHARGRILLED YUAN CHICKEN

4 whole chicken legs, boned
8 large scallions, white part only
lime or lemon wedges, to garnish
MARINADE:
⅓ cup sake or white wine
⅓ cup mirin or 1 tablespoon sugar
⅓ cup shoyu
rind of 1 lemon or lime, in large pieces

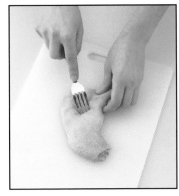

Place chicken legs on a cutting board, skin side up. Using a fork, pierce the skin in a few places. Cut scallions crosswise into 1½-in. lengths.

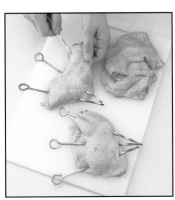

In a dish, mix all the marinade ingredients, add chicken and scallions and leave to marinate for 30 minutes. Thread 3–4 long stainless steel skewers through each chicken leg, parallel with the skin in a fan shape. Grill on a rack over hot coals, skin side down, for 6–7 minutes until golden brown, then turn and cook the other side for 3–4 minutes. Thread scallions, 6–8 pieces to a skewer, and grill. Remove skewers and serve 1 chicken leg and a quarter of the scallion on each serving plate.

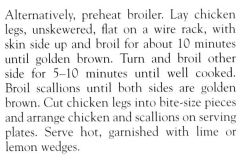

Alternatively, preheat broiler. Lay chicken legs, unskewered, flat on a wire rack, with skin side up and broil for about 10 minutes until golden brown. Turn and broil other side for 5–10 minutes until well cooked. Broil scallions until both sides are golden brown. Cut chicken legs into bite-size pieces and arrange chicken and scallions on serving plates. Serve hot, garnished with lime or lemon wedges.

Serves 4.

MALAY CHICKEN

8 boneless chicken thighs, total weight about 1½ lb.
1 bunch of scallions, white part finely chopped
2 tablespoons chopped fresh cilantro
2 oz. creamed coconut, chopped
1 clove garlic, crushed and finely chopped
½ fresh red chili, cored, seeded, and chopped
2 teaspoons sunflower oil
1 teaspoon sesame oil
2 tablespoons lime juice
2 teaspoons each ground roasted cumin seeds and
    coriander seeds
salt
lime slices
cilantro sprigs, to garnish

Open out chicken thighs. Mix together scallions and cilantro and spoon an equal quantity on each opened chicken thigh. Reform thighs. Put in a single layer in a nonreactive dish. Put coconut in a bowl and stir in scant 1 cup boiling water until dissolved. Stir in garlic, chili, oils, lime juice, spices, and salt. Pour over chicken, turn to coat in marinade, then cover and refrigerate overnight.

Transfer chicken to room temperature. Soak bamboo skewers in water for 30 minutes. Remove chicken from marinade, reserving marinade, and thread 1 or 2 chicken thighs on to each skewer with a lime slice. Grill on a rack over hot coals for about 20 minutes, basting with remaining marinade, until chicken juices run clear when tested with the point of a sharp knife. Garnish with cilantro sprigs.

Serves 4.

CHINESE GRILLED CHICKEN

4 chicken quarters, about 8 oz. each
2 cloves garlic, finely chopped
1-in. piece fresh ginger, peeled and finely chopped
¼ cup hoisin sauce
2 tablespoons dry sherry
1 teaspoon chili sauce
1 tablespoon dark soy sauce
1 tablespoon brown sugar
1 tablespoon chopped fresh chives, to garnish

Remove skin and fat from chicken quarters. Rinse and pat dry with paper towels. Using a sharp knife, score top of quarters in diagonal lines.

Place chicken in a shallow dish. Mix together all the remaining ingredients except chives, and spoon over prepared chicken. Cover and refrigerate overnight.

Grill chicken on a rack over hot coals for about 20 minutes, turning once, or until chicken juices run clear when tested with the point of a sharp knife. Garnish with chives and serve.

Serves 4.

INDONESIAN CHICKEN

2 tablespoons peanut oil
1 large onion, finely chopped
3 cloves garlic, finely chopped
7 oz. creamed coconut
2 tablespoons lemon juice
2 teaspoons salt
1 teaspoon ground cardamom
½ teaspoon ground ginger
2 teaspoons turmeric
⅔ cup unsalted peanuts, roasted and skinned
1½ lb. chicken, cut into 1-in. cubes
lemon wedges and cilantro sprigs, to garnish

In a food processor, finely grind peanuts.

Heat oil and gently fry onion and garlic until soft. In a large bowl, blend coconut with 2 cups hot water and add lemon juice, salt, cardamom, ginger, turmeric, and ground peanuts. Add cooked onion and garlic, including any oil left in pan. Add cubed chicken and stir well. Cover bowl and leave to marinate in the refrigerator for 4 hours.

Remove cubed chicken from marinade and thread on to 8 metal skewers. Grill on a rack over hot coals for 10–12 minutes, turning frequently and basting with remaining marinade. Serve garnished with lemon and cilantro.

Serves 8.

Note: This dish is delicious served with shrimp crackers which are obtainable from larger supermarkets, delicatessens, Chinese, Japanese, and Asian food shops.

GINGER CHICKEN PATTIES

1 lb. lean ground chicken
1 clove garlic, finely chopped
1-in. piece fresh ginger, peeled and finely chopped
4 tablespoons chopped fresh cilantro
1 tablespoon cornstarch
2 cups cooked long-grain white rice
salt and freshly ground black pepper
1 egg white, lightly beaten
2 teaspoons sunflower oil
cilantro leaves, to garnish
DIP:
2 tablespoons light soy sauce
2 tablespoons dry sherry
½-in. piece fresh ginger, peeled and grated

In a bowl, mix together chicken, garlic, ginger, and cilantro. Stir in cornstarch, rice, salt, and pepper. Stir in egg white. Divide mixture into 8 portions and shape into 3-in. diameter patties, dusting hands with extra cornstarch if needed. Place on a plate, cover, and refrigerate for 30 minutes.

Brush patties lightly with oil and grill over hot coals for 4 minutes. Brush again with oil, turn patties over, and cook an additional 3–4 minutes or until cooked through. Drain on paper towels. Mix dip ingredients together. Garnish patties with cilantro and serve with the dip.

Serves 4.

CHICKEN SAINT LUCIA

⅔ cup creamed coconut, grated
1 teaspoon ground cumin
1 teaspoon ground cardamom
4 tablespoons mango chutney
½ cup corn oil
1½–2 teaspoons salt
4 teaspoons turmeric
4 chicken quarters, 10–12 oz. each

Heat ¼ cup water in a small saucepan, stir in grated coconut and when well blended, remove from heat. Stir in cumin, cardamom, and mango chutney. Spoon mixture into a bowl, cover, and set aside.

Mix together oil, salt, and turmeric, and brush generously all over chicken quarters. Grill chicken quarters on a rack over medium-hot coals for 12–15 minutes on each side, basting frequently with remaining seasoned oil. Pierce through to bone with a metal skewer to make sure that the juices run clear and chicken is fully cooked.

Serve with a tiny pot of sauce on the side of each plate.

Serves 4.

CHICKEN WITH CILANTRO

6 cilantro sprigs
1 tablespoon black peppercorns, crushed
2 cloves garlic, chopped
juice 1 lime
2 teaspoons fish sauce
4 large or 6 medium chicken drumsticks or thighs
scallions, to garnish
lime wedges, to serve

Using a mortar and pestle or small blender, pound or mix together cilantro, peppercorns, garlic, lime juice, and fish sauce; set aside.

Using a sharp knife, cut slashes in chicken. Spread spice mixture over chicken. Cover and set aside in the refrigerator for 2–3 hours, turning occasionally.

Grill chicken on a rack over hot coals, basting and turning occasionally, for about 10 minutes or until cooked through and golden. Garnish with scallions and serve with wedges of lime.

Serves 2–6.

FIVE-SPICE CHICKEN

2 skinless, boneless chicken breast halves, each
    about 6 oz., trimmed
2 small red bell peppers, halved and seeded
2 small yellow bell peppers, halved and seeded
chopped fresh chives, to garnish
MARINADE:
1 clove garlic, crushed
1 fresh red chili, cored, seeded, and chopped
3 tablespoons light soy sauce
1 teaspoon five-spice powder
1 teaspoon brown sugar
2 teaspoons sesame oil

Using a small sharp knife, score chicken
breast halves on both sides in a crisscross
pattern, taking care not to slice all the way
through. Place in a shallow dish with bell
peppers. Mix together marinade ingredients,
pour over chicken and bell peppers and turn
to coat. Cover and chill 1 hour.

Remove chicken and bell peppers from
marinade, place on a rack over hot coals, and
grill, basting with marinade, for 4 or 5
minutes on each side or until chicken is
cooked through. Slice chicken breast halves
and serve with a piece of red and yellow bell
pepper, garnished with chives.

Serves 3.

SPICY CHICKEN DRUMSTICKS

8 chicken drumsticks
2 tablespoons tomato sauce
1 tablespoon honey
1 tablespoon barbecue spice
2 oz. plain potato chips

Using a sharp knife, remove skin from
chicken drumsticks.

Mix tomato sauce, honey, and barbecue
spice together and brush over drumsticks
until coated.

Lightly crush potato chips and roll chicken
in them to coat. Barbecue on a rack over
medium-hot coals for about 30 minutes,
turning occasionally, until golden and
chicken juices run clear when tested with
the point of a sharp knife.

Makes 8.

CHILI CHICKEN DRUMSTICKS

1–2 cloves garlic, chopped
1–2 stalks lemongrass, chopped
2 shallots, chopped
1–2 small fresh red or green chilies, cored, seeded, and chopped
1 tablespoon chopped fresh cilantro
¼ cup fish sauce
6–8 chicken drumsticks, skinned
lettuce leaves
Spicy Fish Sauce (see page 128), to serve

Using a mortar and pestle, pound garlic, lemongrass, shallots, chilies, and cilantro to a paste.

In a medium bowl, thoroughly blend pounded mixture with the fish sauce to a smooth paste. Add drumsticks and coat well with the paste. Cover the bowl and leave to marinate 2–3 hours in the refrigerator, turning drumsticks every 30 minutes or so.

Grill drumsticks on a rack over hot coals for 10–15 minutes, turning frequently and basting with remaining marinade for first 5 minutes only. Serve hot on a bed of lettuce leaves with the Spicy Fish Sauce as a dip.

Serves 4–6.

DEEP SOUTH DRUMSTICKS

12–16 chicken drumsticks
1-in. slice whole-wheat bread
6 tablespoons tomato paste
3 tablespoons full-bodied red wine
juice ½ lemon
2 tablespoons Worcestershire sauce
2 tablespoons molasses
1 teaspoon salt
½ teaspoon freshly ground black pepper
1 teaspoon French mustard
½ teaspoon chili powder
1 teaspoon paprika
2 tablespoons vegetable oil
parsley sprigs, to garnish

Wash and dry drumsticks and set aside.

Remove crusts, then dice bread. Put in a large shallow dish, with all remaining ingredients, except parsley. Stir with a fork until bread is incorporated. (The mixture will be thick.) Put drumsticks into sauce, turning to coat evenly. Leave in a cool place for 1 hour, turning drumsticks occasionally.

Wrap drumsticks individually in oiled, single thickness foil. Grill on a rack over medium-hot coals for 30–40 minutes, turning the packages from time to time. Test 1 drumstick for doneness by pricking with the point of a sharp knife; the juices should run clear and flesh touching the bone be fully cooked. Garnish with parsley and serve in the foil packages.

Serves 12–16.

CHICKEN TIKKA

1½ lb. skinless, boneless chicken breast halves
⅔ cup plain yogurt
1-in. piece fresh ginger, grated
2 cloves garlic, crushed
1 teaspoon chili powder
1 tablespoon ground coriander
salt
2 tablespoons lime juice
2 tablespoons vegetable oil
lime slices, to garnish

Rinse chicken, pat dry with paper towels, and cut into ¾-in. cubes. Thread on to short skewers.

Put skewered chicken into a shallow nonmetal dish. In a small bowl, mix together yogurt, ginger, garlic, chili powder, ground coriander, salt, lime juice, and oil. Pour over chicken and turn to coat completely in marinade. Cover and refrigerate 6 hours or overnight to allow chicken to absorb flavors.

Place skewered chicken on a rack over hot coals and grill for 5–7 minutes, turning skewers and basting occasionally with any remaining marinade. Serve hot, garnished with lime slices.

Serves 4.

Note: If using bamboo or wooden skewers, soak in water 30 minutes before using.

CHICKEN & OKRA SKEWERS

8 chicken thighs, with skins, boned
8 scallions, white part only
24 okra, trimmed
lemon wedges, sansho pepper, and chili powder, to
  garnish
TARE SAUCE:
3 tablespoons sake
⅓ cup shoyu
1 tablespoon each mirin and sugar

Cut chicken thighs into 1-in.-square pieces and scallions crosswise into 1-in. lengths. Mix ingredients for the tare sauce in a saucepan and bring to a boil. Remove from heat and set aside.

Thread 4 pieces of chicken and 3 okra alternately on to a 8-in. bamboo or stainless steel skewer. (If using bamboo skewers, soak in water 30 minutes before using.) Repeat with another 7 skewers. Thread another 8 skewers with 4 pieces of chicken and 3 pieces of scallion. Thread any remaining ingredients on to extra skewers. Grill the skewers on a rack over hot coals, turning frequently. Brush with tare sauce 2–3 times during cooking, until chicken is well cooked and golden brown.

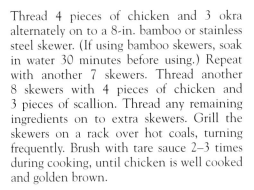

Alternatively, broil on a well-oiled wire rack, spacing chicken pieces apart and broiling until both sides are golden brown. Dip pieces in tare sauce and broil for an additional 30 seconds on each side. Set aside. Lightly broil scallions and okra. Thread 4 chicken pieces alternately with 3 scallions on 8 skewers and with okra on another 8. Serve on a platter, garnished with lemon, sansho peppers, and chili powder.

Serves 4–8 as an appetizer.

HICKORY-SMOKED CHICKEN

2 handfuls hickory smoking chips
handful of mixed fresh herbs
3–4 lb. oven-ready chicken
salt

Cook this dish in a kettle grill or wet smoker. Soak hickory chips in hot water. Light grill and when coals are hot, sprinkle with well-drained hickory chips.

Put herbs in a shallow metal dish of hot water. Place on a rack over coals. Season surface of chicken with salt and place on a metal rack over water pan. Close grill lid.

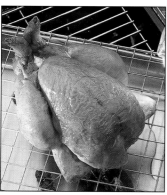

Reduce heat and cook chicken over low coals for about 3 hours, turning every 30 minutes. The pan of hot water may need topping up during cooking. To do this, move chicken to one side and add water with extreme caution. The cooked chicken will be moist with faintly pink-tinged flesh and a distinctive smoky flavor.

Serves 4–6.

VIETNAMESE CHICKEN SKEWERS

1 lb. skinless, boneless chicken breast halves
1 teaspoon very finely chopped garlic
2 shallots or 1 small onion, finely chopped
1 tablespoon ground coriander
1 teaspoon sugar
1 tablespoon mild curry powder
2 tablespoons fish sauce
1 tablespoon lime juice or vinegar
salt and freshly ground black pepper
vegetable oil, for brushing
chopped onion and cucumber, to garnish
Fresh Mint Sambal (see page 130), to serve

Cut chicken breast halves into 1-in. cubes.

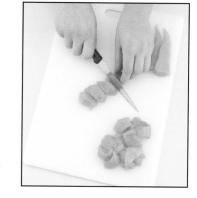

In a bowl, mix chicken with garlic, shallots or onion, coriander, sugar, curry powder, fish sauce, lime juice or vinegar, salt, and pepper, then marinate 2–3 hours in the refrigerator. Meanwhile, soak 16 bamboo skewers in hot water for 30 minutes.

Thread 4 chicken cubes on to one end of each skewer. Brush each filled skewer with a little oil and grill on a rack over hot coals for 5–6 minutes, turning frequently. Garnish with chopped onion and cucumber, and serve hot with Fresh Mint Sambal or the dipping sauce of your choice.

Serves 8.

Variation: Pork fillet, beef steak, or lamb can be prepared and cooked in the same way.

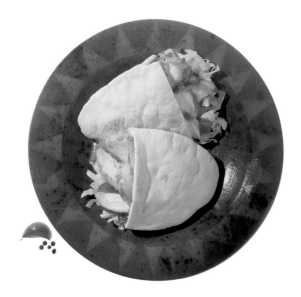

HUMMUS & CHICKEN

2 skinless, boneless chicken breast halves
juice ½ lemon
⅓ cup olive oil
salt and freshly ground black pepper
2 teaspoons toasted sesame seeds
1 teaspoon ground cumin
½ teaspoon paprika
8 slices ciabatta-style bread
salad leaves, to garnish
HUMMUS:
15 oz. canned chickpeas, drained
4 tablespoons tahini
4 tablespoons Greek-style yogurt
2 cloves garlic, crushed
1 tablespoon olive oil
juice 1 lemon

Place chicken breast halves in a shallow dish. In a bowl, mix together lemon juice, 2 tablespoons of the olive oil, salt, and pepper and pour over chicken. Cover and leave in a cool place for 1 hour. To make the hummus, place chickpeas, tahini, yogurt, garlic, olive oil, lemon juice, salt, and pepper in a blender or food processor and process to form a slightly grainy paste.

Grill chicken breast halves on a rack over hot coals for 15 minutes, turning once, until cooked through. Cut into slices and keep warm. Mix together sesame seeds, cumin, paprika, and salt. Drizzle bread on both sides with olive oil and toast on the grill. Spread some hummus on each piece of toast, top with chicken slices, and sprinkle with sesame seed mixture. Drizzle with remaining olive oil and serve garnished with salad leaves.

Serves 4–8.

MOROCCAN CHICKEN IN PITA

scant ½ cup Greek-style yogurt
2 teaspoons harissa
2 teaspoons each ground cumin and ground coriander
2 cloves garlic, crushed
1 tablespoon olive oil
salt and freshly ground black pepper
4 skinless, boneless chicken breast halves
pita bread, shredded lettuce, and chopped tomatoes, to serve

In a bowl, mix together yogurt, harissa, cumin, coriander, garlic, olive oil, salt, and pepper. Spread over chicken breast halves and place in a dish. Cover dish and place in the refrigerator for 2 hours.

Grill chicken breast halves on a rack over hot coals for 25 minutes until browned and the juices run clear when pierced with the point of a sharp knife. Place pita bread on the barbecue rack for last 5 minutes of cooking, to warm through, turning once.

To serve, cut chicken into thin slices. Cut pita bread in half across width and open to form pockets; fill pockets with sliced chicken, shredded lettuce, and chopped tomatoes.

Serves 4–6.

CHICKEN TARTLETS

2¼ lb. skinless, boneless chicken breast halves
olive oil, for brushing
bay leaves, to garnish
PÂTÉ:
8 oz. chicken livers, rinsed, trimmed, and halved
¼ cup full-bodied sherry
¼ teaspoon ground mace
¼ teaspoon bay leaf powder
¼ teaspoon freshly ground black pepper
1 teaspoon salt
½ cup butter, roughly cut up
2 teaspoons brandy

A few hours in advance, brush a 12 section bun pan with oil. Do not use a nonstick pan. Beat chicken breast halves between sheets of plastic wrap or waxed paper until flattened to ⅛ in. in thickness, without creating holes. Cut flattened chicken into rounds to fit into oiled pans. Trim away surplus to use in pâté. Put a small piece of oiled foil into each tartlet. Cover and refrigerate while preparing pâté. Put chicken trimmings and livers in a saucepan.

Add sherry to pan with 2 tablespoons water, spices, and seasonings. Cover and cook gently for 5–7 minutes until chicken and livers are cooked. Purée hot mixture in blender with butter and brandy. Pour into a 1¼ cup dish. Chill until firm. Put bun pan on a barbecue rack over medium-hot coals. Cook until chicken is opaque and underside of tartlet is slightly brown. Loosen from pan, remove foil, and fill with pâté. Top each one with bay leaves.

Serves 12.

CHICKEN & SAFFRON SAUCE

1½ oz. fresh ginger, peeled and chopped
1 clove garlic, crushed
2 teaspoons each ground cumin and coriander
4 cardamom pods, cracked and seeds crushed
finely grated rind and juice ½ lemon
½ teaspoon garam masala
⅔ cup Greek-style yogurt
4 skinless, boneless chicken breast halves
pinch saffron strands
1 shallot, finely chopped
¼ cup dry white wine
⅔ cup chicken stock
⅓ cup heavy cream
1 tablespoon chopped fresh cilantro

In a blender or food processor, purée ginger with garlic, cumin, coriander, crushed cardamom seeds, lemon rind, and garam masala. Add two-thirds of yogurt, mix well, and put to one side. Cut each chicken breast into 8 strips, put into shallow dish, and spoon yogurt mixture over. Cover and marinate for 1½-2 hours. Meanwhile, soak saffron strands in 1 tablespoon hot water. Put shallot in a small pan with wine and boil rapidly until reduced by half. Add stock, saffron and water, and boil until reduced to about ⅔ cup.

Add cream and simmer for about 2 minutes until sauce starts to thicken. Leave to cool, then add remaining yogurt and season with a little lemon juice, salt, and pepper. Remove chicken strips from marinade and place on a barbecue rack, leaving a slight gap between the strips to ensure even cooking. Grill over hot coals for 5 minutes until browned, turning halfway through cooking. Arrange on a serving dish and allow to cool. Drizzle sauce over and sprinkle with chopped cilantro.

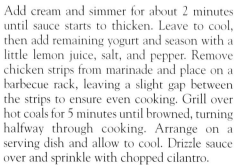

Serves 4.

GINGER & APRICOT CHICKEN

8–10 chicken thighs
14½ oz. canned apricot halves in natural juice
about 1 cup natural orange juice
1 tablespoon walnut oil
1 small onion, ground
1 teaspoon grated fresh ginger
salt and freshly ground black pepper
16 red cherries, pitted

Deeply slash the chicken thighs to the bone in 2 or 3 places.

Remove apricot halves from juice, set aside 16 for garnish, and mash remainder. Make apricot juice up to 1½ cups with orange juice. Pour into a large bowl, add oil, mashed apricots, onion, ginger, and salt and pepper. Mix in chicken thighs, cover and leave in a cool place for 2 hours, stirring occasionally.

Grill chicken thighs on an oiled rack over hot coals for 25–30 minutes, turning them 2 or 3 times and basting with remaining marinade. Place reserved apricot halves on a foil tray on barbecue rack for 3–5 minutes to warm. Fill with cherries and serve with the chicken thighs.

Serves 4.

GAME HEN AIOLI

5 cloves garlic, peeled
2 egg yolks
½ cup olive oil
1 teaspoon lemon juice
salt and freshly ground black pepper
2 oven-ready game hens
lemon slices and parsley sprigs, to garnish

In a glass bowl, pound garlic to a pulp with a pestle. Gradually beat in egg yolks.

Beat oil into mixture drop by drop until it starts to thicken. Mix lemon juice with 1 teaspoon water and beat in alternate drops of juice and oil until well incorporated. Season with salt and pepper.

Loosen skin of game hens and, using a spoon handle, spread garlic mayonnaise close to flesh. Brush mixture inside each cavity and over outside of birds. Separately wrap each game hen in double thickness foil. Grill on a rack over medium-hot coals for 30 minutes. Remove game hens from foil, grill on a rack for an additional 15–20 minutes, turning and basting occasionally. Serve game hens, whole or halved, garnished with lemon and parsley.

Serves 2–4.

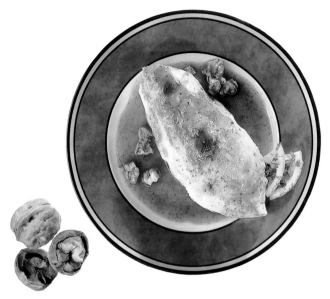

PEPPERED CHICKEN SKEWERS

1 lb. skinless, boneless chicken breast halves, cubed
1 tablespoon rice wine
1 tablespoon dark soy sauce
grated rind and juice 1 lime
2 teaspoons soft brown sugar
1 teaspoon ground cinnamon
1 teaspoon sunflower oil
1 teaspoon Szechuan peppercorns, toasted and
  crushed
strips lime rind, to garnish

Place chicken in a shallow dish. Mix rice wine, soy sauce, lime rind and juice, sugar, and cinnamon. Pour over chicken.

Cover chicken and chill 1 hour. Meanwhile, soak 8 bamboo skewers in cold water for 30 minutes. Remove chicken pieces from marinade, reserving marinade, and thread chicken on to skewers.

Brush skewers with marinade and sprinkle with peppercorns. Grill on a lightly oiled rack over hot coals for 3 minutes, turn, brush again, and cook for an additional 2 or 3 minutes or until cooked through. Drain on paper towels. Garnish with lime rind and serve.

Serves 4.

CHICKEN WITH WALNUT SAUCE

6 boneless chicken breast halves
salt and freshly ground black pepper
juice 1 orange
1¼ cups walnut halves
2 cloves garlic, chopped
⅓ cup walnut oil
⅓ cup olive oil
squeeze lemon juice
chopped fresh parsley and orange slices, to serve

Season chicken breast with salt and pepper and place in a large shallow bowl. Pour orange juice over chicken; set aside.

On a baking tray, spread out walnuts. Bake until lightly browned, 5–10 minutes. Transfer to a blender or food processor with a metal blade. Add garlic, 2 tablespoons water, and a pinch of salt. Process to a paste. With motor running, slowly pour in walnut and olive oils to make a smooth, mayonnaise-like sauce. Transfer to a bowl; add lemon juice and pepper and set aside.

Grill chicken on a rack over hot coals for 5–7 minutes on each side until juices run clear when thickest part is pierced with the point of a sharp knife. Sprinkle orange slices with chopped parsley; use to garnish chicken, then serve with the sauce.

Serves 6.

SPATCHCOCKED CHICKEN

2 oven-ready game hens or spring chickens, 1 lb.
  each
3 tablespoons butter
¾ teaspoon grated lemon rind
¾ teaspoon dry mustard
⅓ cup heavy cream
parsley sprigs, to garnish

On a wooden chopping board, and using poultry shears or a heavy, sharp-bladed knife, cut birds through backbone. With skin-sides uppermost, flatten each bird to 1-in. thickness using a mallet or rolling pin.

Soften butter and blend in lemon rind, mustard, and cream. Spread split chickens with half the mixture. Diagonally insert 2 long metal skewers through both thighs and breast, crossing them over in the center.

Grill on a rack over hot coals for 20 minutes, basting occasionally with remaining butter cream, and turning once. Reduce heat and move birds to side of grill. Continue cooking for about 20 minutes, or until juices run clear when pierced with the point of a sharp knife, turning once. Remove skewers and halve birds; serve garnished with parsley sprigs.

Serves 4.

CHICKEN WITH GARLIC SAUCE

4 chicken portions
salt and freshly ground black pepper
6 tablespoons olive oil
3 tablespoons fresh lemon juice
2 tablespoons finely chopped scallions
2 tablespoons chopped fresh parsley
2 lemons, quartered, to serve
GARLIC SAUCE:
6–9 cloves garlic
about ⅔ cup olive oil

Rub chicken with salt and pepper, then place in a single layer in a nonmetallic dish

Pour oil and lemon juice over chicken and let stand 1 hour, turning chicken over once or twice. Meanwhile, make garlic sauce. Using a mortar and pestle, crush garlic with a little salt. Work in oil a drop at a time; as the sauce thickens oil can be added more quickly. Season with salt and pepper.

Place chicken on a rack over medium-hot coals and grill slowly 8–10 minutes on each side, basting occasionally with oil and lemon mixture, until crisp on the outside and tender throughout. Transfer to a warm serving plate and sprinkle onions and parsley over the top. Serve with garlic sauce and lemon quarters.

Serves 4.

DOLCELATTE & PEAR TOASTS

4 muffins
¼ cup garlic and herb-flavored butter
2 small cooked skinless, boneless chicken breast
  halves
⅔ cup dolcelatte cheese
1 small dessert pear, cored and sliced
freshly ground black pepper
watercress sprigs, to garnish

Split muffins in half and toast on a rack over hot coals, turning once, until lightly browned.

Spread with a little flavored butter. Cut chicken and cheese into thin slices. Arrange alternate pieces of chicken, cheese, and pear on top of each muffin half.

Sprinkle with black pepper and return to the barbecue until cheese has melted. Serve at once, garnished with sprigs of watercress.

Serves 4.

CHICKEN WINGS & COLE SLAW

½ cup soy sauce
¼ cup tomato sauce
¼ cup white wine vinegar
¼ cup honey
1 clove garlic, crushed
1 teaspoon ground ginger
pinch chili powder
12 chicken wings
COLE SLAW:
1½ cups finely shredded red cabbage
1½ cups finely shredded white cabbage
1 carrot, grated
1 tablespoon chopped fresh parsley
2 teaspoons chopped fresh dill
¼ cup olive oil
1 tablespoon soy sauce

Put soy sauce, tomato sauce, vinegar, honey, garlic, ginger, and chili powder in an oven-proof dish and mix well. Add chicken wings and turn to coat thoroughly. Cover and marinate overnight in the refrigerator. To make cole slaw, place red cabbage, white cabbage, carrot, parsley, dill, olive oil, and soy sauce in a bowl and mix together. Set aside.

Grill chicken wings on a rack over medium-hot coals for 35–40 minutes, turning occasionally and brushing with reserved marinade, until brown and crisp. Serve with the cole slaw.

Serves 4.

ASIAN BACON ROLLS

8 oz. chicken livers
2 teaspoons soy sauce
1 teaspoon finely chopped fresh ginger
2 tablespoons honey
4 teaspoons dry sherry
8 bacon slices
8 canned water chestnuts, drained

Soak chicken livers in cold water for 1 hour, drain and remove cores. Cut chicken livers into 16 pieces.

Mix together soy sauce, ginger, 2 teaspoons honey, and sherry. Add prepared chicken livers and leave to marinate for 25 minutes. Using the back of a knife, stretch each slice of bacon and cut in half.

Cut water chestnuts in half, place at the end of a slice of bacon, top with a piece of liver, and roll up in the bacon. Secure with a wooden toothpick. Continue until all the ingredients are used. Grill bacon rolls on a rack over hot coals, basting with remaining marinade and drizzling with remaining honey, until bacon is crisp and brown, and honey has caramelized.

Makes 16.

PIQUANT SPRING CHICKEN

2 spring chickens, 1 lb. 2 oz. each
1½ cups tomato juice
¼ cup Worcestershire sauce
2 teaspoons lemon juice
juice ½ orange
salt and freshly ground black pepper
4 heads Belgian endive
small piece of butter
1 orange, thinly sliced, to garnish

Halve chickens so that each piece has a wing and a leg. Place cut-side up in a shallow dish.

Combine tomato juice, Worcestershire sauce, and citrus juice. Season generously with pepper. Pour over chicken, cover and refrigerate for 12 hours, basting occasionally. Put endive heads on individual pieces of double thickness foil. Dot with butter and season with salt and pepper. Wrap tightly.

Grill chickens on an oiled rack over medium-hot coals for 30–40 minutes until well cooked, brushing occasionally with marinade. Cook endive pockets over or in medium-hot coals during the final 10–12 minutes. Garnish chicken halves with orange slices, and serve with the endive pockets.

Serves 4.

CHICKEN SUNDAY BRUNCH

8 oz. chicken livers
¼ cup vegetable oil
salt and freshly ground black pepper
4 skinless, boneless chicken breast halves, 4 oz. each
4 eggs
3 tablespoons milk
3 teaspoons butter, melted
hot buttered toast, to serve (optional)

Rinse and trim chicken livers and pat with paper towels to remove surplus moisture. Thread on to metal skewers, leaving a small gap between each liver. Season the oil with salt and pepper and brush over livers.

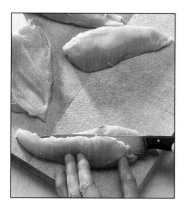

Slit chicken breast halves with a sharp knife, cutting horizontally through chicken, but not quite severing in two. Open out to a butterfly shape and brush with seasoned oil. Grill chicken on a rack over hot coals for 6–10 minutes on each side, basting occasionally. Add skewered livers for last 8–10 minutes of cooking time, brushing with oil and turning skewers frequently.

Meanwhile, beat eggs and milk together, season with salt and pepper, and scramble in melted butter in a small saucepan on the side of the barbecue rack. Spoon scrambled egg over chicken and top with livers removed from skewers with a fork. Serve with hot buttered toast, if desired.

Serves 4.

Note: If using bamboo or wooden skewers, soak in water 30 minutes before using.

CRANBERRY BALLOTINE

4 lb. oven-ready chicken
1 onion, chopped
2 tablespoons oil
½ cup long-grain rice
⅞ cup stock
½ cup raisins
grated rind and juice 1 lemon
salt and freshly ground black pepper
1 egg, beaten
½ cup cranberries, cooked and drained
½ teaspoon sugar

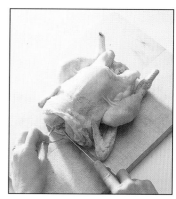

Remove chicken wings at second joint and set aside. Loosen skin at neck, cut around wishbone and remove.

Cut through skin and flesh along backbone. Follow contour of carcass carefully; fillet flesh away from bone without damaging skin. Sever shoulder joint, ease carcass out from skin and flesh, and push back skin from thighs. Cut away flesh and turn inside out to free bone from skin. Repeat for wing bones. Spread skin out and cover evenly with flesh. Use carcass and bones to make stock. Fry onion in oil until soft. Add rice, hot stock, raisins, lemon rind, and lemon juice. Cover; simmer for 20 minutes until stock is absorbed.

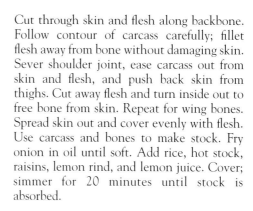

Season rice mixture with salt and pepper. Allow to cool, then beat in egg. Spread over flesh side of chicken, leaving a ¾-in. border. Sweeten cranberries; spoon lengthwise along center of rice. Reshape and sew chicken. Roast on a rack over low coals, in a covered grill, for 1–1¼ hours until chicken is dark golden brown. Leave to stand for 10–15 minutes before carving.

Serves 4.

CHICKEN SATAY

juice 1 lime
stalk lemongrass, finely chopped
1 clove garlic, finely chopped
2 tablespoons sunflower oil
1 teaspoon ground coriander
1 lb. skinless, boneless chicken breast halves
lime slices and chili rings, to garnish
PEANUT SAUCE:
3 tablespoons smooth peanut butter
⅔ cup coconut milk
2 teaspoons Thai red curry paste
1 tablespoon Thai fish sauce
1 tablespoon soft brown sugar

Mix together lime juice, lemongrass, garlic, sunflower oil, and ground coriander.

Cut chicken into ¾-in. cubes and add to marinade. Turn to coat, cover and leave to marinate for at least 1 hour. Meanwhile, make peanut sauce. Mix together peanut butter, coconut milk, red curry paste, fish sauce, and sugar, and set aside. Soak 12 bamboo skewers in water for 30 minutes.

Thread chicken on to skewers. Grill on a rack over hot coals, turning frequently, for 8–10 minutes, until cooked through and browned on the outside. Garnish with lime slices and chili rings, and serve with the peanut sauce.

Serves 6.

CHICKEN LIVER KABOBS

1¼ lb. chicken livers, rinsed and trimmed
¼ cup sunflower oil
1 onion, finely chopped
1 clove garlic, crushed
¼ cup red wine
½ teaspoon Tabasco sauce
1½ teaspoons dark soft brown sugar
12 black peppercorns
salt
18 canned water chestnuts
1 large red bell pepper, seeded and sliced into rings

Halve or quarter chicken livers, depending on size.

Heat oil in a small saucepan and gently fry onion until soft. Add garlic, wine, Tabasco sauce, sugar, and peppercorns, and season with salt. Bring to a boil, add prepared livers, and simmer for 1 minute to firm liver. Remove from heat and leave to marinate for 2 hours.

Using a slotted spoon, remove livers from marinade. Thread alternately on to 6 skewers, with the water chestnuts. Discard peppercorns from marinade. Grill on rack over hot coals for 6–8 minutes, turning frequently, and basting occasionally with marinade. Serve with red bell pepper rings, dressed with remaining marinade.

Serves 6.

Note: If using bamboo or wooden skewers, soak in water 30 minutes before using.

MANGO TURKEY

TANDOORI TURKEY

1 clove garlic, crushed
1 teaspoon dried oregano
½ teaspoon ground allspice
salt and freshly ground black pepper
4 turkey steaks
7 oz. canned mango slices with their syrup
7 oz. canned chopped tomatoes
1–2 teaspoons hot pepper sauce
1 tablespoon oil
1 tablespoon butter
1 small mango, peeled and sliced, to garnish

In a dish, mix together garlic, oregano, all-spice, and salt and pepper. Turn turkey in mixture to coat. Cover and leave in a cool place for 1 hour.

Meanwhile, place canned mango slices with their syrup, and the tomatoes, in a blender or food processor and blend until smooth. Pour into a saucepan, and add hot pepper sauce, and salt and pepper. Bring to a boil, cover, and simmer gently for 3 minutes. The sauce should be quite thick.

Grill turkey steaks on a rack over hot coals for about 5 minutes on each side until cooked through, basting with mango sauce and turning frequently. Grill fresh mango slices until lightly browned. Serve turkey with remaining mango sauce, garnished with mango slices.

Serves 4.

6 skinless, boneless turkey breast halves, 6 oz. each
juice 3 small lemons
¾ cup plain yogurt
½ cup vegetable oil
4 cloves garlic, crushed
2 teaspoons paprika
2 teaspoons ground cumin
4 teaspoons turmeric
½ teaspoon ground ginger
2 teaspoons salt
Cucumber Raita (see page 132), to serve

Deeply slash turkey breast halves on both sides. Place in a single layer in a large, shallow, nonporous dish.

Mix together lemon juice, yogurt, oil, garlic, paprika, cumin, turmeric, ginger, and salt; blend well. Pour over turkey breast halves, then turn turkey breast halves to ensure both sides are coated. Cover and marinate in refrigerator for at least 12 hours.

Remove turkey breast halves from marinade and grill on an oiled rack over hot coals for 10 minutes each side until cooked through, basting frequently with marinade. Serve with Cucumber Raita.

Serves 6–8.

SPIT-ROAST DUCKLING

4½-lb. oven-ready duckling
salt and freshly ground black pepper
⅔ cup pineapple juice
SAUCE:
2½–3 cups pitted black cherries
1 clove garlic, unpeeled
⅔ cup port
1¾ cups well-flavored beef stock
1 tablespoon fecule or potato flour
2 tablespoons butter
1 tablespoon red currant jelly

Prick duck skin in several places. Season inside and out with salt and pepper. Sprinkle inside with a little pineapple juice.

To make sauce, put cherries, garlic, port, and stock in a saucepan and poach until cherries are tender. Remove cherries with a slotted spoon and set aside. Discard garlic. Blend fecule or potato flour with 2 tablespoons cold water, stir into liquid in pan and bring to a boil, stirring continuously, until thickened. Mix in butter and red currant jelly, and season with salt and pepper. Add cherries and cook until hot. Reheat on side of barbecue when duck is cooked.

When barbecue coals are hot, move them toward side and place a roasting pan in center. This must be large enough to catch drips (which are considerable). Fix duck on to a spit or put in a roasting basket. Grill over medium-hot coals for 2½–3 hours until well cooked. Foil tenting or covering with grill lid will hasten cooking. Do not open for 30 minutes, then baste every 10 minutes with pineapple juice. Pour away fat; mix juices into sauce and serve with duck.

Serves 6–8.

CHINESE DUCK

3 duck breast quarters, 1 lb. each
hoisin sauce, for serving
bunch scallions, trimmed and shredded
MARINADE:
2 teaspoons miso paste
⅓ cup dry sherry or saki
¼–½ teaspoon five-spice powder
CHINESE PANCAKES:
2 cups strong white flour
sesame oil

Deeply score the duck flesh through to the bone in a crisscross fashion. Thoroughly blend marinade ingredients together.

Put duck in a dish; add marinade. Cover; chill for 12 hours, basting occasionally. Make pancakes. Put flour in bowl; add ¼ cup boiling water and mix to a dough. Knead for 10 minutes. Cover with damp cloth and leave for 30 minutes. Knead for 5 minutes; divide into 16 pieces. Work with 2 pieces at a time; press out to 2-in. diameter. Oil one side of each piece; sandwich oiled sides together. With a rolling pin, press out to 7-in. circles. Cook in an ungreased pan over low heat for 1–1½ minutes each side until opaque and pale yellow. Peel apart.

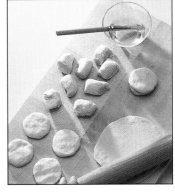

Grill duck quarters on a rack over low coals in a covered barbecue for about 1 hour, turning them over 3 times during cooking and basting with any remaining marinade. If using an unlidded barbecue, tent with foil, and allow extra time. Shred the meat from the bone while duck is still hot. Serve a portion of shredded duck with 3 or 4 pancakes, a tiny dish of hoisin sauce, and the onions. The pancakes are eaten spread with sauce, and filled with duck and onions.

Serves 3–4.

DUCK WITH KIWI FRUIT

2 boneless duck breast halves, about 8 oz. each
½-in. piece fresh ginger, peeled and finely chopped
1 clove garlic, finely chopped
2 tablespoons dry sherry
2 kiwi fruit
1 teaspoon sesame oil
SAUCE:
¼ cup dry sherry
2 tablespoons light soy sauce
4 teaspoons honey

Remove skin and fat from duck breast halves. With a sharp knife, score flesh in diagonal lines. Beat with a meat tenderizer until ½ in. thick.

Place duck breast halves in a shallow dish and add ginger, garlic, and sherry. Cover and chill 1 hour. Peel and thinly slice kiwi fruit and halve crosswise. Cover and chill until required. Drain duck breast halves and place on barbecue rack. Brush with sesame oil and grill over hot coals for 8 minutes. Turn and brush again with oil. Cook 8–10 minutes until tender and cooked through.

Meanwhile, put sauce ingredients in a saucepan, bring to a boil, and simmer 5 minutes or until syrupy. Drain duck breast halves on paper towels and slice thinly. Arrange duck slices and kiwi fruit on serving plates. Pour sauce over duck and serve.

Serves 4.

APPLEJACK DUCK

4 duck breast quarters, 1 lb. each
1¼ cups apple juice concentrate
2 teaspoons ground cloves
2 teaspoons dried oregano
1 teaspoon salt
½ teaspoon freshly ground black pepper
Walnut Apple Crescents (see page 101), to serve

Using a sharp knife, diagonally score through skin and flesh of duck quarters, creating a diamond pattern. Place in a glass dish, skin-side down.

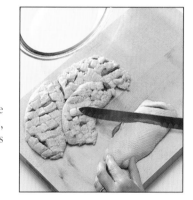

Mix together apple juice concentrate, ground cloves, oregano, salt, and pepper, and add 1¼ cups water. Pour over duck quarters. Cover and marinate in the refrigerator for at least 6 hours, or preferably overnight.

Remove duck quarters from marinade; set aside marinade. Grill on a rack over medium-hot coals for about 1¼ hours, turning every 20 minutes and basting with marinade. Cooking will be hastened if dish is tented with foil or cooked in a covered grill. Serve with Walnut Apple Crescents.

Serves 4.

SPICY GRILLED QUAIL

1 clove garlic
salt
1 teaspoon ground cumin
1 teaspoon ground coriander
½ small onion
1 tablespoon chopped fresh cilantro
pinch red pepper
¼ cup olive oil
8 quail
vine leaves, parsley, and lemon slices, to garnish

Put all the ingredients except quail and garnish in a food processor. Process to make a paste.

Spread the paste over quail. Cover and leave to marinate in a cool place for 2 hours.

Grill quail on a rack over hot coals for 10–15 minutes, turning frequently, until cooked and slightly charred on the outside. Serve quail on vine leaves, garnished with parsley and lemon slices.

Serves 4.

Variation: Baby game hens or chicken portions can be cooked in this way.

QUAIL & ARAB SALAD

8 quail
⅓ cup olive oil
juice 2 lemons
4 cloves garlic, crushed
salt and freshly ground black pepper
2 tablespoons chopped fresh parsley
ARAB SALAD:
1 teaspoon harissa
5 tablespoons olive oil
2 tablespoons lemon juice
8 oz. cherry tomatoes, halved
1 small or ½ large cucumber, cut into cubes
1 bunch scallions, chopped
1 bunch watercress, washed and dried

With a pair of kitchen scissors, cut quail down the backbone, turn them over, and press down on the breastbone to flatten them out. Pat dry with paper towels. Pass 2 skewers through each quail. Place them in a glass dish. In a bowl, mix together olive oil, lemon juice, garlic, salt, pepper, and parsley. Pour over quail. Cover and marinate in the refrigerator for 4–6 hours.

To make the salad, in a bowl, mix together harissa, olive oil, lemon juice, salt, and pepper. Add tomatoes, cucumber, scallions, and watercress. Mix lightly. Remove quail from marinade and grill on a rack over hot coals for 10–15 minutes, turning during cooking and brushing with marinade. Serve with the salad.

Serves 4.

Note: If using bamboo or wooden skewers, soak in water 30 minutes before using.

CLARET & PEPPER STEAKS

1¼ cups red wine
½ cup olive oil
2 tablespoons green peppercorns, ground
2 tablespoons coriander seeds
8 sirloin steaks, 1 in. thick, trimmed
cilantro sprigs, to garnish
lightly salted, whipped cream, to serve (optional)

In a large bowl, mix together red wine, olive oil, ground peppercorns, and coriander seeds.

Prick steaks deeply, then immerse them in marinade and leave for at least 2 hours.

Grill steaks on a rack over hot coals. Initially grill for 1 minute on each side to seal, then continue cooking, turning steaks occasionally and basting frequently with marinade until cooked as desired. As a general rule, a rare steak will require 3–4 minutes on each side; a medium steak 6–7 minutes and a well-done steak 8–10 minutes. Garnish with sprigs of cilantro and serve plain or with a spoonful of lightly salted whipped cream, if desired.

Serves 8.

SURPRISE BEEFBURGERS

1¼ lb. lean ground beef
1 small onion, finely chopped
1 teaspoon dried mixed herbs
⅔ cup rolled oats
1 egg, beaten
salt and freshly ground black pepper
3-oz. piece cheese, such as Gouda
1 tablespoon oil

Put beef, onion, herbs, and oats into a bowl and mix together to break up beef. Add the beaten egg, salt, and pepper, and bind together.

With floured hands, divide the mixture into 6, then flatten each piece on a board or counter. Cut cheese into 6 and place a piece in the middle of each round of meat.

Carefully enclose cheese in meat mixture and form into a burger shape. Brush with oil and grill on a rack over medium-hot coals for about 4–5 minutes on each side until golden.

Serves 6.

RUM-GRILLED STEAK

⅔ cup rum
2 cloves garlic, crushed
1 teaspoon chili powder
1 tablespoon finely chopped fresh cilantro
½ teaspoon Tabasco sauce
2¼-lb. piece rump or sirloin steak, 2 in. thick

Mix together rum, garlic, chili powder, cilantro, and Tabasco sauce.

Rinse steak under cold water and dry. Place in a shallow, ovenproof dish and pour rum mixture over. Cover, and leave for at least 30 minutes, but preferably in a refrigerator overnight. Remove steak from dish; set aside marinade.

Grill steak on a rack over hot coals for 5 minutes a side, or longer if desired, turning occasionally and basting frequently with marinade. Carve steak into thin slices and serve.

Serves 4.

Note: If steak has been in refrigerator overnight, transfer to room temperature 45 minutes before cooking.

VIETNAMESE BEEF WRAPS

2 cloves garlic, chopped
3 shallots, chopped
2 tablespoons chopped lemongrass
1 tablespoon sugar
1 tablespoon fish sauce
1 tablespoon sesame oil
½ teaspoon freshly ground black pepper
1-lb. beef fillet, cut across the grain into thin slices about 2 in. long
8 sheets dried rice paper, halved if large
mint and cilantro leaves, to serve
Spicy Fish Sauce (see page 128), to serve

Using a mortar and pestle, pound garlic, shallots, lemongrass, and sugar to a paste.

Place paste in a medium bowl with fish sauce, sesame oil, and pepper. Blend well. Add beef and marinate 1 hour, or longer in the refrigerator. Grill beef on a rack over hot coals for about 1 minute, turning once.

To serve, dip each piece of dried rice paper in warm water to soften it, then place a slice of beef on one end of the paper, put a mint leaf and some cilantro on top of the beef, and roll into a neat wraps. Dip the wraps in the Spicy Fish Sauce before eating.

Serves 4 as a main course or 6–8 as an appetizer.

BEEF & BACON SATAY

12 oz. lean beef
12 oz. unsmoked bacon slices
1 onion, finely chopped
finely grated rind and juice 2 lemons
4 tablespoons ground coriander
2 tablespoons ground cumin
¾ cup crunchy peanut butter
½ cup peanut oil
2 tablespoons honey
4 zucchini
scallions, to garnish

Cut beef into 1-in. cubes. Put in a shallow dish. Halve bacon slices lengthwise.

Stretch bacon slices on a counter with a round-bladed knife drawn flat along each slice. Roll each up tightly along its length and add to dish with cubed beef. Mix together onion, lemon rind and juice, coriander, cumin, peanut butter, oil, and honey. Pour over beef and bacon and marinate for at least 1 hour, basting occasionally.

Soak 18 bamboo skewers in water for 1 hour. Peel zucchini, cut in half lengthwise, and then into ½-in. chunks. Alternately thread beef cubes, bacon rolls, and zucchini chunks on to skewers. Grill on a rack over hot coals for about 20 minutes, turning frequently. Garnish with scallions and serve.

Makes 18.

SKEWERED BEEF KABOBS

1½ lb. lean ground beef
1 onion, finely chopped
2-in. piece fresh ginger, grated
3 cloves garlic, crushed
1 teaspoon chili powder
1 tablespoon garam masala
1 tablespoon chopped fresh cilantro
1 tablespoon ground almonds
1 egg, beaten
¼ cup chickpea flour
6 tablespoons plain yogurt
2 teaspoons vegetable oil
onion rings and thin lemon wedges, to garnish

Mix together beef, onion, ginger, garlic, spices, cilantro, almonds, egg, and flour in a large bowl. Cover beef mixture and refrigerate up to 4 hours to allow flavors to blend. Shape into 16 to 20 long ovals; thread on to 4 long skewers. (If using bamboo or wooden skewers, soak in water 30 minutes before using.)

Mix together yogurt and oil, and brush over kabobs. Grill kabobs on a rack over medium-hot coals for 20–25 minutes, until well browned and cooked through. Brush kabobs with remaining yogurt and oil mixture, and turn occasionally during cooking. Serve hot, garnished with onion rings and lemon wedges.

Serves 4.

Note: The meatball mixture can be made up to 12 hours in advance and refrigerated.

LIGHT BEEF SATAY

1 lb. lean beef round or sirloin steak
MARINADE:
1 shallot, finely chopped
1-in. piece fresh ginger, peeled and finely chopped
2 cloves garlic, finely chopped
rind and juice 1 lemon
2 teaspoons garam masala
salt and freshly ground black pepper
1 teaspoon light soy sauce
SAUCE:
6 tablespoons unsweetened shredded coconut
2 tablespoons crunchy peanut butter
1 tablespoon soft brown sugar
1 teaspoon sunflower oil
2 cloves garlic, finely chopped
1 fresh red chili, cored, seeded, and chopped
1 tablespoon dark soy sauce
strips fresh red chili, to garnish

Soak 8 bamboo skewers in cold water. Trim any fat from beef and cut into ¼-in. strips. Place in a shallow dish.

Mix together marinade ingredients and pour over beef. Mix well, cover and chill 2 hours.

Meanwhile, make the sauce. Place shredded coconut in a bowl and pour 1 cup boiling water over coconut. Leave for 30 minutes. Place a fine strainer over a bowl and pour mixture through strainer, pressing coconut with a spatula or spoon to extract all the water. Discard coconut.

Blend coconut water with peanut butter and brown sugar. Heat oil in a nonstick or well-seasoned wok and stir-fry garlic and chili 1 minute. Stir in peanut butter mixture and soy sauce, and bring to a boil. Reduce heat and simmer sauce 10 minutes, stirring occasionally, until thickened. Set aside.

Thread beef strips along each skewer in the shape of an S. Cover ends of skewers with foil to prevent burning. Grill beef on a rack over hot coals for 3 or 4 minutes on each side. Drain on paper towels. Reheat peanut sauce. Garnish with strips of red chili. Serve skewers on a bed of rice with the peanut sauce and lime wedges.

Serves 4.

STEAK & SEAFOOD PLATTER

4 large sirloin steaks, about 1 in. thick
8 oz. cooked peeled shrimp
2 cloves garlic
¼ teaspoon salt
½ cup butter
4 teaspoons paprika
¼ teaspoon Tabasco sauce
¼ cup heavy cream
4 cooked unpeeled jumbo shrimp, to garnish

Pierce steaks on both sides with a fork. Spread out shrimp on a plate and cover with a double sheet of paper towels to absorb excess moisture.

Crush garlic with salt and put in a small saucepan with butter, paprika, and Tabasco. Warm gently over low heat until butter is very soft but not melted. Stir in cream and remove pan from heat.

Brush steaks on both sides with butter mixture, then fold peeled shrimp into mixture remaining in the pan. Grill steaks on a rack over hot coals, turning them over frequently. When steaks are nearly cooked, heat pan of shrimp on side of the grill for 2–3 minutes. To serve, pile shrimp on top of steaks and garnish with unpeeled shrimp.

Serves 4.

STEAKS WITH SHERRY DIP

4 lean beef fillets, about 4 oz. each
freshly ground black pepper
1 tablespoon dry sherry
1-in. piece fresh ginger, peeled and finely chopped
1 teaspoon sesame oil
4 scallions, finely chopped, and scallion strips, to garnish
DIP:
2 teaspoons sunflower oil
4 scallions, finely chopped
½-in. piece fresh ginger, peeled and finely chopped
¼ cup dry sherry
2 tablespoons dark soy sauce

Make the dip. Heat oil in a nonstick or well-seasoned wok and stir-fry scallions and ginger 2 minutes or until soft. Drain well on paper towels and place in a bowl. Mix in sherry and soy sauce. Set aside.

Trim fat from steaks and lightly tenderize with a meat tenderizer. Season both sides with pepper. Mix together sherry, ginger, and sesame oil. Place steaks on barbecue rack and brush with sherry mixture. Grill on the rack over hot coals for 3 or 4 minutes on each side, basting to prevent drying out. Drain on paper towels. Garnish steaks with chopped scallions and scallion strips and serve with the dip.

Serves 4.

MOROCCAN BROCHETTES

1 onion, roughly chopped
2 cloves garlic, roughly chopped
1 fresh red chili, cored, seeded, and cut into strips
1½ lb. ground beef
4 tablespoons chopped fresh parsley
½ teaspoon dried oregano
1 teaspoon each paprika and ground cumin
1 teaspoon salt
½ teaspoon freshly ground black pepper
yogurt and chopped scallions, to serve

Place onion, garlic, and chili in a food processor and process briefly. Add ground beef, parsley, oregano, paprika, cumin, salt and pepper, and blend to a paste.

Transfer mixture to a bowl, cover, and leave to stand for 30 minutes. With damp hands, take an egg-size piece of mixture and press it into a long sausage shape around a skewer. (Skewers made from rosemary twigs may be used to add extra fragrance. If using bamboo or wooden skewers, soak in water 30 minutes before using.) Continue until all the meat mixture is used.

Grill the brochettes on a rack over hot coals for 6–7 minutes, turning frequently, until well browned on the outside but still moist inside. To serve, spoon yogurt over the brochettes and sprinkle with chopped scallions.

Serves 6.

STEAKS WITH CHILI SAUCE

4 lean beef fillets, about 4 oz. each
1 teaspoon dark soy sauce
1 clove garlic, finely chopped
1 teaspoon sesame oil
2 tablespoons chopped fresh chives, to garnish
SAUCE:
1 teaspoon sunflower oil
1 fresh green chili, cored, seeded, and finely chopped
1 shallot, finely chopped
1 teaspoon chili sauce
2 tablespoons red rice vinegar
¼ cup dry sherry
1 teaspoon brown sugar

Trim any fat from steaks. Tenderize lightly with a meat tenderizer or rolling pin.

Mix together soy sauce, garlic, and sesame oil and brush over steaks. Grill steaks on a rack over hot coals 3 or 4 minutes on each side, brushing with the soy sauce mixture to prevent drying out.

Meanwhile, make the sauce. Heat oil in a nonstick or well-seasoned wok and stir-fry chili and shallot over a low heat 1 minute. Add remaining ingredients and simmer 2 or 3 minutes. Drain cooked steaks on paper towels. Sprinkle with chives and serve with the sauce.

Serves 4.

PLOWMAN'S BURGERS

3 eggs
½ teaspoon freshly ground black pepper
3 lb. freshly ground lean beef
4–6 tablespoons bottled fruity sauce
8 oz. Emmental cheese
shredded iceberg lettuce, to garnish

Beat eggs in a large bowl, season with pepper, and mix in ground beef.

Form mixture into 24 thin burgers. Spread 12 of the burgers with sauce, leaving a border to that the sauce does not quite reach the edges.

Slice cheese thinly and cut out 12 circles smaller than the burgers. Lay slices of cheese over the sauce, topping with cheese trimmings. Cover with remaining burgers and press edges together to seal. Grill on a rack over hot coals for 8–10 minutes on each side. Garnish with shredded lettuce and serve with the relish of your choice.

Makes 12.

BEEF IN TAHINI PASTE

1¼ lb. beef fillet
4 tablespoons tahini
8 tablespoons sesame oil
½ teaspoon garlic salt
1 tablespoon lemon juice
8 scallions, finely chopped
freshly ground black pepper
3 tablespoons sesame seeds, toasted
scallions, to garnish

Slice beef across the grain into 20–25 thin slices.

In a bowl, combine tahini, sesame oil, garlic salt, lemon juice, and onions; season with pepper. Using tongs, dip beef slivers, one at a time, into tahini baste, then spread them out on a board or tray. Cover with plastic wrap or foil and leave for at least 1 hour for the flavors to impregnate the meat. Set aside the tahini baste.

Prepare a hot barbecue and press the meat slices, basted-sides down, on to the rack. Using barbecue tongs, turn the slices over after 30 seconds and brush with the remaining baste. Grill for an additional 1–1½ minutes. Arrange on a hot platter and sprinkled with toasted sesame seeds. Garnish with scallions.

Serves 6–7.

MEATBALL KABOBS

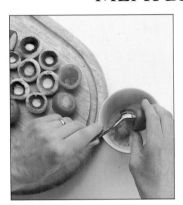

4 oz. cherry tomatoes
1 cup button mushrooms
4 small zucchini
8 oz. ground beef or lamb
1 small onion, finely chopped
1 tablespoon finely chopped fresh cilantro
¼ teaspoon ground cumin
generous pinch red pepper
1 egg, beaten
salt and freshly ground black pepper
oil, for brushing

Slice tops off tomatoes; using a teaspoon carefully scoop out seeds. Remove mushroom stalks, finely chop, and set aside.

Cut zucchini into 1-in. chunks, then steam for 5 minutes. Drain. Using a teaspoon scoop out ½ in. of flesh from one end. In a medium bowl, combine meat, onion, cilantro, cumin, red pepper, egg, and mushroom stalks. Season with salt and pepper.

Fill tomatoes, mushroom caps, and zucchini with meat mixture, and thread alternately on to metal skewers so they are touching closely. Brush with olive oil and grill on a rack over hot coals for 10 minutes each side, making sure they do not burn.

Serves 6.

Note: Any left-over mixture can be fried and served with tortilla chips.

MINI ROASTS

2½ lb. rolled topside of beef
Skewered Potato Crisps (see page 95), to serve
MARINADE:
1 red onion, chopped
1 small green bell pepper, seeded and chopped
1 green eating apple, peeled, cored and chopped
1¼ cups beef stock
2 tablespoons olive oil
2 tablespoons red currant jelly
1 tablespoon tomato paste
1 tablespoon Worcestershire sauce
1 teaspoon arrowroot
1 tablespoon crushed lemon verbena leaves

Cut beef through grain into 4 cylindrical chunks. Discard string. Remove fat and cut it into 4 strips. Shape each piece of meat into a barrel by rolling with the hands, if necessary. Place one strip of fat lengthwise down one side of each piece. Tie with string in 1 or 2 places. To make the marinade, in a food processor or blender purée onion, bell pepper, and apple with remaining marinade ingredients.

Heat mixture in a heavy-based saucepan, stirring occasionally until boiling; simmer, uncovered, for 10 minutes until reduced by a quarter. Leave to cool, then marinade the beef pieces for 12 hours. Grill beef on an oiled rack over hot coals for about 20 minutes if using a covered barbecue, or 35–40 minutes on an open barbecue. Turn frequently and baste with the marinade. Serve with Skewered Potato Crisps and the relish of your choice.

Serves 4–8.

GRILLED STEAK

20-oz. piece sirloin steak
2 tablespoons sunflower oil
1 tablespoon chopped fresh cilantro
salt and freshly ground black pepper
⅓ cup fresh orange juice
1 tablespoon fresh lime juice
2 teaspoons cider vinegar
orange slices, to garnish

With a sharp knife, trim excess fat from steak.

Wipe meat with damp paper towels. Put in a shallow dish. Put oil, cilantro, salt, pepper, orange juice, lime juice, and vinegar in a bowl and mix well. Pour over steak, cover and marinate in the refrigerator overnight.

Transfer to room temperature 45 minutes before cooking. Lift steak from marinade, allowing excess to drain off; set aside marinade. Cut steak into 4 equal size pieces. Grill steaks on rack over hot coals for 5 minutes each side, or longer if desired, basting with marinade. Cook for a little longer if a more well-cooked meat is preferred. Garnish with orange slices.

Serves 4.

FILLET STEAK ENVELOPES

4 fillet steaks, 6 oz. each
6 oz. veal escalope
½ cup butter, softened
4 cloves garlic, crushed
1 teaspoon dried basil
salt and freshly ground black pepper

Using a rolling pin, flatten steaks between sheets of waxed or nonstick paper to ½-in. thickness. Beat veal escalope thinly and cut into 4 equal pieces.

Make a deep horizontal slit through each steak to form a pocket. Mix butter, garlic and basil thoroughly together and season with salt and pepper. Spread half the butter mixture inside each pocket, then insert a piece of veal into each.

Spread outside of steaks with remaining butter mixture. Grill on a rack over hot coals for 2 minutes on each side to seal. Position steaks away from fierce heat and cook over medium-hot coals for an additional 6–8 minutes on each side, depending on taste.

Serves 4.

VITELLO SIROTTI

8 veal escalopes, 6 oz. each
3 tablespoons butter
12 black olives, pitted and chopped
scant ½ cup pine nuts, finely chopped
1¼ cups soft bread crumbs
salt and freshly ground black pepper
SAUCE:
14 oz. canned tomatoes
1 clove garlic, peeled
1 handful parsley sprigs
1 tablespoon olive oil
6 tablespoons Cinzano Rosso

Beat escalopes thinly between sheets of waxed or nonstick paper.

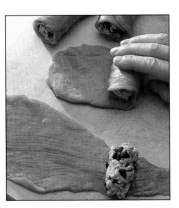

Beat butter until soft, then mix in chopped olives, pine nuts, and bread crumbs. Season with salt and pepper. Divide mixture into 8 portions, place along one edge of each escalope, and roll up.

Securely wrap each escalope individually in well-oiled, double thickness foil. Purée all sauce ingredients together. Strain through a nylon sieve into a saucepan and cook over moderate heat, stirring continuously, until sauce thickens. Keep warm. Grill veal rolls on a rack over medium-hot coals for 30–45 minutes, or for 20 minutes in a covered barbecue. Turn pockets over halfway through cooking. Unwrap veal pockets and serve with the sauce.

Serves 8.

PITA BURGERS

2 eggs, beaten
1 teaspoon turmeric
1 teaspoon cumin
¼ teaspoon red pepper
2 cloves garlic, very finely chopped
2¼ lb. freshly ground lean beef
2 cups fresh bread crumbs
8 pitted green olives, chopped
6 pita breads, halved
lettuce and stuffed green olives, sliced, to garnish

In a large bowl, beat eggs with turmeric, cumin, and red pepper. Stir in garlic.

Mix meat, bread crumbs, and chopped olives into egg mixture and form into 12 burger shapes. Grill burgers on a rack over hot coals for 8–10 minutes on each side.

When burgers are nearly ready, warm the halved pita breads on the side of the rack. Open cut sides of each pita and insert a burger. Serve wrapped in a paper napkin. Garnish with lettuce and sliced stuffed olives.

Makes 12.

GRILLED PORK WITH MISO

4 pork loin steaks
lemon wedges, to garnish
MISO SAUCE:
3 tablespoons red miso
3 scallions, finely chopped
2 teaspoons sake
2 teaspoons fresh ginger juice

Remove any fat from pork. If pork is more than ⅔ in. thick, slice in half horizontally.

Grill pork on a well-oiled rack over medium-hot coals for 3–4 minutes on each side or until both sides are golden brown and pork is just cooked.

Make the miso sauce. In a bowl, mix all the sauce ingredients. Spoon miso sauce evenly on to center of pork steaks and continue cooking for 1 minute until the miso sauce is fairly dry. Transfer pork steaks to 4 individual plates, garnish with lemon wedges, and serve.

Serves 4.

MEXICAN MUFFINS

4 fillet steaks, ½-in. thick, 3 oz. each
1 large or 2 small ripe but firm avocados
2 teaspoons fresh lemon juice
2 oz. Gorgonzola cheese, crumbled
2 muffins
red pepper

Grill steaks on an oiled rack over hot coals according to desired doneness.

Meanwhile, split muffins in half and toast on both sides on the barbecue rack. Halve avocado and remove pit. Scoop out flesh and, using a stainless steel fork, mash with lemon juice and cheese.

When steaks are cooked, spread with half avocado mixture, cover with toasted muffin halves, then invert on to hot serving plates so that muffins form a base. Top with a dollop of remaining avocado mixture and sprinkle with red pepper.

Serves 4.

Note: The avocado mixture should not be prepared in advance or it will discolor.

STICKY RIBS

1½ lb. pork spare ribs
5 tablespoons tomato sauce
2 tablespoons honey
1 tablespoon soy sauce
1 tablespoon wine vinegar
1 tablespoon Worcestershire sauce
2 tablespoons orange juice

Cut ribs into single rib pieces, if necessary. Grill the ribs on a rack over medium-hot coals for about 5 minutes, turning once.

Meanwhile, mix remaining ingredients together. Brush ribs on both sides with the glaze, and continue cooking ribs for an additional 5 minutes.

Turn the ribs over, brush again with the glaze and cook for an additional 5 minutes or until richly golden and cooked through. Serve hot.

Serves 6.

GRILLED SPARE RIBS

2 tablespoons chopped fresh cilantro stalks
3 cloves garlic, chopped
1 teaspoon black peppercorns, cracked
1 teaspoon grated kaffir lime peel
1 tablespoon green curry paste
2 teaspoons fish sauce
1½ teaspoons crushed palm sugar
¾ cup coconut milk
2 lb. pork spare ribs, trimmed
scallions, to garnish

Using a mortar and pestle or small blender, pound or mix together cilantro, garlic, peppercorns, lime peel, curry paste, fish sauce, and sugar. Stir in coconut milk. Place spare ribs in a shallow dish and pour spiced coconut mixture over. Cover and marinate in the refrigerator for 3 hours, basting occasionally.

Grill ribs on a rack over medium heat for about 5 minutes a side, until cooked through and brown, basting occasionally with coconut mixture. Garnish with scallions.

Serves 4–6.

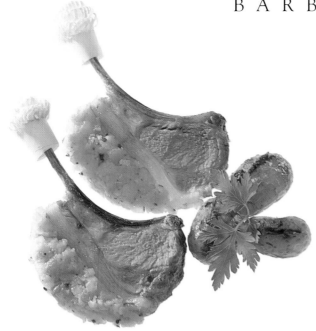

JUNIPER CROWN ROAST

2¼ lb. crown roast of lamb
STUFFING:
3 tablespoons butter
1 small onion, finely chopped
½ cup well-seasoned hot stock
1 cup soft bread crumbs
½ cup dried apricots, finely chopped
8 juniper berries, finely ground

Make the stuffing. Melt butter and cook onion until transparent; remove from heat. Add stock and remaining stuffing ingredients and mix to form a soft mixture. Leave for 10 minutes.

Place crown roast, bone ends uppermost, on a circle of well-oiled, double thickness foil. Press stuffing into center cavity.

Grill on a rack over medium-hot coals in a lidded barbecue, or make a foil tent to enclose joint if using an open barbecue. The crown roast will take 35–50 minutes depending on which type of barbecue is used. Place a cutlet frill over each bone before serving.

Serves 4–5.

ASIAN SPARE RIBS

6 lb. lean pork spare ribs
scallions, to garnish
SAUCE:
½ cup hoisin sauce
½ cup miso paste
1¼ cups tomato paste
1½ teaspoons ground ginger
1½ teaspoons Chinese five-spice powder
1 cup dark soft brown sugar
3 cloves garlic, crushed
1 teaspoon salt
2 tablespoons saki or dry sherry

Separate the ribs and trim away most of the fat.

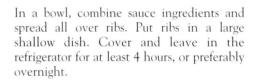

In a bowl, combine sauce ingredients and spread all over ribs. Put ribs in a large shallow dish. Cover and leave in the refrigerator for at least 4 hours, or preferably overnight.

Place a drip pan in medium-hot coals and grill ribs on a rack above the pan for 45–60 minutes, turning occasionally and basting with sauce. Heat any remaining sauce gently and serve separately. Garnish ribs with scallions.

Serves 8.

Note: Offer guests warmed damp cloths or sachets of finger wipes.

PORK WITH HERB SAUCE

SPICY PORK KABOBS

½ cup fresh white bread crumbs
2 tablespoons white wine vinegar
2 cloves garlic
2 canned anchovy fillets, drained
4 tablespoons chopped fresh parsley
2 teaspoons capers, drained
1 hard-boiled egg yolk
1 cup extra-virgin olive oil
salt and freshly ground black pepper
4 boneless pork loin chops, about 1 in. thick

In a small bowl, soak bread crumbs in vinegar.

1 lb. boned pork loin
lemon slices and fresh bay leaves, to garnish
MARINADE:
2 teaspoons paprika
1 teaspoon finely crushed coriander seeds
1½ teaspoons ground cumin
1 teaspoon finely chopped fresh oregano
¼ teaspoon ground ginger
generous pinch each ground cinnamon, red pepper,
  and grated nutmeg
1 bay leaf, finely crumbled
2 tablespoons olive oil
salt and freshly ground black pepper

Cut pork into 1-in. cubes.

Meanwhile, using a mortar and pestle, crush garlic with anchovy fillets, parsley, capers, and egg yolk. Squeeze vinegar from bread crumbs, then mix bread crumbs into garlic-anchovy mixture. Slowly stir in oil to make a creamy sauce. Season with salt and pepper. Set aside.

In a bowl, mix together all the marinade ingredients. Add pork cubes to marinade and stir to coat evenly. Cover bowl and refrigerate 8–12 hours, turning pork occasionally.

Grill pork chops on a rack over hot coals for about 12 minutes on each side until lightly browned and cooked through but still juicy in center. Season chops with salt and pepper, and top with some of the sauce. Serve immediately with remaining sauce.

Serves 4.

Thread pork on to small skewers. Grill on a rack over hot coals for about 7 minutes, turning occasionally, or until pork is cooked through but still juicy. Garnish with lemon slices and bay leaves, and serve hot.

Serves 4.

Note: If using bamboo or wooden skewers, soak in water 30 minutes before using.

GRILLED PORK

1½ lb. pork loin, cut into long strips
shredded Chinese cabbage, to serve
MARINADE:
⅔ cup soft brown sugar
1 tablespoon dark soy sauce
1 tablespoon oyster sauce
2 tablespoons rice wine or dry sherry
1 teaspoon sesame oil
½ teaspoon sea salt
½ teaspoon edible red food coloring (optional)

Make marinade; in a small bowl, stir together sugar and 3 tablespoons boiling water until sugar dissolves, then stir in remaining ingredients. Cool slightly.

Place pork in a medium bowl. Pour marinade over, turning pork several times to coat evenly. Refrigerate for 8 hours, turning pork several times. Lift pork from marinade, allowing excess to drain off; set aside marinade.

Thread meat on to meat skewers and grill on a rack over hot coals for about 8 minutes until crisp and cooked, basting several times with reserved marinade. Remove pork from skewers, cut into bite-size pieces, and serve on a bed of shredded Chinese cabbage.

Serves 4–6.

Note: If using bamboo or wooden skewers, soak in water 30 minutes before using.

JEWELED PORK CHOPS

3 shallots
½ small red bell pepper
½ small green bell pepper
6 tablespoons shelled pistachio nuts
6 large pork chops, 1 in. thick
2 tablespoons walnut oil
2 tablespoons lemon juice
salt and freshly ground black pepper
12 tiny pearl onions; 3 cocktail gherkins, thickly
   sliced and 6 cherries, pitted, to garnish

Peel and roughly chop shallots. Seed and finely dice bell peppers. Halve nuts.

Put shallots, bell peppers, and nuts in a bowl and cover with boiling water. Leave to stand for 10 minutes, then drain and discard liquid.

Using the tip of a sharp knife, make several small incisions into both sides of chops. Insert pieces of shallot, bell pepper, and nut to stud surfaces. Mix together oil and lemon juice and use to brush over both sides of chops. Season with salt and pepper. Grill on a rack over medium-hot coals for 15–18 minutes on each side, basting occasionally with oil mixture. Garnish with pearl onions, gherkins, and cherries, threaded on to wooden toothpicks.

Serves 6.

DANISH PATTIES

6 oz. trimmed pork fillet
6 oz. cooked ham
6 oz. Danish salami, skinned
parsley or cilantro sprigs, to garnish
DOUGH:
3 cups all-purpose flour
pinch salt
1 teaspoon baking powder
¼ cup shortening
⅔ cup milk

Using a food processor, finely chop all meats together.

Sift flour, salt, and baking powder into a bowl. Rub in shortening and mix to a soft dough with milk. Divide dough into 12 balls. On a lightly floured surface, flatten each ball into a 5-in. circle. Put an equal quantity of meat filling on the center of each circle. Dampen edges and seal by drawing them together. Press well to seal. Flatten slightly with the palm of the hand.

Thoroughly grease individual pieces of double thickness foil. Place one patty, seam side down, on each piece of foil, flattening slightly with the palm of the hand. Wrap up securely. Grill on a rack over medium-hot coals for about 10 minutes, turning foil packages over once during cooking. To test that the filling is completely cooked, insert a sharp-tipped knife into the center—no juices should escape. Garnish with sprigs of parsley or cilantro.

Makes 12.

VERMONT PORK CHOPS

4 pork chops, 1 in. thick
8–12 shelled pecan nuts, dipped in maple syrup, and scallions, to garnish
MARINADE:
4 scallions, trimmed and finely sliced
2 cloves garlic, very finely chopped
4 tablespoons maple syrup
4 teaspoons tomato sauce
1 cup unsweetened apple juice
generous pinch chili powder
generous pinch ground cinnamon
generous pinch freshly ground black pepper
1 teaspoon salt

Trim any surplus fat; pierce chops on both sides.

Combine marinade ingredients in a large shallow dish, stirring briskly with a fork to thoroughly blend in tomato sauce. Add chops, turning them over to coat both sides. Cover and refrigerate for at least 2 hours, turning the chops over once or twice during this time.

Grill chops on a rack over medium-hot coals for 15–20 minutes on each side, basting frequently with marinade. Just before serving, spoon remaining marinade over chops, evenly distributing any scallions that may still be in the bottom of the dish. Top each chop with 2 or 3 pecans and garnish with scallions.

Serves 4.

DRUNKEN ROAST PORK

3 lb. joint pork, boned and rolled
2 tablespoons butter
1 large onion, chopped
2 carrots, thinly sliced
2 sticks celery, finely sliced
1 large leek, sliced
⅔ cup red wine
1 tablespoon fresh thyme leaves
2 teaspoons fresh tarragon leaves
salt and freshly ground black pepper
2 tablespoons dry sherry
few thyme sprigs
2 tablespoons brandy
thyme and tarragon sprigs, to garnish

Score skin of joint; secure with string.

Place pork on a rack in a covered grill, and roast over low coals for about 2 hours. Unless using a spit, turn joint every 15 minutes to ensure even cooking. While roast is cooking, prepare sauce. In a saucepan, melt butter and gently fry onion until brown. Add carrots, celery, leek, wine, and herbs. Cover and simmer, stirring occasionally, until vegetables are very soft. Pass through a sieve or purée mixture in a food processor or blender. Return to pan and season with salt and pepper. Stir in sherry.

When the joint is thoroughly cooked in the center (and registers a temperature of 170F on a meat thermometer), pierce meat in several places and insert sprigs of fresh thyme. Place on a hot flameproof serving platter. Pour brandy into a metal ladle and heat gently over barbecue for a few seconds until warm. Pour over joint and immediately ignite. Spoon brandied juice into reheated sauce. Slice meat, garnish with herb sprigs, and serve with brandied sauce.

Serves 6–8.

PORK KABOBS

1 lb. lean pork
1 onion, cut into quarters
1 green bell pepper, seeded and cut into squares
8 cherry tomatoes
shredded lettuce, orange slices and thyme sprigs, to
  garnish
MARINADE:
juice ½ orange
2 tablespoons olive oil
1 clove garlic, crushed
1 teaspoon chopped fresh thyme
1 teaspoon coriander seeds, crushed
salt and freshly ground black pepper

To make the marinade, in a bowl, mix together orange juice, olive oil, garlic, thyme, coriander seeds, salt, and pepper. Cut pork into ¾-in. cubes and add to marinade. Mix thoroughly, cover, and leave in a cool place for 2 hours. Soak 8 bamboo satay skewers in water 30 minutes before using.

Alternately thread pieces of pork, onion, bell pepper, and the tomatoes on to satay skewers. Grill on a rack over hot coals, turning from time to time, for 10–15 minutes until pork is cooked through. Serve on a bed of shredded lettuce, garnished with orange slices and thyme.

Makes 8.

PORK & BANANA KABOBS

BROCHETTES MEXICANA

1¼ lb. lean pork, cut into 1½-in. cubes
3 bananas
12 bacon slices
1 red bell pepper, seeded and cut into 1½-in. pieces
1 green bell pepper, seeded and cut into 1½-in. pieces
1 small pineapple, cubed
MARINADE:
1 teaspoon honey
1 teaspoon soy sauce
2 cloves garlic, crushed
¼ cup pineapple juice
1 tablespoon hot pepper sauce

12 oz. trimmed rump steak
12 oz. pork fillet
1 large red bell pepper, seeded
1 large green bell pepper, seeded
Spicy Almonds (see page 137), to serve (optional)
MARINADE:
2 fresh green chilies, cored and seeded
8 oz. canned tomatoes
8 oz. canned pimentos, drained
2 tablespoons lemon juice
2 tablespoons olive oil
1 clove garlic, crushed
1 teaspoon turmeric
½–1 teaspoon salt
½ teaspoon freshly ground black pepper

To make marinade, in a bowl, mix together honey, soy sauce, garlic, pineapple juice, and hot pepper sauce. Place pork in a dish and pour marinade over. Cover and leave in a cool place for at least 2 hours, turning occasionally. Cut each banana into 4 equal pieces. Roll each piece in a slice of bacon.

Cut meat into 1-in. cubes and cut bell peppers into similar-size pieces. Purée the marinade ingredients in a food processor or blender, then simmer in a saucepan until reduced by half. Leave until cold. Stir in meat and bell peppers. Cover and marinate in the refrigerator for 12 hours.

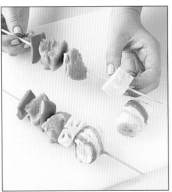

Thread 6 skewers with alternate pieces of red bell pepper, pork, green bell pepper, pork, pineapple, banana, and so on. Grill skewers on a rack over hot coals for 10–15 minutes, turning occasionally and brushing with marinade, until pork is cooked through.

Thread meat on to skewers, alternating with red and green bell pepper pieces. Grill on a rack over hot coals for about 20 minutes, turning frequently and basting with marinade. Serve with Spicy Almonds, if desired.

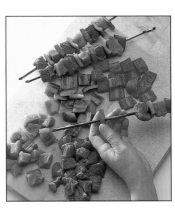

Serves 6.

Serves 5–6.

Note: If using bamboo or wooden skewers, soak in water 30 minutes before using.

Note: If using bamboo or wooden skewers, soak in water 30 minutes before using.

PORK SATAY

12 oz. lean pork, cubed
juice 1 lime
1 stalk lemongrass, finely chopped
1 clove garlic, chopped
2 tablespoons vegetable oil
SAUCE:
¼ cup vegetable oil
½ cup raw shelled peanuts
2 stalks lemongrass, chopped
2 fresh red chilies, cored, seeded, and sliced
3 shallots, chopped
2 cloves garlic, chopped
1 teaspoon fish paste
2 teaspoons crushed palm sugar
1¼ cups coconut milk
juice ½ lime

Meanwhile, make the sauce. Over a high heat, heat 1 tablespoon oil in a wok, add peanuts and cook, stirring constantly, for 2 minutes. Using a slotted spoon, transfer to paper towels to drain. Using a mortar and pestle or small blender, grind to a paste. Remove and set aside.

Divide pork between 4 skewers and place them in a shallow dish. (If using bamboo or wooden skewers, soak in water 30 minutes before using.) In a bowl, mix together lime juice, lemongrass, garlic, and oil. Pour over pork and turn to coat; cover and set aside in a cool place for 1 hour, turning occasionally.

Using a mortar and pestle or small blender, pound or mix lemongrass, chilies, shallots, garlic, and fish paste to a smooth paste.

Remove pork from dish, allowing excess liquid to drain off. Grill pork skewers on a rack over hot coals for 8–10 minutes, turning and basting frequently.

Heat remaining oil in wok, add spice mixture and cook, stirring, for 2 minutes. Stir in peanut paste, sugar, and coconut milk. Bring to a boil, stirring, then adjust heat so sauce simmers. Add lime juice and simmer, stirring, for 5–10 minutes until thickened. Serve in a warmed bowl to accompany pork.

Serves 4.

PORKIES WITH CREAMY DIP

8–12 low-fat, thick pork or beef sausages
oil, for brushing
CREAMY DIP:
3 tablespoons grated horseradish
¼ cup cream cheese
2 tablespoons lemon juice
½ teaspoon sugar
½ teaspoon salt
⅔ cup thick sour cream

To make dip, blend horseradish, cream cheese, lemon juice, sugar, and salt together. Gradually stir in thick sour cream. Cover and chill until required.

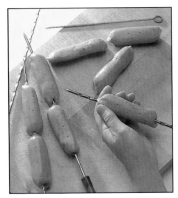

Prick sausages and thread on to skewers. (If using bamboo or wooden skewers, soak in water 30 minutes before using.) Brush with oil. Grill on a rack over medium-hot coals for 12–15 minutes until cooked through, turning frequently.

Arrange hot sausages in a circle on a wooden platter and place the prepared dip in the center.

Serves 8–12.

BACON LATTICE STEAKS

4 sirloin steaks, 1 in. thick, 7½ oz. each
4 thin smoked bacon slices
freshly ground black pepper
¼ cup olive oil
6 oz. cole slaw
parsley sprigs, to garnish (optional)

Make 3 deep diagonal slashes lengthwise and 3 slashes crosswise on each side of the steaks but do not cut right through.

Cut bacon into thin strips and insert into the slashes to form a lattice. Press with the palm of the hand. Season the steaks with pepper and brush all over with oil.

Grill steaks on a rack over hot coals, turning immediately the underside is sealed (this is important to ensure juicy steaks). Turn steaks over frequently during cooking until desired doneness is reached, about 5 minutes on each side for rare. Garnish with sprigs of parsley, if desired, and serve with the cole slaw.

Serves 4.

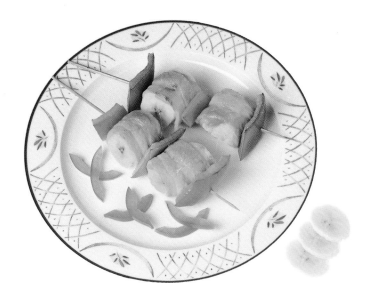

SAUSAGE TWISTS

8 bacon slices
2–3 tablespoons barbecue relish
8 frankfurters
8 long bread rolls
tomato sauce or extra barbecue relish, to serve

BANANA & BACON ROLLS

4 large, slightly under-ripe bananas
8 lean bacon slices, halved
1 red bell pepper, seeded and cut into pieces
1 green bell pepper, seeded and cut into pieces
1 tablespoon sunflower oil
1 tablespoon soy sauce
1 teaspoon honey

Spread each bacon slice with relish and wrap around a frankfurter.

Soak bamboo or wooden skewers in water for 30 minutes before using. Peel bananas and cut each into 4 pieces. Wrap each piece of banana in a halved bacon slice.

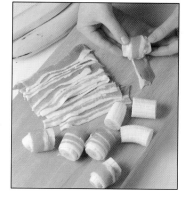

Secure each end of bacon with a wooden toothpick. Place on a barbecue rack over medium-hot coals.

Thread the bacon rolls on to bamboo skewers with the pepper pieces.

Grill sausage twists until bacon is crisp and just lightly browned, turning frequently during cooking. Serve in split, long bread rolls with extra tomato sauce or barbecue relish.

Makes 8.

Mix oil, soy sauce, and honey together and brush over kabobs. Grill on a rack over hot coals, turning during cooking and brushing with oil mixture, until bacon is golden.

Serves 4.

HOT DOGS WITH MUSTARD DIP

12–16 frankfurters
salt and freshly ground black pepper
DIP:
3 tablespoons dry mustard
1 cup light cream

To make the dip, blend dry mustard and cream together in a bowl. Cover and leave in a cool place for 15 minutes for the flavor to develop.

Prick frankfurters and grill on an oiled rack over medium-hot coals for 6–10 minutes, turning frequently. Season with salt and pepper.

Wrap a twist of colored foil round one end of each frankfurter to make it easier to hold and arrange on a platter with a bowl of dip in the center. If preferred, cooked frankfurters can be coated with dip and inserted into long soft rolls.

Makes 12–16.

PORK NUGGETS

1¾ lb. boneless lean pork, cut into 1-in. cubes
1 oz. cilantro leaves
3 cloves garlic, peeled
1¼-in. piece fresh ginger, sliced
1 lemongrass stalk, outer layers removed
grated rind 1 lime
large bunch scallions
2 large fresh red chilies, cored and seeded
2 tablespoons soy sauce
2 tablespoons honey
2 tablespoons white wine vinegar
2 tablespoons Thai fish sauce
2 tablespoons sesame oil
14 fl oz. canned coconut milk
lime wedges, to serve

Put pork in a shallow nonmetallic dish. Place half the cilantro, the garlic, ginger, 1¼ in. lemongrass, lime rind, and remaining ingredients except coconut milk in a blender and process finely. Scrape over pork and stir pork to coat thoroughly. Cover and refrigerate overnight. Remove pork from marinade; set aside marinade.

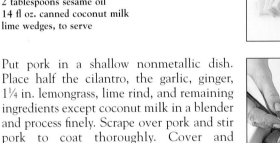

Grill pork on a rack over hot coals for 4–5 minutes a side, brushing occasionally with marinade. Meanwhile, scrape remaining marinade into a skillet, add coconut milk and remaining lemongrass. Boil briskly until thick. Discard lemongrass. Chop remaining cilantro and add to sauce. Thread pork nuggets on to wooden toothpicks and serve with the hot dipping sauce, accompanied by lime wedges.

Makes about 30.

PORK & MANGO SATAY

SKEWERED MEAT ROLLS

1 lb. lean pork, cut into bite-size cubes
2 tablespoons soy sauce
2 teaspoons sesame oil
1 teaspoon each ground cumin, cilantro, cardamom,
  and grated fresh ginger
2 ripe mangoes
SATAY SAUCE:
1 small onion, very finely chopped
2 cloves garlic, crushed
2½ teaspoons grated fresh ginger
1 teaspoon very finely chopped lemongrass
2 oz. creamed coconut, chopped
4 tablespoons crunchy peanut butter

1¾ lb. fillet of beef, pork, or lamb
8 oz. mozzarella cheese
salt and freshly ground black pepper
basil or sage leaves
2 corn cobs
1 eggplant, cut into large cubes
3 zucchini, cut into 1-in. lengths
olive oil, for basting

Soak 6 or 12 bamboo skewers in cold water
for 30 minutes. Cut meat into thin slices,
then place between sheets of plastic wrap
and beat out thinly without tearing. Slice
cheese thinly.

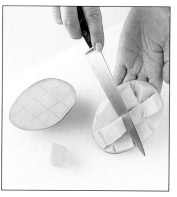

Put pork in a bowl. Mix together soy sauce,
sesame oil and spices. Stir into pork. Cover
and marinate for at least 4 hours, stirring
occasionally. To make sauce, in a saucepan,
slowly bring all the ingredients plus 1¼ cups
water to a boil, stirring until coconut
dissolves. Add more water if necessary. Keep
sauce warm.

Season meat with salt and pepper and lay a
piece of cheese on top of each escalope with
a sage or basil leaf. Roll up each escalope like
a sausage. Place in a dish, cover, and chill in
the refrigerator.

Cut mangoes into same size pieces as pork,
removing pits and peel. Remove pork from
marinade and thread a cube each of pork and
mango on to small skewers. Grill pork and
mango skewers on a rack over hot coals for
about 10 minutes, turning once. Serve with
the satay sauce in a bowl.

Makes about 25.

Note: If using bamboo or wooden skewers,
soak in water 30 minutes before using.

Meanwhile, cook corn cobs in boiling salted
water for 10 minutes; drain and refresh in
cold water. Slice corn cobs into 1 in. thick
rounds. Thread meat rolls and vegetables on
to skewers. Brush lightly with olive oil, place
on a rack over hot coals, and grill for 3–4
minutes per side.

Serves 6.

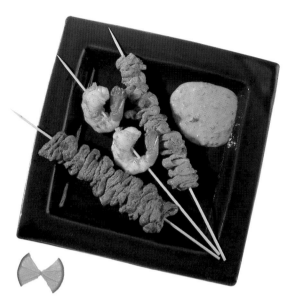

MIXED SATAY

12 oz. pork fillet, chilled and thinly sliced
12 oz. steak, chilled and thinly sliced
½ lime
2 teaspoons each ground coriander and ground cumin
1 teaspoon ground turmeric
1 tablespoon soft light brown sugar
¼ cup coconut milk
12 large raw shrimp, peeled, tails left on, deveined
Satay Sauce (see page 125), to serve

Lay each pork slice between sheets of plastic wrap film and beat with a rolling pin until fairly thin. Cut slices into 1-in.-wide strips.

Cut steak into strips about same size as pork. Put meats into a nonreactive bowl. Squeeze lime juice over. In a small bowl, mix together coriander, cumin, turmeric, sugar, and coconut milk to make a fairly dry paste. Add shrimp to dish with meat and spoon coconut mixture over to coat thoroughly. Cover and marinate for 1 hour, or overnight in the refrigerator. Soak bamboo skewers in water for 30 minutes.

Thread pork strips, steak strips, and shrimp on to separate skewers. Brush with oil and grill on a rack over very hot coals for 10 minutes, turning frequently. Shrimp should have turned opaque with bright pink tails, pork should be cooked through, and beef still be pink in the center. Meanwhile, heat Satay Sauce. Serve the skewers with the hot sauce.

Serves 6.

LAMB KUMQUAT KABOBS

2 large oranges
1¼ lb. lean lamb, cut into cubes
4 oz. cooked, short-grain rice
8–10 mint leaves
salt and freshly ground black pepper
15 kumquats, rinsed, wiped, and stalks removed
olive oil, for basting
mint sprigs, to garnish
SAUCE:
1 teaspoon arrowroot
¼ teaspoon sweet paprika
1 teaspoon maple syrup
2 teaspoons Cointreau

Squeeze juice from oranges and make up to 1 cup with water.

Pare orange rind and snip into pieces with kitchen scissors. Using a food processor, blend rind, lamb, rice, and mint to a smooth paste; season with salt and pepper. This may need to be done in 2 batches. Divide the mixture into 20 equal portions, allowing 4 portions and 3 kumquats per skewer. Mold meat paste into lozenge shapes around 5 skewers, interspersing with kumquats. (If using bamboo or wooden skewers, soak in water 30 minutes before using.)

Grill kabobs on a rack over hot coals for 10–12 minutes, turning frequently and basting with olive oil. To make the sauce, smoothly blend reserved orange juice and arrowroot together in a small saucepan. Bring to a boil, stirring continuously, until sauce thickens. Stir in paprika, maple syrup, and Cointreau. Keep sauce warm and use to coat kabobs just before serving. Garnish with mint sprigs.

Serves 5.

CHINESE GRILLED LAMB

2 small eggs, beaten
¾ cup all-purpose flour
1 teaspoon sea salt
½ teaspoon freshly ground black pepper
1 teaspoon ground Szechuan pepper
4 scallions, finely chopped
2 tomatoes, peeled and finely chopped
1 lb. lamb fillet, cut into cubes
4 teaspoons sesame seeds

In a bowl, mix together all ingredients, except lamb and sesame seeds. Stir in lamb to coat; cover and marinate in the refrigerator for 4 hours.

Spread sesame seeds out on a plate. Roll lamb cubes in sesame seeds to coat evenly.

Thread coated lamb on to skewers and sprinkle on any remaining sesame seeds. Grill skewers on a rack over hot coals for 4–5 minutes, turning frequently, until tender.

Serves 4.

Note: If using bamboo or wooden skewers, soak in water 30 minutes before using.

LAMB KABOBS WITH SALSA

2 cloves garlic, crushed
¼ cup lemon juice
2 tablespoons olive oil
1 dried red chili, crushed
1 teaspoon ground cumin
1 teaspoon ground coriander
1¼ lb. lean lamb, cut into 1½-in. cubes
salt and freshly ground black pepper
8 bay leaves
peel ½ preserved lemon, cut up
TOMATO & OLIVE SALSA:
1¼ cups mixed pitted olives, chopped
1 small red onion, finely chopped
4 plum tomatoes, peeled and chopped
1 fresh red chili, cored, seeded, and finely chopped
2 tablespoons olive oil

Mix garlic, lemon juice, olive oil, chili, cumin, and coriander in a large shallow dish. Add lamb cubes and season with pepper. Mix well. Cover and leave to marinate in the refrigerator for 2 hours. To make the salsa, put olives, onion, tomatoes, chili, olive oil, salt, and pepper in a bowl. Mix well, cover and set aside.

Remove lamb from marinade and divide among 4 skewers, adding bay leaves and lemon rind at intervals. Grill on a rack over hot coals, turning occasionally, for 10 minutes until lamb is browned and crisp outside and pink and juicy inside. Serve with the salsa.

Serves 4.

Note: If using bamboo or wooden skewers, soak in water 30 minutes before using.

LAMB CHOPS TAMARIND

3 tablespoons butter
1 onion, finely chopped
2 tablespoons tamarind concentrate
2 tablespoons tomato paste
1-in. piece fresh ginger, finely grated
2 teaspoons dark soft brown sugar
2 tablespoons olive oil
grated peel and juice 1 large orange
6 double loin lamb chops
orange segments, orange peel, and parsley sprigs, to garnish

Melt butter in a saucepan and cook onion until transparent.

Add tamarind concentrate, tomato paste, ginger, sugar, oil, and orange peel and juice, and simmer gently, uncovered, for 7–8 minutes until reduced by a quarter. Leave to cool. Coat lamb chops thoroughly in the sauce, then cover, and refrigerate overnight.

Grill the chops on a rack over hot coals for 15–20 minutes, turning twice during cooking and basting frequently with remaining sauce. If there is insufficient sauce for basting use a little olive oil instead. Serve garnished with orange segments and peel, and parsley.

Serves 6.

SOUVLAKIA

1½ lb. lean lamb
1½ tablespoons sea salt
6 tablespoons chopped oregano leaves
¼ cup olive oil
bay leaves
1 large onion, finely chopped
6–8 cherry tomatoes, halved
1 small cucumber, peeled and sliced
2 lemons, cut into wedges
1¼ cups natural Greek-style yogurt
oregano sprigs, to garnish

Cut the lamb into 1-in. cubes and toss in sea salt.

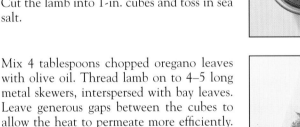

Mix 4 tablespoons chopped oregano leaves with olive oil. Thread lamb on to 4–5 long metal skewers, interspersed with bay leaves. Leave generous gaps between the cubes to allow the heat to permeate more efficiently. Brush with oil mixture.

Grill skewers on a rack over hot coals for 20 minutes, turning occasionally. Arrange salad ingredients in sections on individual plates including a pool of yogurt at one side. Sprinkle with remaining oregano leaves. Remove meat from skewers using a fork and arrange in a line across the salad. Garnish with oregano.

Serves 4–5.

MURGHAL MASALA CHOPS

8 lamb loin chops
¼ teaspoon chili powder
1 clove garlic, crushed
1 tablespoon lemon juice
frisée and cherry tomatoes, to garnish
MURGHAL MASALA SPICE MIX:
¼ cup green cardamom pods
2 3-in. cinnamon sticks, crushed
1 tablespoon whole cloves
1 tablespoon black peppercorns
1 teaspoon grated nutmeg

Wipe lamb chops with a damp paper towel; trim off any excess fat. Slash meaty parts two or three times on each side and set aside.

Make the Murghal Masala spice mix. Remove seeds from cardamom pods and discard pods. Grind seeds, cinnamon sticks, cloves, peppercorns, and nutmeg to a fine powder in a spice grinder, or with a mortar and pestle. Put 1 tablespoon spice mix, chili powder, garlic, and lemon juice in a small bowl; mix to a smooth paste. Rub paste into chops, cover, and refrigerate 2–3 hours to allow meat to absorb flavors. Set aside remaining spice mix for other recipes.

Grill chops on a rack over hot coals for 12–15 minutes, until browned on outside and just pink in center, turning over halfway through cooking. Press point of a sharp knife into center of chops; juices should be just faintly pink. Serve hot, garnished with frisée and tomatoes.

Serves 4.

Note: The Murghal Masala spice mix will keep in a screw top jar for 6–8 weeks.

CARIBBEAN BURGERS

2 tablespoons vegetable oil
1 large onion, finely chopped
1 clove garlic, crushed
1 green bell pepper, seeded and finely chopped
2¼ lb. freshly ground lean beef
1 teaspoon dried mixed herbs
2 eggs, beaten
2 cups fresh bread crumbs
1 tablespoon tomato paste
salt and freshly ground black pepper
1 small pineapple
melted butter, for brushing
Singed Spiced Plantains (see page 102), to serve

Heat oil in a saucepan. Add onion, garlic, and pepper; cook for 5 minutes.

Transfer mixture to a large bowl and mix in meat, herbs, eggs, bread crumbs, and tomato paste; season with salt and pepper. Form mixture into 12 burger shapes and grill on an oiled rack over hot coals for 8–10 minutes on each side.

Peel pineapple and slice thinly. Brush pineapple rings on both sides with melted butter and grill on a rack over hot coals for 3–6 minutes, turning once, until golden brown. Place a pineapple ring on top of each burger, and serve accompanied by Singed Spiced Plantains.

Makes 12.

LAMB & LANCASHIRE SAUCE

12 oz. ground lamb
1 egg, beaten
1 teaspoon dried rosemary
½ cup fresh white bread crumbs
1 small red bell pepper, seeded and finely chopped
1 teaspoon Tabasco sauce
½ teaspoon onion salt
½ teaspoon freshly ground black pepper
SAUCE:
1½ teaspoons butter
½ cup milk
1 egg yolk
⅓ cup thick sour cream
2 oz. Lancashire cheese, crumbled
rosemary sprigs and red bell pepper rings, to garnish
    (optional)

Thoroughly mix lamb, egg, rosemary, bread crumbs, chopped bell pepper, Tabasco, onion salt, and pepper. Shape mixture into about 16 rectangular fingers and refrigerate for 30 minutes (see above left). Meanwhile make the sauce. Melt butter in a small saucepan, stir in flour, remove from the heat, and thoroughly blend in milk. Cook over moderate heat, stirring continuously, until sauce thickens to the consistency of light cream. Remove pan from heat. Blend egg yolk with cream and pour into pan. Mix in cheese. Cook gently until cheese has just melted.

Grill lamb fingers on an oiled rack over hot coals for 5–6 minutes on each side, reducing heat if they become too brown. Arrange 4 neat fingers in a fan shape on each plate and spoon some sauce over the tips, allowing it to form a pool. Garnish with red bell pepper rings or sprigs of rosemary, if desired.

Serves 4.

BLUEBERRY VENISON

6 venison steaks
grated peel and juice 2 oranges
juice 1 lemon
3 tablespoons whisky
8 tablespoons olive oil
1 teaspoon rosemary leaves
3 bay leaves, crumbled
1 teaspoon celery salt
2 cups blueberries
1 cup soft brown sugar
1 tablespoon lemon juice
bay leaves, fresh blueberries, and orange slices, to
    garnish (optional)

Trim venison steaks and place on a chopping board. Flatten with a mallet or rolling pin.

Mix together orange peel, citrus juices, whisky, oil, rosemary, bay leaves, and celery salt in a large, shallow dish. Place venison steaks in marinade, turning over to coat both sides. Leave in refrigerator for 6–8 hours, basting occasionally. Remove stalks from blueberries. In a heavy-based saucepan, combine sugar, 1 tablespoon lemon juice, and ⅔ cup water. Heat gently, stirring until sugar dissolves. Add blueberries and bring to a boil. Reduce heat and cook until pulpy. Keep warm.

Remove venison steaks from marinade and grill on an oiled rack over hot coals for about 10 seconds on each side to seal meat. Brush with marinade and continue cooking for 5–7 minutes on each side until tender. Garnish with a few bay leaves, fresh blueberries, and orange slices, if desired. Serve with the blueberry sauce.

Serves 6.

CAPERED NEW POTATOES

1 lb. new potatoes
3 tablespoons capers
⅓ cup butter, softened
parsley sprigs, to garnish

Scrub potatoes well, then boil in their skins in salted water for 10 minutes. Drain and leave to cool slightly.

Finely chop capers and blend with butter. Make a deep slit in each potato and fill with caper butter.

Tightly wrap each potato in separate squares of single thickness foil and grill on a rack over hot coals for 10–15 minutes. Garnish with sprigs of parsley.

Serves 4–6.

Note: These grilled potatoes are ideal as an accompaniment to plain grilled fish or poultry.

SPICED GRILLED SQUASH

2 small butternut squash, cut into quarters and seeded
2 cloves garlic, finely chopped
2 teaspoon ground cumin
2–3 tablespoons vegetable oil
½ lime
salt and freshly ground black pepper

Using a small, sharp knife make shallow crisscross cuts in the flesh of each squash quarter.

In a bowl, mix together garlic, cumin, oil, a good squeeze of lime juice, and salt and pepper. Brush over flesh side of each piece of squash, working it well into the cuts.

Grill squash quarters on a rack over hot coals for 10–15 minutes until lightly browned and flesh is tender. Brush occasionally with any remaining cumin mixture.

Serves 4.

SESAME-DRESSED ENDIVE

6 heads of Belgian endive, trimmed and halved
    lengthwise
4 oz. French beans, trimmed
1 tablespoon sesame seeds, toasted
DRESSING:
⅓ cup light olive oil
½ teaspoon sesame oil
2 teaspoons orange juice
1 teaspoon balsamic vinegar
1 teaspoon grated fresh ginger
½ teaspoon grated orange rind
½ teaspoon honey
salt and freshly ground black pepper

To prepare dressing, place all the ingredients in a screw top jar and shake vigorously. Leave in a cool place for the flavors to develop.

Wash and dry Belgian endive, brush with a little dressing, and grill on a rack over hot coals for 3–4 minutes on each side until leaves become lightly charred. Meanwhile, blanch beans in boiling water for 1–2 minutes until just tender. Drain, refresh under cold water, and pat dry. Arrange 3 Belgian endive halves on each plate, add the beans, drizzle dressing over, and sprinkle with sesame seeds. Serve at once.

Serves 4.

SAGE & CREAM JACKETS

6 baking potatoes
vegetable oil
2 tablespoons white wine vinegar
1 bunch scallions, finely sliced
1 egg yolk
pinch dry mustard
salt and freshly ground black pepper
1 teaspoon finely chopped sage leaves
⅔ cup thick sour cream
sage leaves, to garnish

Scrub potatoes and dry on paper towels. Prick deeply through skins and rub with oil.

Wrap potatoes separately in double thickness foil and bake in coals of barbecue for 45 minutes to 1 hour, turning occasionally until soft. Put vinegar in a small saucepan, add scallions, and cook over low heat until vinegar has almost evaporated. Remove pan from heat. Beat together egg yolk, mustard, and salt and pepper, and stir into scallions.

Cook over very low heat for 1 minute, beating continuously until mixture thickens. Care must be taken not to overheat or sauce may curdle. Remove from heat; stir in chopped sage and cream. Cut a deep cross through foil into cooked potatoes and squeeze sides to open out. Spoon in a little sauce. Garnish with sage leaves.

Serves 6.

SKEWERED POTATO CRISPS

2 baking potatoes, 8 oz. each
salt
¼ cup sunflower oil

Peel potatoes. Carefully cut into paper thin slices lengthwise, following the curve of the potato.

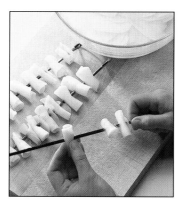

Immediately plunge potato slices into hot, salted water. Stir to separate, then leave for 3–4 minutes until pliable. Carefully coil each potato slice, then thread on to long skewers, leaving at least a ½-in. space between each one. (If using bamboo or wooden skewers, soak in water 30 minutes before using.)

Brush potato coils with oil and grill on a rack over hot coals for 10–15 minutes, turning frequently until potato coils are crisp. Briefly lay skewers on paper towels to drain before serving.

Serves 4–6.

Note: The recipe may be doubled, but it will then be better to soak potato slices in separate bowls of hot, salted water.

FENNEL WITH FETA & PEARS

2 fennel bulbs
¼ cup olive oil
6 oz. feta cheese
1 ripe pear
4 sun-dried tomatoes in oil, drained and sliced
¼ cup pitted black olives
basil leaves
1 teaspoon lemon juice
½ teaspoon honey
salt and freshly ground black pepper

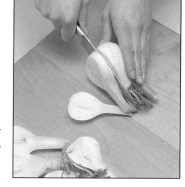

Trim fennel, discarding any damaged outer leaves. Cut each bulb, lengthwise, into 6 thin slices.

Brush with a little olive oil and grill on a rack over hot coals for 2–3 minutes until browned. Turn fennel, brush with oil, and grill for an additional 2–3 minutes until charred and just tender. Leave to cool slightly.

Slice feta into thin slabs and quarter, core, and thinly slice the pear. Arrange fennel, cheese, and pear on serving plates and top with tomatoes, olives, and basil. Blend remaining oil, lemon juice, honey, and salt and pepper together, drizzle over salad and serve.

Serves 4.

HOT HOT ALOO

1 lb. small new potatoes
12 teaspoons lime pickle
¼ cup vegetable oil
2 teaspoons tomato paste
2 teaspoons ground cardamom
2 tablespoons plain yogurt
lime slices, to garnish

Wash and scrub potatoes. Cook in salted water until tender but firm. Drain. Leave until cold, then thread on to 4–6 skewers. (If using bamboo or wooden skewers, soak in water 30 minutes before using.)

Put lime pickle in a glass bowl and, using kitchen scissors, cut up any large pieces of the pickle. Blend in oil, tomato paste, cardamom, and yogurt.

Spoon pickle mixture over skewered potatoes so that each potato is well coated. Grill on a rack over hot coals for about 10 minutes, turning frequently. Garnish with slices of lime.

Serves 4–6.

Note: Use mild lime pickle, if preferred.

PEANUT BEEFSTEAK TOMATOES

4 beefsteak tomatoes
salt and freshly ground black pepper
few drops Worcestershire sauce
2 teaspoons chopped fresh basil
2 teaspoons chopped fresh parsley
4 teaspoons grated Parmesan cheese
2 oz. roasted unsalted peanuts, finely ground
knob of butter
8 'bracelets' of fried bread (see Note below)
basil or parsley sprigs, to garnish

Rinse and dry tomatoes and halve crosswise. Season cut surfaces of tomatoes with salt and pepper.

Sprinkle with a few drops of Worcestershire sauce. Top with basil and parsley mixed together, then sprinkle with grated Parmesan cheese. Cover with ground peanuts and add a small piece of butter to each one. Loosely wrap tomato halves separately in single thickness foil. Place cut-sides up on a rack and grill over hot coals for 20–25 minutes until tomatoes are soft.

Remove from foil wrappings and place each tomato in center of a fried croûton 'bracelet'. Garnish with basil or parsley sprigs.

Serves 4–8.

Note: The 'bracelets' can be prepared ahead of time and will store in the freezer. Recrisp on barbecue at the last minute. To make the 'bracelets', cut out 8 rounds of bread from a sliced loaf and use a slightly smaller cutter to remove centers. Fry in shallow oil. Drain thoroughly.

GREEK GRILLED VEGETABLES

4 oz. feta cheese, cut into cubes
2 baby eggplants, halved lengthwise
4 baby zucchini, halved lengthwise
1 red bell pepper, seeded and cut into quarters
1 yellow bell pepper, seeded and cut into quarters
1 fennel bulb, cut into quarters and sliced
1 tablespoon lemon juice
salt and freshly ground black pepper
zucchini flowers, to garnish (optional)
MARINADE:
⅔ cup olive oil
2 cloves garlic, crushed
1 teaspoon chopped fresh parsley
1 teaspoon chopped fresh mint
1 teaspoon chopped fresh oregano

To make marinade, mix together olive oil, garlic, parsley, mint, and oregano. Put feta in a bowl. Add a little of the marinade and mix gently. Put vegetables in another bowl with remaining marinade, mix together, and leave for 1 hour.

Grill the vegetables on a rack over hot coals for 10 minutes, turning and brushing with marinade every few minutes, or until tender and flecked with brown. Leave to cool. Arrange the vegetables on a serving plate. Drizzle with lemon juice, and season with salt and pepper. Sprinkle with the feta, garnish with zucchini flowers, if desired, and serve.

Serves 4.

WHOLE TOMATOES IN WINE

8 firm tomatoes
8 teaspoons red wine
salt and freshly ground black pepper
watercress or lettuce leaves, to serve (optional)

Cut 8 large squares of double thickness foil. Cup each tomato in foil but do not completely enclose.

Pour 1 teaspoon wine over, and season with salt and pepper. Mold foil around tomatoes securely to prevent juices escaping.

Put foil pockets on side of rack over medium-hot coals and grill for about 10–15 minutes. Unwrap and transfer to serving plates, spooning wine-flavored juices over tomatoes. Serve on a bed of watercress or lettuce leaves, if desired.

Serves 8.

Note: The tomatoes are particularly delicious as an accompaniment to grilled steaks or burgers which can be cooked at the same time.

GREEK VEGETABLES

1 fennel bulb
1 red bell pepper, seeded and cut into quarters
2 baby zucchini, halved lengthwise
2 baby eggplants, halved lengthwise
8 baby corn
salt and freshly ground black pepper
zucchini flowers and basil sprigs, to garnish
MARINADE:
⅔ cup olive oil
2 cloves garlic, crushed
1 teaspoon chopped fresh parsley
1 teaspoon chopped fresh mint
1 teaspoon chopped fresh oregano

SWEET & SOUR EGGPLANTS

2 eggplants
3 tablespoons tarragon vinegar
3 tablespoons olive oil
1 small clove garlic, crushed
pinch salt
½ teaspoon French mustard
½ teaspoon dried marjoram
pinch red pepper
1 tablespoon sugar
marjoram sprigs, to garnish

Peel eggplants, cut in half, then slice and cut into 1-in. cubes.

To make marinade, in a bowl mix together olive oil, garlic, parsley, mint, and oregano. Cut fennel bulb into quarters. Put pepper, zucchini, eggplants, fennel, and corn into bowl with marinade. Leave for at least 1 hour.

Combine remaining ingredients, except garnish, in a large bowl, add cubed eggplant and mix well. Leave for 15 minutes, stirring occasionally.

Grill the vegetables on a rack over hot coals for about 10 minutes, brushing frequently with marinade. Season with salt and pepper. Garnish with zucchini flowers and basil sprigs.

Serves 4.

Variation: A wide variety of vegetables can be grilled. Try mushrooms, tomatoes, Belgian endive, onions, and squashes.

Thread eggplant cubes on to 8 skewers and grill over hot coals for 15 minutes, turning occasionally. (If using bamboo or wooden skewers, soak in water 30 minutes before using.) Garnish with sprigs of marjoram.

Serves 8.

Note: These are extremely good served with grilled steaks or chops.

ZUCCHINI WITH HERBS

8–10 young zucchini, about 5 in. long
1 teaspoon finely chopped lemon verbena leaves
4–5 finely chopped mint leaves
1 teaspoon finely chopped marjoram leaves
2 bay leaves, finely chopped
½ teaspoon salt
2 tablespoons medium white wine
2 tablespoons lemon juice
¼ cup sunflower oil
lemon slices and fresh herbs, to garnish

Rinse and dry zucchini and pierce at either end in one or two places along length.

In a large bowl, mix together herbs, salt, wine, lemon juice, and oil. Add zucchini, turning over to coat thoroughly. Cover and marinate for 4–5 hours, tossing occasionally.

Remove zucchini from marinade and grill on a rack over hot coals for 8–10 minutes, until tender but not soft, turning frequently, and basting with remaining marinade. Serve skewered with wooden skewers. Garnish with lemon slices and fresh herbs.

Serves 8–10.

GRILLED VEGETABLES

1 cup couscous
1 red bell pepper, seeded and cut into quarters
2 baby zucchini, halved lengthwise
2 baby eggplants, halved lengthwise
1 fennel bulb, cut into quarters
4 patty pan squashes
2 tablespoons olive oil
mint sprigs and lemon slices, to garnish
MARINADE:
⅔ cup olive oil
1 tablespoon lemon juice
2 clove garlic, crushed
salt and freshly ground black pepper
1 teaspoon chopped fresh parsley
1 teaspoon chopped fresh mint

Place couscous in a bowl and cover with boiling water. Leave for 10 minutes to absorb water, then fluff up with a fork and spread out in a dish. Leave for 1 hour to dry. To make marinade, in a large bowl, mix together olive oil, lemon juice, garlic, salt, pepper, parsley, and mint. Place red bell pepper in the bowl with marinade. Add zucchini, eggplants, fennel bulb, and squashes. Marinate for 1 hour.

Grill vegetables on a rack over hot coals, turning and brushing with marinade every few minutes, for 10 minutes, or until tender and lightly browned. Heat olive oil in a skillet. Add couscous and fry, stirring, until golden and crisp. Transfer vegetables to a heated serving dish and sprinkle with couscous. Serve, garnished with mint leaves and lemon slices.

Serves 4.

EGGPLANT SALAD

1 small eggplant
3 tablespoons olive oil
1½ cups thinly sliced shiitake mushrooms
6 cups torn mixed salad leaves
1½ tablespoons chopped fresh cilantro
¼ cup hazelnuts, toasted and coarsely chopped
DRESSING:
⅓ cup olive oil
1 teaspoon sesame oil
2 teaspoons light soy sauce
1 tablespoon balsamic vinegar
½ teaspoon sugar
freshly ground black pepper

Cut eggplant into thin slices, brush with oil and grill on a rack over hot coals for 2–3 minutes on each side, until charred and softened. Allow to cool. Heat remaining oil in a small skillet and stir-fry mushrooms over a medium heat for 3–4 minutes until tender. Drain on paper towels and leave to cool.

Place salad leaves in a large bowl. Sprinkle cilantro and nuts over. Blend all the dressing ingredients together until well mixed. Add eggplant and mushrooms to the salad, pour the dressing over, toss well, and serve at once.

Serves 4.

SPANISH CHARCOALED ONIONS

2 large Spanish or red onions
garlic salt
4 tablespoons heavy cream, half-whipped
1 tablespoon crushed black peppercorns
2 tablespoons butter
rosemary sprigs, to garnish

Peel onions and cut into ½-in.-thick slices. Do not separate into rings.

Season with garlic salt. Brush one side with heavy cream and sprinkle with crushed peppercorns.

Grill in a tented, hinged wire basket and cook peppered-side up first. Grill over hot coals for 5–8 minutes on each side until beginning to char. Put dabs of butter on onion slices while first sides are cooking. Serve peppered-sides up, garnished with sprigs of rosemary.

Makes 8–10.

Note: Serve with meat dishes, or as an appetizer.

STUFFED EGGPLANTS

6 small eggplants, about 6 oz. each
2 tablespoons butter
1 onion, finely chopped
1 clove garlic, crushed
8 oz. canned tomatoes with their juice
⅓ cup fresh bread crumbs
½ cup grated cheddar cheese
1 teaspoon dried oregano
salt and freshly ground black pepper
oregano sprigs, to garnish

Cut off a thin slice along length of eggplants and set aside. Scoop out flesh from eggplants, leaving a ¼-in. wall. Finely chop flesh.

Melt butter in a saucepan and gently fry onion and garlic until soft. Add chopped eggplant and continue frying until tender. Switch off heat, stir in tomatoes, bread crumbs, cheese, and oregano, and season with salt and pepper.

Pack filling into eggplant shells. Replace lids and wrap separately in lightly oiled, double thickness foil. Grill on a rack over medium-hot coals, or cook directly in coals, for 20–30 minutes. Garnish with sprigs of oregano.

Serves 6.

WALNUT APPLE CRESCENTS

2 small, red-skinned eating apples
⅓ cup shelled walnuts
1-oz. block dried dates
¼ cup apple juice
1 teaspoon grated orange rind
strips of orange rind, to garnish

Rinse and dry apples and remove core, keeping apples whole. Cut each apple in half lengthwise. (Each half will have a tubular shaped hollow along center.)

Roughly chop walnuts and dates. Put apple juice and grated orange rind in a small saucepan. Add walnuts and dates, bring to a boil, then simmer for 2–3 minutes until liquid has been absorbed. Cool slightly, then fill apple hollows with mixture.

Wrap each apple half separately in double thickness foil. Grill on a rack over hot coals for about 30 minutes, turning occasionally until apples are tender. Garnish with strips of orange rind.

Serves 4.

Note: Serve as an accompaniment to poultry or game.

SINGED SPICED PLANTAINS

6 plantains or under-ripe bananas
2 tablespoons butter
2 tablespoons lemon juice
½ teaspoon quatre épices
pinch ground ginger
lemon slices, to garnish

Without peeling, grill the plantains or bananas on a rack over medium-hot coals, turning them over until the skin blackens.

Soften butter, mix in lemon juice, quatre épices, and ginger.

Cut cooked plantains or bananas lengthwise to separate into halves and spoon the spicy butter over the surface. Garnish with lemon slices.

Serves 6–12.

Notes: Quatre épices is a spicy mixture of ground pepper, cloves, nutmeg, and either cinnamon or ginger. It is obtainable from many delicatessens.
Singed Spiced Plantains are delicious served with chicken, gammon, or veal dishes.

CHARBROILED ARTICHOKES

⅓ cup olive oil
1 clove garlic, crushed
2 tablespoons, chopped fresh parsley
salt and freshly ground black pepper
6 baby artichokes
flat-leaf parsley sprigs, to garnish
RED BELL PEPPER SAUCE:
1 tablespoon olive oil
1 small onion, chopped
2 red bell peppers, seeded and diced
1 cup vegetable stock

Mix together olive oil, garlic, parsley, and salt and pepper. Set aside.

To make red bell pepper sauce, heat oil in a saucepan. Add onion and cook for 5 minutes until soft. Add red bell peppers and cook over a low heat for 5 minutes. Pour in stock, bring to a boil, and simmer for 10 minutes. Push through a sieve or purée in a food processor or blender. Season with salt and pepper.

Trim bases of artichokes and remove any tough outer leaves. Cut artichokes in half lengthwise and immediately brush with seasoned oil. Grill artichokes on a rack over medium-hot coals for 10 minutes, turning once, until browned on both sides. Reheat sauce. Drizzle artichokes with remaining seasoned oil, garnish with parsley, and serve with the red bell pepper sauce.

Serves 3–4.

CRUSTY GARLIC POTATOES

1 lb. new potatoes
8–10 large cloves garlic
2 eggs, beaten
6–8 tablespoons yellow cornmeal
parsley sprigs, to garnish

Scrub potatoes well. Peel garlic, leaving the cloves whole.

Boil potatoes and garlic in salted water for 12–15 minutes until just cooked. Drain, reserving garlic. Skin potatoes as soon as they are cool enough to handle. Roughly chop garlic and, using a small skewer, insert pieces deeply into potatoes.

Dip potatoes first in beaten egg and then in cornmeal. Press cornmeal on well with a round-bladed knife, then dip in beaten egg once more. Grill on a well-oiled rack over hot coals for 10–15 minutes until crusty and golden. Serve in a basket lined with a clean napkin. Garnish with sprigs of parsley.

Serves 5–6.

VEGETABLE BAR

8 oz. even-shaped carrots
1 cauliflower
8 oz. snow peas
8 oz. baby onions
3 slim corn cobs
1 tablespoon milk
vegetable oil, for brushing

Using a small paring knife, cut carrots into chunks and shape into barrels. Separate cauliflower into flowerets.

Top and tail snow peas, removing any tough strings. Peel onions. Using a heavy, sharp knife, cut corn into 1-in. slices. Plunge vegetables into boiling water to which 1 tablespoon milk has been added. Cook to slightly soften or until al dente. Drain in a colander under cold running water, then drain again.

Have ready 8–10 skewers and oil for brushing. Thread a selection of vegetables on to skewers, baste with oil, and grill on a rack over hot coals for 5 minutes, turning skewers frequently. Serve with the dip or relish of your choice.

Serves 8–10.

Note: If using bamboo or wooden skewers, soak in water 30 minutes before using.

GREEN LENTIL ZUCCHINI

3 large zucchini
2 scallions, finely sliced
1 small green bell pepper, seeded and finely chopped
1 tomato, skinned and chopped
⅓ cup green lentils, cooked
1 teaspoon fresh basil leaves, snipped
salt and freshly ground black pepper
3 tablespoons grated, roasted hazelnuts
basil sprigs, to garnish

Halve zucchini lengthwise. Scoop pulp into a bowl, leaving ¼-in.-thick shells to prevent zucchini from collapsing. Set aside shells.

Add the scallions, green bell pepper, and tomato to the bowl of zucchini pulp and mix in lentils and basil. Season with salt and pepper. Pile mixture high into reserved zucchini shells.

Place filled zucchini halves individually on large squares of double thickness foil. Wrap up securely, leaving a space above the stuffing for steam to circulate. Grill on a rack over hot coals for about 20 minutes until zucchini are tender, but firm. Open pockets and sprinkle hazelnuts over stuffing. Garnish with sprigs of basil.

Serves 6.

ROAST CORN ON THE COB

6 corn cobs, with husks
½ cup butter, melted
HERBED BUTTER PATS:
¼ cup butter
1 teaspoon lemon juice
2 tablespoons chopped fresh parsley
1 tablespoon chopped fresh chives
salt and freshly ground black pepper

Fold back corn husks, pull out silk from corn, and rewrap husks over corn. Soak in cold water for at least 1 hour. Drain cobs and shake off surplus water.

While cobs are soaking, prepare butter pats. Beat all ingredients together until softened and well blended. Shape into a 1-in.-wide roll and wrap tightly in greaseproof paper, maintaining cylindrical shape. Chill in freezer until firm, then slice. Arrange in a single layer on a plate and refrigerate until needed.

Pull back corn husks and brush corn with melted butter. Re-wrap corn in husks and grill on a rack over medium-hot coals for 30–40 minutes, turning frequently until the husks are well browned. Remove husks and serve corn with the butter pats.

Serves 6.

Variation: After brushing corn cobs with melted butter, corn cobs may also be spread with peanut butter, if desired.

COUNTY MUSHROOMS

12 open, flat mushrooms, about 2 oz. each
¾ cup virgin olive oil
¼ cup lemon juice
5 teaspoons grated horseradish
¼ teaspoon salt
¼ teaspoon freshly ground black
1 tablespoon chopped fresh parsley, to garnish

Wipe mushrooms and, if necessary, cut stalks to ½-in. lengths.

Thoroughly mix olive oil, lemon juice, grated horseradish, and salt and pepper in a large shallow dish. Add mushrooms, spooning liquid over to coat completely. Leave to stand for at leave 30 minutes, basting occasionally.

Grill on a rack over hot coals for about 10 minutes, turning mushrooms and spooning marinade over occasionally. Garnish open sides of mushrooms with chopped parsley.

Serves 6–12.

BROCCOLI PANCAKE ROLLS

8 oz. broccoli spears
⅓ cup natural Greek-style yogurt
freshly ground black pepper
2 tablespoons all-purpose flour
3 tablespoons milk
4 extra large eggs
1 tablespoon soy sauce
butter, for greasing
vegetable oil, for brushing

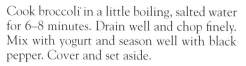

Cook broccoli in a little boiling, salted water for 6–8 minutes. Drain well and chop finely. Mix with yogurt and season well with black pepper. Cover and set aside.

Sift flour into a mixing bowl and blend in milk. Beat eggs and soy sauce together and add gradually to flour mixture, beating well to form a smooth, thin batter. Pour into a jug. Heat a small omelet pan, add a knob of butter, and make six or eight 6-in.-thin pancakes, browning them on one side only. (If necessary, grease pan with a little butter after making each pancake.) Remove pancakes carefully (they set as they cool) and spread out, cooked-sides up, on nonstick paper.

Spoon a little broccoli filling on one edge of the browned side of each pancake. Fold over to enclose filling, tucking in sides, and fold again to form a wrap. Brush cool pancake rolls with oil and grill on a rack, starting with seam-sides down, over hot coals for 3–4 minutes on each side.

Serves 6–8.

Note: These pancake rolls taste delicious served with a green salad.

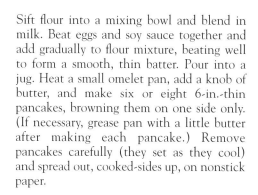

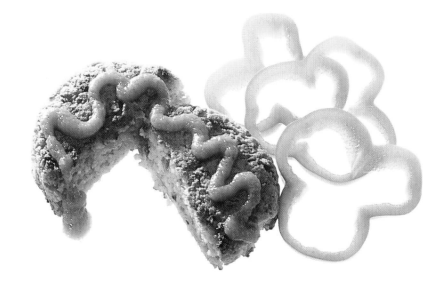

EGGPLANT STACKS

⅓ cup olive oil
1 onion, finely chopped
1 clove garlic, crushed
1 red bell pepper, seeded and chopped
14 oz. canned chopped tomatoes
1 oz. sun-dried tomatoes in oil, drained and chopped
1 tablespoon raisins
½ teaspoon sugar
2 teaspoons balsamic vinegar
salt and freshly ground black pepper
1 teaspoon dried mint
4 long-shaped eggplants
mint sprigs, to garnish

In a saucepan, heat 2 tablespoons of olive oil. Add onion and garlic, and cook for 10 minutes or until soft. Add pepper, canned tomatoes, sun-dried tomatoes, raisins, sugar, vinegar, salt, pepper, and mint. Simmer gently, uncovered, for 20 minutes or until mixture thickens. Meanwhile, cut eggplants into ¼-in.-thick slices. Brush each slice on both sides with remaining olive oil.

Grill eggplant slices on a rack over hot coals for 3–4 minutes on each side until soft and browned. Keep hot while cooking remaining slices. Spoon a little of the tomato mixture on half the eggplant slices. Top with a second slice. Serve garnished with mint sprigs.

Serves 6.

BRAZIL NUT BURGERS

3 tablespoons butter
1 onion, finely chopped
1 stick celery, finely chopped
½ small green bell pepper, seeded and finely chopped
8 oz. shelled Brazil nuts, finely ground
1 carrot, grated
1 teaspoon yeast extract
1¼ cups vegetable stock
⅜ cup bulgar
salt and freshly ground black pepper
2 eggs, beaten
flour, for dusting
vegetable oil , for greasing
green bell pepper rings, to garnish
Fiery Chili Baste (see page 116), to serve (optional)

In a heavy-based saucepan, melt butter and fry onion, celery, and green bell pepper until soft. Stir in nuts and cook for 3–4 minutes, stirring continuously to bring out flavor. Stir grated carrot, yeast extract, and vegetable stock into mixture and bring to a boil, then simmer for 5 minutes. Mix in bulgar wheat and season with salt and pepper. Leave mixture to cool, then bind together with beaten eggs to consistency of thick paste.

Shape mixture into 6 or 7 burgers and dust with flour. Put burgers on a well-oiled foil tray. Place on a rack and grill over hot coals for 10 minutes, turning burgers once during cooking. Carefully remove burgers from grill and garnish with green bell pepper rings. Serve with Fiery Chili Baste, if desired.

Serves 6–7.

CELERY & STILTON AVOCADO

3 ripe avocados
2 tablespoons lemon juice
salt and freshly ground black pepper
2 sticks celery, cooked and chopped
3 tablespoons brown rice, cooked
3 oz. white Stilton cheese, crumbled
1 tablespoon vegetable or tomato paste
pinch chili powder
celery leaves and halved and seeded black grapes, to
    garnish

Halve avocados and remove pits. Mix lemon
juice with salt and pepper and brush over cut
surfaces.

Combine celery, brown rice, and Stilton; stir
in vegetable or tomato paste and chili
powder, and mix well. Pile on to avocado
halves, then arrange on an oiled foil tray.

Place foil tray on a rack and loosely tent with
foil, or cook in a lidded barbecue, over
medium-hot coals for 15–20 minutes until
heated through. Garnish with celery leaves
and grape halves.

Serves 6.

GRILLED VINE LEAVES

4 scallions, finely chopped
1 small nectarine or peach, pit removed and finely
    chopped
1 tablespoon chopped fresh mint
¼ teaspoon ground coriander
pinch ground cumin
salt and freshly ground black pepper
4 oz. goat cheese
8 large vine leaves in brine, drained
olive oil, for brushing

Place onions, nectarine or peach, mint, and
spices in a small bowl, season, and stir well
until combined. Cut cheese into 4 equal
slices.

Wash and dry vine leaves, arrange in pairs,
and brush top leaves with oil. Place a slice of
cheese at one end of each leaf and top with
nectarine mixture. Carefully fold leaves over
cheese until completely covered, and secure
with wooden toothpicks.

Brush the pockets with oil and grill on a rack
over hot coals for 3–4 minutes on each side
until leaves are lightly charred. Transfer to
serving plates, carefully removing
toothpicks, and serve at once with a crisp
green salad.

Serves 4.

Variation: Use a low-fat cream cheese
instead of the goat cheese, if preferred.

PEACHES & BUTTERSCOTCH

6 peaches
angelica, to decorate (optional)
BUTTERSCOTCH SAUCE:
½ cup light soft brown sugar
⅔ cup maple syrup
3 tablespoons butter
pinch salt
⅔ cup light cream
few drops vanilla extract
FILLING:
½ cup ground almonds
2 tablespoons finely chopped angelica

Wash, dry, and halve peaches; remove pits.

To make sauce, combine sugar, maple syrup, butter, and salt in a heavy-based saucepan. Bring to a boil, stir once, then boil for 3 minutes to form a thick syrup. Stir in cream, bring back to a boil, and immediately remove from heat. Stir in vanilla extract to taste. Pour into a jug and keep warm.

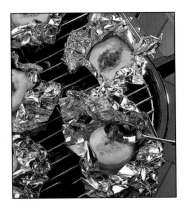

Put peach halves, cut-sides down, on individual squares of double thickness foil. Curl up sides of foil but do not seal. Grill on a rack over hot coals for 5 minutes. Turn peaches over on the foil; spoon almonds and angelica into cavities and pour 1 tablespoon of butterscotch sauce over each. Draw up edges of foil and twist above peaches to seal. Grill for 10 minutes until tender. Decorate with angelica, if desired, and serve hot with remaining sauce.

Serves 6–12.

PRALINE BANANAS

½ oz. unskinned almonds
½ oz. unskinned hazelnuts
¼ cup granulated sugar
6 under-ripe bananas
whipped cream, to serve

Put almonds, hazelnuts, and sugar in a small, heavy-based skillet. Heat gently, stirring constantly until sugar dissolves. Raise heat and cook to a deep brown syrup. Immediately, pour on to a sheet of nonstick paper placed on a metal baking tray on a wooden board. The toffee-like mixture will be very hot. Leave until cold and brittle; crush finely.

Lay unpeeled bananas flat and make a slit through skin along top surface. Slightly open out skin and fill each slit with about 1 tablespoon of nut caramel. Reshape the bananas and wrap each tightly in double thickness foil, sealing along the top.

Grill directly on medium-hot coals for 8–10 minutes, turning packages over halfway through cooking time. To serve, unfold foil wrapping and slightly open banana skins. Serve with whipped cream.

Serves 6.

RUM & RAISIN PERSIMMONS

6 firm persimmons
2 tablespoons mixed dried fruit
1 glacé cherry
3 unskinned almonds
2 teaspoons dark soft brown sugar
1 teaspoon dark rum
pinch ground cinnamon
½ teaspoon lemon juice
6 small strawberries

Remove stalks from persimmons and, using a teaspoon, scoop out pulp, leaving fleshy wall intact. Put pulp in a bowl.

Using a sharp, lightly-floured knife, very finely chop dried fruit, cherry, and almonds. Mix into fruit pulp, adding sugar, rum, cinnamon, and lemon juice. Carefully pack filling into persimmon shells and wrap separately in lightly oiled, double thickness foil.

Grill foil pockets directly in medium-hot coals and cook for 25–30 minutes until fruit is soft. To serve, unwrap and top each one with a strawberry.

Serves 6.

VODKA-SOUSED PINEAPPLE

4 large, fresh, ¾-in.-thick pineapple slices
3 tablespoons vodka
⅓ cup unsalted butter
¼ cup heavy cream
1 teaspoon ground cardamom
2 tablespoons confectioners' sugar
12 bottled morello cherries
confectioners' sugar, for dusting

Peel pineapple and remove central core. Pour vodka into a shallow dish, add pineapple slices, then turn slices over once. Cover dish and leave to marinate for 20 minutes.

Melt butter in a small saucepan. Stir in cream, cardamom, and confectioners' sugar.

Dip pineapple slices into melted butter mixture and grill on a rack over hot coals for 5 minutes on each side, until golden brown. Serve on warm plates, with pineapple centers filled with morello cherries. Dust lightly with confectioners' sugar.

Serves 4.

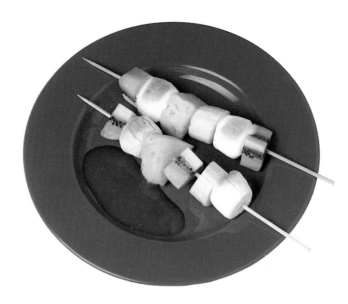

MARSHMALLOW FRUIT KABOBS

2 firm bananas
2 thick slices pineapple, trimmed
2 kiwi fruit, cut into ¾-in. pieces
24 marshmallows
1 tablespoon honey
1 tablespoon lemon juice
RASPBERRY SAUCE:
1½ cups raspberries, fresh or frozen, thawed if
    frozen
juice 1 orange
1 tablespoon confectioners' sugar

Make the sauce. Put all the sauce ingredients in a food processor or blender and blend until smooth. Press through a sieve.

Cut bananas into thick slices and pineapple into chunks. Thread all the fruit on to 12 oiled bamboo skewers with the marshmallows. Mix the honey and lemon juice together and brush over the fruit.

Grill the kabobs on a rack over medium-hot coals until marshmallows begin to color, turning once during cooking. Serve with the raspberry sauce.

Makes 12.

Note: When using bamboo or wooden skewers, soak in water 30 minutes before using.

HOT TROPICANAS

3 pink grapefruits
3 lychees
2 kumquats, rinsed and dried
1 guava
1 papaya
1 small mango
4 tablespoons golden syrup
2 tablespoons butter
2 tablespoons dried coconut, toasted
sprigs of mint, to decorate (optional)

Halve grapefruit, separate and remove segments, and drain. Scrape out grapefruit shells, discarding membranes.

Peel and pit lychees. Slice kumquats. Halve guava and papaya. Scoop out seeds, then peel and dice flesh. Peel mango, pare flesh away from pit, and cut into strips. Combine all fruits in a bowl. Melt syrup, pour over fruits, and mix gently.

Spoon fruits into grapefruit shells. Top each with a small knob of butter. Wrap grapefruit in large individual pieces of double thickness foil and grill on a rack over medium-hot coals for 7–10 minutes, until fruit is warm but not cooked. Remove grapefruit from foil, place in individual dishes, and top with toasted coconut. Decorate with sprigs of mint, if desired.

Serves 6.

PEAR & PEACH APPLES

2 dried pear halves
2 dried peach halves
1 tablespoon sultanas
generous pinch ground cloves
pinch mixed spice
⅓ cup light soft brown sugar
2 tablespoons butter
4 cooking apples
whipped cream, to serve

Put pear and peach halves in a saucepan. Add sufficient water to just cover fruits, then bring to a boil and cook for 5 minutes. Drain thoroughly, then chop. Mix with sultanas, spices, sugar, and butter.

Wash and core apples. Put on individual squares of double thickness foil. Stuff cavities with fruit filling, packing it in firmly. Draw up edges of foil and twist to secure over apples.

Grill on a rack over medium-hot coals for 45–50 minutes. Using twisted foil as an aid, turn apples on their sides from time to time. Alternatively, cook directly in coals without turning for 20–30 minutes. To serve, snip off foil stalks and fold foil back to expose apples. Serve with whipped cream.

Serves 4.

FIGS WITH CINNAMON CREAM

9 large ripe figs
¼ cup unsalted butter
4 teaspoons brandy
1 tablespoon soft brown sugar
almond flakes, to decorate
CINNAMON CREAM:
⅔ cup heavy cream
1 teaspoon ground cinnamon
1 tablespoon brandy
2 teaspoons honey

Prepare the cinnamon cream. Combine all the ingredients in a small bowl, cover, and refrigerate for 30 minutes to allow time for flavors to develop.

Halve figs and thread on to 6 skewers. (If using bamboo or wooden skewers, soak in water 30 minutes before using.) Melt butter in a small pan and stir in brandy.

Brush figs with brandy butter and sprinkle with a little sugar. Grill on a rack over hot coals for 4–5 minutes until softened and bubbling. Whip cinnamon cream until just holding its shape, decorate with almond flakes, and serve with the grilled figs.

Serves 6.

SPICED HOT FRUIT KABOBS

2¼ lb. prepared mixed fresh fruits such as mango,
  papaya, pineapple, nectarine, plum, banana,
  lychees, cherries
⅔ cup unsalted butter
3 tablespoons grated fresh ginger
1 tablespoon confectioners' sugar
1 tablespoon lime juice

Soak about 20 bamboo skewers in water for
30 minutes. Cut fruit into bite-size chunks.
Thread a selection of fruits on each skewer.

Melt butter and stir in ginger, confectioners'
sugar, and lime juice.

Brush butter mixture over kabobs. Grill
kabobs on a rack over hot coals, turning
frequently and brushing with butter mixture,
for about 5 minutes until beginning to
caramelize. Serve warm.

Makes about 20.

COCONUT PINEAPPLE

4 tablespoons unsweetened flaked coconut
1 pineapple
2 tablespoons rum
⅓ cup soft brown sugar

Line a broiler pan with foil and spread
coconut over. Broil under a low heat, stirring
frequently, until just toasted. Alternatively,
spread coconut on a baking tray and grill
over low coals. Remove and set aside.

Using a sharp knife, cut pineapple,
lengthwise, into 8 wedges, cutting right
through leaves and leaving them intact. Cut
away core. Sprinkle rum evenly over flesh.

Sprinkle brown sugar over pineapple wedges.
Grill pineapple on a rack over a medium
heat until sugar begins to melt and pineapple
is hot and beginning to soften. Sprinkle
reserved coconut over before serving.

Serves 4.

GRAND MARNIER KABOBS

3 firm apricots
3 firm fresh figs
2 trimmed pineapple slices, 1 in. thick
2 satsumas
2 firm bananas
2 eating apples
1 tablespoon lemon juice
⅓ cup unsalted butter
½ cup confectioners' sugar
1 tablespoon Grand Marnier
1 tablespoon fresh orange juice
1 tablespoon finely grated orange rind

Halve apricots and remove pits. Remove stalks and quarter figs lengthwise.

Remove any woody core and cut pineapple slices into chunks. Peel satsumas and quarter but do not remove membranes. Peel bananas and cut into 1-in.-thick slices. Peel apples, cut into quarters, remove cores, and halve each apple piece crosswise. Sprinkle apples and bananas with lemon juice to prevent discoloration.

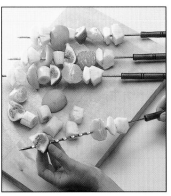

Thread fruit on to 6–8 metal skewers, making sure that each has a mixture of fruit, and starting and finishing with apple and pineapple. Melt butter, stir in confectioners' sugar, then add Grand Marnier, orange juice and rind. Brush kabobs with sauce, and grill on a rack over medium-hot coals for 5–6 minutes, frequently basting with sauce. Serve any remaining sauce with kabobs. Serve hot.

Serves 6–8.

KIWIS & STEM GINGER

6 pieces preserved stem ginger in syrup
6 firm kiwi fruit, unpeeled
5–6 tablespoons preserved stem ginger syrup
⅔ cup heavy cream
1 tablespoon confectioners' sugar
1 tablespoons chopped shelled pistachio nuts

Cut pieces of stem ginger in half lengthwise. Rinse and dry kiwi fruit and halve lengthwise. Remove firm cores, chop, and set aside. Spoon a little ginger syrup over kiwi flesh and pierce with a skewer to help absorption. Stiffly whip cream with sugar and refrigerate until required.

Place ginger in cavities in kiwi fruit. Place filled kiwi halves, skin-sides down, on to squares of foil and pour a little more ginger syrup over ginger. Wrap up securely.

Grill on a rack over medium-hot coals for 10–15 minutes, turning packages over toward end of cooking time. Serve in open packages, cut-sides of fruit uppermost. Sprinkle with nuts and reserved chopped cores. Serve with the sweetened whipped cream.

Serves 6.

Note: This dish can also be served as an appetizer, in which case omit the cream and sugar.

ACCOMPANYING DISHES

MARINADES AND BASTES

RICH TOMATO BASTE

1 large red bell pepper, seeded and finely chopped
1 lb. tomatoes, peeled and chopped
1 small onion, finely chopped
1 clove garlic, finely chopped
2/3 cup dry white wine
large rosemary sprig
2 tablespoons sunflower oil
salt and freshly ground black pepper

Put first 6 ingredients in a saucepan. Simmer, uncovered, until thickened; purée. Add oil and season with salt and pepper.

COGNAC MARINADE

1/4 cup brandy
2/3 cup dry white wine
2 tablespoons olive oil
scant 1 cup finely sliced button mushrooms
2 shallots, finely chopped
1 teaspoon thyme leaves
4 bay leaves
1 small clove garlic, crushed
10 peppercorns, crushed
1 teaspoon salt

Combine ingredients in a lidded container. Leave for 24 hours. Strain.

SWEET & SOUR MARINADE

grated rind and juice 1 orange
2/3 cup honey
2/3 cup red wine vinegar
3 tablespoons soy sauce
3 tablespoons Worcestershire sauce
1 tablespoon sesame oil

Combine all ingredients in a saucepan. Bring to a boil, then simmer, uncovered, for 5 minutes until sauce reduces by about one-third.

WARMLY-SPICED BASTE

1/4 cup, plus 1 tablespoon dark soft brown sugar
2 tablespoons red wine vinegar
1/4 teaspoon ground cloves
1/4 teaspoons ground allspice
1 tablespoon cornstarch
1 small eating apple, peeled, cored, and finely chopped

Place ingredients in a saucepan. Add 7/8 cup water. Bring to a boil, stirring; simmer for 5 minutes or until thickened.

FIERY CHILI BASTE

2 tablespoons dark soft brown sugar
2/3 cup tomato sauce
3/4 cup cider vinegar
2 tablespoons Worcestershire sauce
2 teaspoons chili powder
1/4 onion, finely chopped

Put sugar and 2/3 cup water in a heavy-based saucepan. Stir until dissolved. Add remaining ingredients; bring to a boil. Simmer until reduced by about one-third.

CITRUS SHARP MARINADE

grated rind and juice 4 limes
grated rind and juice 1 lemon
2 teaspoons salt
6 tablespoons sunflower oil
12 white peppercorns, bruised

Mix all ingredients together in a bowl, cover and leave to infuse for 8 hours, or overnight. Strain marinade before using.

Note: All the recipes given here make 1¼ cups.

SPICED GARLIC MAYONNAISE

WARM ARTICHOKE DIP

2 unpeeled bulbs garlic, separated into cloves
extra-virgin olive oil
1 cup good-quality mayonnaise
1 tablespoon Dijon mustard
1 tablespoon white wine vinegar or lemon juice
salt
red pepper

Put cloves of garlic into a small roasting pan and drizzle with 2–3 tablespoons olive oil, toss well to coat evenly. Roast for 35–40 minutes, stirring occasionally, until very tender when pierced with the tip of a knife.

2 13-oz. cans artichoke hearts in brine, drained
1 cup garlic-flavored mayonnaise
2 scallions, finely chopped
1–2 tablespoons lemon juice
1 cup freshly grated Parmesan cheese, plus extra for
  sprinkling
2 tablespoons chopped fresh parsley
½ teaspoon dried thyme
½ teaspoon dried oregano
red pepper
paprika or mild chili powder, to garnish
toasted French bread, to serve

Transfer to a plate to cool, then squeeze each clove of garlic out of its skin into a food processor fitted with a metal blade. Process until smooth, scraping the side of the bowl once of twice. Add mayonnaise, mustard, vinegar or lemon juice, and process to blend. Season with a little salt and red pepper.

Lightly oil a 4½ cup shallow baking dish. Dry artichokes on paper towels; cut any large artichoke hearts into halves or quarters. Mix with mayonnaise, scallions, lemon juice, Parmesan cheese, parsley, thyme, and oregano; season with red pepper.

With the machine running, gradually add about ½ cup of the oil in a thin steady stream, until oil is incorporated and mayonnaise is thick and creamy. Add more salt and red pepper if necessary. If not using immediately, add about 2 tablespoons boiling water and process to blend; this helps prevent mayonnaise from separating when refrigerated. Cover and refrigerate for up to 3 days. To serve, bring to room temperature and stir.

Serves 8–10.

Spread artichoke mixture evenly in baking dish and sprinkle with a little Parmesan cheese and paprika or chili powder. Bake for about 20 minutes until hot and lightly browned on top. Serve immediately with toasted French bread.

Serves 6–8.

SMOKY EGGPLANT DIP

1 extra large eggplant
¼ cup lemon juice
3–4 cloves garlic, crushed
3–4 tablespoons sesame seed paste or mayonnaise
salt and freshly ground black pepper
2–4 tablespoons olive oil
2 tablespoons chopped fresh parsley
TO SERVE:
crudités
warm pita bread

Preheat broiler to medium. Place eggplant on a baking tray and pierce with a knife in several places.

Broil eggplant for about 30 minutes until well charred on all sides, turning frequently. Allow to cool. Cut lengthwise in half and scoop flesh into a food processor fitted with a metal blade. Add lemon juice, garlic, sesame seed paste or mayonnaise, and salt and pepper. Process until smooth, scraping down bowl once or twice.

With machine running, slowly add olive oil until mixture is smooth and very creamy. Set aside 1 tablespoon parsley and add remaining parsley to food processor. Using pulse button, process until well blended. Spoon into a serving bowl, cover, and refrigerate until ready to serve. Garnish with remaining parsley and serve with a selection of crudités and warm pita bread.

Serves 6–8.

RED BELL PEPPER & PINE NUT DIP

2 large red bell peppers
3–4 tablespoons olive oil
1–2 red chilies, pierced
2 unpeeled cloves garlic, lightly crushed
1 teaspoon soft light brown sugar
1 teaspoon balsamic vinegar
¾ cup cream cheese or mascarpone cheese or ½ cream cheese and ½ mascarpone cheese
2–3 tablespoons thick plain yogurt or mayonnaise
2 tablespoons chopped fresh cilantro
2 tablespoons pine nuts, lightly toasted
TO SERVE:
crudités
selection of crispbreads, or toast

Preheat oven to 400°F. Put red bell peppers in a baking dish and brush generously with olive oil on all sides. Bake for 15 minutes. Oil chilies and add to bell peppers, with cloves of garlic. Bake for 15–20 minutes longer until skins are blistered and beginning to char. Remove bell peppers, chilies, and garlic to a large plastic bag and twist to seal. When cool enough to handle, peel bell peppers, chilies, and garlic then discard the stems, seeds, and any membranes.

Put bell peppers, chilies, and garlic in a food processor fitted with a metal blade, and process until smooth, scraping down bowl. Add sugar and vinegar and, using pulse button, process to blend. Add cream cheese and yogurt, and process until smooth. Spoon into a serving dish, stir in cilantro, cover, and refrigerate. About 20 minutes before serving, transfer to room temperature. Sprinkle with pine nuts and serve with accompaniments.

Serves 4–6.

SUN-DRIED TOMATO-BASIL DIP

1 tablespoon pine nuts
3 oz. sun-dried tomatoes in olive oil
½ cup mascarpone cheese or cream cheese
½ cup cup mayonnaise
2 cloves garlic, crushed
1 tablespoon balsamic vinegar
2–3 tablespoons oil from sun-dried tomatoes
1 tablespoon chopped fresh oregano or marjoram
2 tablespoons fresh basil, torn into pieces
fresh basil leaves, to garnish

In a dry skillet over a medium-low heat, toast pine nuts for 5 minutes or until golden, tossing frequently. Allow to cool.

Coarsely chop sun-dried tomatoes. Put into a food processor fitted with a metal blade. Add mascarpone cheese or cream cheese, mayonnaise, garlic, balsamic vinegar, and sun-dried tomato oil. Process until nearly smooth and scrape down bowl of processor.

Add oregano and basil and process until smooth, scraping down bowl again. If mixture is too thick, add a little more of the oil or a little boiling water. Spoon into a serving bowl, cover, and refrigerate. About 15 minutes before serving, transfer dip to room temperature. Sprinkle with roasted pine nuts and garnish with basil leaves.

Serves 6–8.

BISSARA

1 lb. frozen fava beans
4 cloves garlic, crushed
3 scallions, roughly chopped
1 teaspoon ground cumin
2 tablespoons each chopped fresh mint, chopped fresh cilantro, and chopped fresh parsley
salt
pinch red pepper
juice ½ lemon
toasted Arab bread, olive oil, and red pepper, to serve

Boil beans for 5 minutes, or until tender. Drain, reserving a little of the cooking liquid, and refresh in cold water. Drain again.

Slip beans out of their skins and place in a food processor or blender with garlic. Process to a rough purée then add scallions, cumin, mint, cilantro, parsley, salt, red pepper, and lemon juice. Process again until thoroughly blended. Add enough of reserved cooking liquid to make a spreading consistency.

To serve, spread purée on toasted bread. Drizzle a little olive oil over and sprinkle with red pepper. Cut toasted bread into smaller pieces, as desired.

Serves 6–8.

Note: Bissara is traditionally made with dried fava beans.

Variation: Add sufficient cooking liquid to make a dipping consistency and serve with raw vegetables.

LOW-FAT WATERCRESS DIP

2 cups watercress
1 cup low-fat Greek or thick yogurt or ½ cup yogurt
    and ½ cup reduced-calorie mayonnaise, mixed
freshly ground black pepper
lemon juice
2 large slices smoked salmon
1 lb. cooked large shrimp
lemon wedges, to serve

Cut coarse stems from watercress. Set aside a few watercress sprigs for garnish.

Put remaining watercress in a food processor fitted with a metal blade, add yogurt and, if using, mayonnaise. Season with pepper and a little lemon juice. Process until smooth, scraping down bowl once or twice. Scrape into a bowl, cover, and refrigerate until required.

Spread salmon slices on counter. Sprinkle with a little pepper and lemon juice. Cut slices lengthwise into 1½-in. strips about 4 in. long. Roll each strip into a log shape. Arrange smoked salmon rolls and shrimp on a plate and garnish with watercress sprigs. About 15 minutes before serving, transfer dip to room temperature. Serve with smoked salmon rolls, shrimp, and lemon wedges.

Serves 4–6.

SPICY CRANBERRY CHUTNEY

2 cups cranberries
2 packed cups light brown sugar
1⅓ cups raspberry vinegar or red wine vinegar
2 large red onions, finely chopped
1 red chili, cored, seeded, and finely chopped
1 lb. seedless black grapes
1 in. fresh ginger, finely chopped or grated
1 teaspoon juniper berries, lightly crushed
seeds from 6–8 cardamom pods
½ teaspoon ground cloves or allspice
freshly ground black pepper

In a large saucepan over a medium-high heat, bring cranberries and ¼ cup water to a boil. Cook until cranberries begin to pop, stirring frequently.

Add sugar and vinegar, reduce heat to medium, and stir until sugar has dissolved. Stir in remaining ingredients and simmer gently, uncovered, for about 45 minutes until mixture is thick and soft. Remove from heat and leave to cool. Spoon into a serving bowl and put in refrigerator until required.

Serves 10–12.

Tip: For longer storage, the hot dip can be bottled in sterilized jars, sealed, and kept for 6 months, or frozen for up to 6 months.

SPICY HAMBURGER RELISH

3 tablespoons olive oil
1 onion, finely chopped
1 red bell pepper, chopped
2–3 cloves garlic, finely chopped
1-in. piece fresh ginger, finely chopped
6 large ripe tomatoes, peeled and cut into ½-in.
  pieces
1 teaspoon dried chili flakes
1 teaspoon ground cinnamon
1 teaspoon ground nutmeg
salt and freshly ground black pepper
⅓ cup balsamic vinegar or cider vinegar
⅓ cup light or dark brown sugar
1–2 tablespoons chopped fresh cilantro or parsley

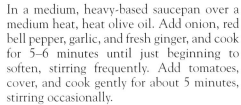

In a medium, heavy-based saucepan over a medium heat, heat olive oil. Add onion, red bell pepper, garlic, and fresh ginger, and cook for 5–6 minutes until just beginning to soften, stirring frequently. Add tomatoes, cover, and cook gently for about 5 minutes, stirring occasionally.

Stir in chili flakes, cinnamon, nutmeg, salt and pepper, vinegar, and sugar, and bring to a boil, stirring to dissolve sugar. Simmer for about 20 minutes until liquid has evaporated and vegetables are tender. Remove from heat and stir in cilantro or parsley. Set aside to cool. Pour into a glass or plastic container with an airtight cover and refrigerate for up to 1 week.

Serves 12–14.

HOISIN RELISH

½ cup hoisin sauce or Chinese plum sauce
¼ cup tomato sauce
2 tablespoons Japanese soy sauce
2 tablespoons Chinese chili sauce
2–4 scallions, thinly sliced diagonally
1-in. piece fresh ginger, finely grated
cilantro leaves, to garnish
asparagus spears, baby corn, or cucumber strips, for
  dipping

Put hoisin sauce or plum sauce in a bowl and blend in tomato sauce, soy sauce, and chili sauce. If too thick, add a little hot water to thin to a dipping consistency.

Stir in scallions and ginger. Spoon into a serving bowl, cover, and refrigerate for about 30 minutes or until required. Garnish with a few cilantro leaves before serving.

Serves 6–8.

Tip: Hoisin sauce is made from soy flour, chilies, ginger, garlic, and sugar. Plum sauce is prepared from plums, apricots, garlic, chilies, sugar, and vinegar. Both can be found in supermarkets or Chinese groceries.

SPANISH GARLIC DIP

ROAST BELL PEPPER RELISH

2 unpeeled heads garlic, separated into cloves
3 tablespoons olive oil
½ cup mayonnaise
½ cup sour cream or thick plain yogurt
1 teaspoon mild, sweet mustard
salt and freshly ground black pepper
TO SERVE:
selection of pepper strips and other Mediterranean
    vegetables such as zucchini and fennel
bread sticks
French bread

1 large red bell pepper
1 large yellow bell pepper
1 large green bell pepper
1 large jalapeño or other medium chili, cored,
    seeded, and chopped
1 small red onion, finely chopped
1–2 cloves garlic, finely chopped
2 tablespoons extra-virgin olive oil, plus extra for
    brushing
1–2 tablespoons balsamic vinegar
2 tablespoons shredded fresh basil
salt and freshly ground black pepper

Preheat oven to 350°F. Put garlic into a small roasting pan and drizzle with olive oil. Toss well to coat evenly. Bake for 35–40 minutes until very tender when pierced with the tip of a knife, stirring occasionally. Transfer garlic to a plate or chopping board to cool slightly. When cool enough to handle, squeeze each clove of garlic out of its skin (most of the skins will have split – if not use a knife to open), on to a chopping board. Using a small knife, chop and crush garlic on board until very smooth. Transfer to a bowl.

Preheat broiler. Arrange bell peppers on a foil-lined broiler pan or baking tray and broil for 8–10 minutes until charred and blistered, turning frequently. Transfer to a plastic bag, twist to seal the top, and leave until bell peppers are cool enough to handle. Alternatively, transfer charred bell peppers to a chopping board and cover with a large inverted bowl. Peel off charred skin and remove stems and seeds. Chop flesh reserving any juices.

Gradually beat mayonnaise into garlic, then stir in sour cream or yogurt, and mustard. Season lightly with salt and pepper. Spoon into a serving bowl, cover, and refrigerate until required. About 30 minutes before serving, transfer dip to room temperature then serve with accompaniments.

Serves 4–6.

Put bell peppers and chili into a bowl with their juices. Stir in onion, garlic, olive oil, balsamic vinegar, basil, and salt and pepper. Cover and refrigerate for about 2 hours or until required.

Serves 6–8.

CRANBERRY & ORANGE RELISH

1 orange, preferably seedless
1 lemon
1 lime
4 cups fresh cranberries
1½ cups sugar, plus extra, if needed
2 tablespoons chopped fresh mint (optional)

CHUNKY GUACAMOLE

2 ripe avocados, pit removed and flesh mashed
juice 1 small lime
2 tablespoons chopped red onion
½ teaspoon ground cumin (optional)
1 ripe tomato, peeled, seeded, and chopped
1–2 jalapeño chilies, cored, seeded, and finely
   chopped
salt
2–4 tablespoons chopped fresh cilantro
sour cream, to garnish
TO SERVE:
4 corn tortillas
vegetable oil, for frying

Grate rind from orange, lemon, and lime. Carefully peel white pith from each fruit and cut flesh into quarters. In a food processor fitted with a metal blade, using pulse button, process cranberries until coarsely chopped.

In a bowl and using a fork, mix together avocado flesh and lime juice. Add onion, cumin, if using, tomato, and jalapeño, and season with salt. Stir in cilantro. Spoon into a serving bowl, cover, and refrigerate until ready to serve. Place tortillas on a counter and cut into 3 strips. Cut each strip into triangle shapes. Over a medium heat, heat a saucepan containing 2 in. vegetable oil. When very hot, carefully add several tortilla triangles and fry for about 1 minute, turning until crisp and brown.

Add grated rind and fruit quarters to cranberries with sugar, and mint, if using. Pulse until mixture is well chopped but still has as even texture. Taste and add more sugar if necessary. Scrape into a bowl, cover, and refrigerate overnight to blend flavors.

Serves 10–12.

Tip: The relish will keep for 2 weeks refrigerated or can be frozen for up to 6 months.

Using a slotted spoon, remove tortilla chips to paper towels to drain. Continue frying and draining tortilla triangles, a few at a time. Garnish dip with a spoonful of sour cream and serve with tortilla chips.

Serves 4–6.

Tip: Pickled jalapeño chilies are available in jars from most supermarkets. If preferred, fresh chilies can be used.

ROMESCO SAUCE

BARBECUE SAUCE

3 cloves garlic, unpeeled
8 oz. beefsteak tomatoes
1 red bell pepper
⅓ cup blanched almonds, lightly toasted
1 dried hot red chili, soaked in cold water
  30 minutes, drained, cored, and seeded
3 tablespoons red wine vinegar
about ⅔ cup olive oil
salt

Preheat oven to 475°F. Roast garlic, tomatoes and bell pepper 20–30 minutes, removing tomatoes and garlic when soft and pepper when soft and lightly browned. Allow to cool.

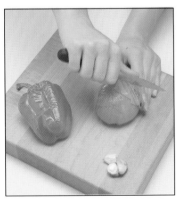

With a sharp knife, peel tomatoes and pepper, and discard seeds. Peel garlic. In a blender or food processor with a metal blade, process vegetables with almonds and chili. With the motor running, slowly pour in vinegar and enough oil to make a thick sauce.

Season with salt. Cover and refrigerate 3–4 hours before serving with meat, fish, and vegetable dishes.

Serves 6.

Variation: True Romesco Sauce is made from romesco peppers. If available, substitute 2 dried romesco peppers for the red bell pepper and chili.

2 cloves garlic
8 oz. canned pineapple in fruit juice
8 oz. canned chopped tomatoes
3 tablespoons cider vinegar
2 tablespoons soft brown sugar
2 tablespoons mango chutney
2 teaspoons Worcestershire sauce
½ teaspoon smooth mustard
½ teaspoon mixed spice
few drops Tabasco sauce
salt and freshly ground black pepper
1 tablespoon cornstarch

Peel and crush cloves of garlic and chop pineapple roughly.

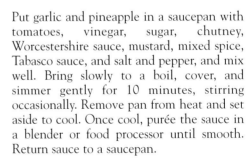

Put garlic and pineapple in a saucepan with tomatoes, vinegar, sugar, chutney, Worcestershire sauce, mustard, mixed spice, Tabasco sauce, and salt and pepper, and mix well. Bring slowly to a boil, cover, and simmer gently for 10 minutes, stirring occasionally. Remove pan from heat and set aside to cool. Once cool, purée the sauce in a blender or food processor until smooth. Return sauce to a saucepan.

In a small bowl, blend cornstarch with 1 tablespoon water. Stir cornstarch mixture into sauce and bring slowly to a boil, stirring continuously. Simmer gently for 3 minutes and adjust seasoning before serving. Serve with grilled meat or poultry such as steaks, chops, or chicken portions.

Makes 1¾ cups.

WARM SALSA VERDE

2–3 jalapeño chilies, cored, seeded, and coarsely
  chopped
6–8 scallions, coarsely chopped
1–2 cloves garlic, crushed
⅓ cup capers, rinsed
1 bunch fresh parsley
½ bunch fresh tarragon, dill, cilantro, or mint
1 cup extra-virgin olive oil
finely grated rind and juice 1 large lemon
salt
julienned lemon rind, to garnish

In a food processor fitted with a metal blade,
process chilies, scallions, and garlic until
blended, scraping down side of bowl once or
twice. Add capers and herbs, and, using
pulse button, process until finely chopped. In
a medium saucepan over a low heat, heat
olive oil until just warm. Stir in herb mixture
and immediately remove pan from heat.

Add lemon rind and juice, and season with a
little salt. Serve warm garnished with
julienned lemon rind.

Serves 6–8.

SATAY SAUCE

⅔ cup roasted peanuts
1 fresh red chili, cored, seeded, and chopped
1 clove garlic, chopped
4 tablespoons red curry paste
scant 1¾ cups coconut milk
squeeze lime juice
2 tablespoons soft light brown sugar

Put peanuts, chili, and garlic in a blender.
Mix together, then add curry paste,
2 tablespoons of the coconut milk, and a
squeeze of lime juice. Mix to blend evenly.

Pour mixture into a saucepan. Stir in
remaining coconut milk and the sugar. Bring
to a boil, stirring, then boil for 2 minutes.

Lower heat and simmer for 10 minutes,
stirring occasionally. Add a little water if
sauce becomes too thick.

Serves 6.

MUSHROOM & SAGE SAUCE

MINTY APPLE SAUCE

2 shallots
12 oz. chestnut mushrooms
2 teaspoons olive oil
1¼ cups vegetable stock
1¼ cups semi-skimmed milk
2 tablespoons chopped fresh sage
1 bay leaf
salt and freshly ground black pepper
1 tablespoon cornstarch

Chop shallots and mushrooms finely. In a saucepan, heat oil for 1 minute. Add shallots and mushrooms, and cook for 8–10 minutes until soft, stirring.

1 small onion
1 lb. cooking apples
small bunch fresh mint
5 teaspoons superfine sugar

Chop onion finely. Peel, core, and slice apples. Put onion and apples in a saucepan with 2 tablespoons water.

Stir in stock and milk. Add chopped sage to saucepan with bay leaf, and season with salt and pepper, mixing well. Bring slowly to a boil, cover,and simmer gently for 30 minutes, stirring occasionally. Remove and discard bay leaf.

Cover saucepan and heat mixture gently until apples and onion are soft. Remove pan from heat and mash apples and onion lightly.

In a small bowl, blend cornstarch with 2 tablespoons cold water. Stir cornstarch mixture into sauce and bring slowly back to a boil, stirring continuously. Simmer gently for 3 minutes and adjust seasoning before serving. Serve with chicken, fish, or veal.

Makes 4 cups.

Chop mint finely and add to the saucepan with the sugar, mixing well. Reheat sauce gently until sugar has dissolved. Serve hot or cold with pork or lamb.

Makes 1¾ cups.

CHILI SAUCE

4 scallions
1 fresh red chili
1 clove garlic
1 tablespoon peanut oil
14 oz. canned chopped tomatoes
1 tablespoon lemon juice
1 tablespoon soft brown sugar
salt and freshly ground black pepper
2 teaspoons cornstarch

Trim and chop scallions finely. Seed and chop chili finely and crush garlic.

In a saucepan, heat oil for 1 minute. Add onions, chili, and garlic, and cook for 5 minutes, stirring. Add tomatoes, lemon juice, sugar, and salt and pepper. Bring slowly to a boil, cover, and simmer gently for 10 minutes, stirring occasionally.

In a small bowl, blend cornstarch with 1 tablespoon water. Stir cornstarch mixture into the chili sauce and bring the sauce to a boil, stirring continuously. Simmer gently for 3 minutes and adjust the seasoning before serving. Serve with fish, seafood, or stuffed vegetables.

Makes 2 cups.

TOMATO SAUCE

2 tablespoons olive oil
½ Spanish onion, finely chopped
½ clove garlic, chopped
1 red bell pepper, seeded and chopped
3 lb. beefsteak tomatoes, peeled, seeded, and chopped
sugar or tomato paste (optional)
salt and freshly ground black pepper

In a skillet, heat oil. Add chopped onion and cook over low heat 5 minutes.

Stir in garlic and pepper, and cook 10 minutes, stirring occasionally.

Stir tomatoes into pan. Simmer 20–30 minutes, stirring occasionally, until thickened. Add sugar or tomato paste, if desired, and season with salt and pepper. Process in a blender or food processor with a metal blade until puréed, or alternatively press through a nonmetallic strainer.

Serves 4–6.

SPICY FISH SAUCE

DIPPING SAUCE & SPICY SAUCE

2 cloves garlic
2 small red or green chilies, cored, seeded, and chopped
1 tablespoon sugar
2 tablespoons lime juice
2 tablespoons fish sauce

DIPPING SAUCE
1 clove garlic, crushed
salt
¼ cup light soy sauce
2½ tablespoons lime juice
1 tablespoon very finely sliced scallion
1 teaspoon soft light brown sugar
1 or 2 drops chili sauce

Mash garlic with a very small pinch of salt. In a small dish, put garlic, soy sauce, lime juice, scallion, and sugar. Add chili sauce to taste. Stir before serving.

Serves 4.

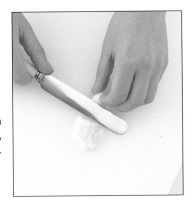

SPICY SAUCE
4 dried red chilies, cored, seeded, and chopped
6 tablespoons peanut oil
4 shallots, finely chopped
8 cloves garlic, finely chopped
1 cup coarsley chopped ripe tomato
1 teaspoon ground coriander seeds
1 teaspoon ground cumin seeds
1 teaspoon light brown sugar

Using a mortar and pestle, pound garlic and chilies until finely ground. Alternatively, very finely chop garlic and chilies.

In a small bowl, soak chilies in 3 tablespoons hot water for 15 minutes. Drain and set aside. Heat oil in a skillet over medium-low heat. Add shallots and fry until softened.

Place mixture in a bowl and add sugar, lime juice, fish sauce, and 2–3 tablespoons water. Blend well. Serve in small dipping saucers.

Serves 4.

Note: This sauce is known as *nuoc cham*. You can make a large quantity of the base for later use by boiling the lime juice, fish sauce, and water with sugar in a pan. It will keep for months in a tightly sealed jar or bottle in the refrigerator. Add very finely chopped garlic and chilies before serving.

Add garlic, tomato, coriander seeds, cumin seeds, and sugar to pan. Bring to a boil then simmer for 3–4 minutes. Pour into a fine sieve placed over a bowl. Press through as much of the contents of sieve as possible. Cover and refrigerate until required.

Serves 6.

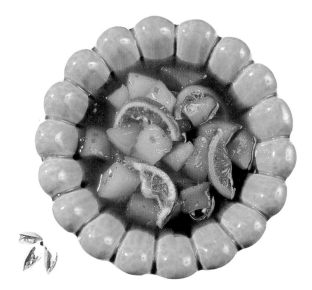

MANGO CHUTNEY

4 lb. unripe mangoes, peeled and cubed
2 limes, sliced into semi-circles
3 fresh red chilies, cored, seeded, and finely chopped
3 cups plus 2 tablespoons white wine vinegar
1 tablespoon ground toasted cardamom seeds
1 teaspoon ground toasted cumin seeds
1 teaspoon ground turmeric
1½ teaspoons salt
1 lb. soft light brown sugar

Put mangoes, limes, chilies, and vinegar into a nonreactive pan. Bring to a boil then reduce heat and simmer, uncovered, for 10–15 minutes until mangoes are just tender.

Add spices, salt, and sugar. Stir until sugar has dissolved then increase heat and bring to a boil. Reduce heat again and simmer, uncovered, for 50–60 minutes, stirring occasionally, until most of the liquid has evaporated and the chutney is quite thick.

Ladle the chutney into hot, very clean jars. Cover top of each jar of chutney with a disc of waxed paper, waxed side down. Close jars with nonreactive lids. Leave chutney for 1 month before using.

Makes 3 lb.

QUICK MIXED PICKLE

2 fresh red chilies, cored, seeded, and chopped
7 shallots, 5 chopped, 2 left whole
6 cloves garlic, 3 chopped, 3 left whole
1½-in. piece fresh ginger, grated
6 oz. cauliflower flowerets
4 small carrots, cut into fine sticks
6 oz. unpeeled cucumber, cut into fine sticks
3 tablespoons vegetable oil
1 tablespoon curry powder
½ teaspoon each black mustard seeds and ground turmeric
2 teaspoons soft light brown sugar
¼ cup rice vinegar
salt
1 tablespoon sesame oil
1 tablespoon toasted sesame seeds

Put chilies, chopped shallots, chopped garlic, and ¾ ginger in a blender. Add 1 tablespoon water and mix to a paste. Bring a large saucepan of water to a boil. Add cauliflower and carrots. Quickly return to a boil. After 30 seconds add cucumber and boil for about 3 seconds. Tip vegetables into a colander and rinse under running cold water.

Heat oil in a large saucepan. Add spice paste and fry for 1 minute. Add whole shallots, whole garlic, and remaining ginger. Stir-fry for 30 seconds. Reduce heat to medium low. Stir in curry powder, mustard seeds, turmeric, and sugar. Add vinegar, blanched vegetables, and 1½ teaspoons salt. Bring to a boil. Remove from heat and stir in sesame oil and sesame seeds. Cool then ladle into a large warm jar. Cover with nonreactive lid. Refrigerate when cold.

Makes 4 cups.

FRESH MINT SAMBAL

COCONUT SAMBAL

1 cup mint leaves
½-in. piece fresh ginger, coarsely chopped
1 small onion, coarsely chopped
¼ cup lime juice
salt

2 oz. dried shrimp
2 cups dried coconut
2 fresh red chilies, cored, seeded, and chopped
1 small onion, chopped
2 cloves garlic, smashed
1 stalk lemongrass, chopped
3 tablespoons vegetable oil

In a mortar or small bowl, pound shrimp with a pestle or end of a rolling pin, until fairly fine. Add coconut and work in lightly.

Put mint, ginger, onion, and lime juice in a blender. Mix to a paste. Season with salt.

Put chilies, onion, garlic, and lemongrass in a blender. Mix to a paste.

Transfer sambal to a serving small bowl. Serve the sambal with Vietnamese Chicken Skewers (page 51).

Makes about 1 cup.

Heat oil in a wok or small skillet over medium heat. Add spice paste and fry, stirring, for about 3 minutes until very fragrant. Add coconut mixture and fry until coconut is crisp and golden. Transfer to a small serving bowl and leave until cold. Store in a covered glass jar in the refrigerator.

Serves 6.

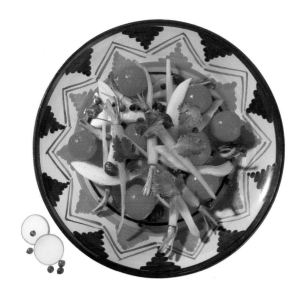

CILANTRO LEAF CHUTNEY

juice 2 lemons
1 cup shredded fresh coconut
1-in. piece fresh ginger, grated
1 fresh green chili, cored and seeded
2 cups cilantro leaves
2 scallions, chopped
2 teaspoons sugar
salt
cilantro leaves and scallions, to garnish

Put lemon juice, coconut, ginger, and chili in a blender or food processor fitted with a metal blade and process until smooth. Spoon into a bowl.

Finely shred cilantro leaves and stir into coconut mixture with scallions, sugar, and salt. Cover and refrigerate at least 1 hour. Serve cold, garnished with cilantro leaves and scallions.

Makes about 1½ cups.

Note: If fresh coconut is unavailable, substitute dried coconut, soaked in ⅓ cup boiling water 10 minutes, then drained and squeezed to remove excess water.

PICKLED VEGETABLES

8 oz. baby carrots
8 oz. radishes, trimmed
1 fennel bulb, sliced
2 teaspoons salt
¼ cup white wine vinegar
4 tablespoons sugar
1 tablespoon green bell peppercorns in brine, drained
1 tablespoon capers
freshly ground black pepper
cilantro leaves, to garnish

Peel and trim carrots, leaving some green leaves attached at the top. Place in a bowl.

Add radishes and fennel slices to carrots in the bowl. Sprinkle salt over and leave for 2 hours. Drain vegetables and rinse with cold water. Pat dry and return to the bowl.

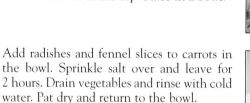

In a saucepan, heat vinegar and sugar, without boiling, until sugar is dissolved. Pour vinegar mixture over vegetables and add peppercorns, capers, and pepper. Leave until cold then cover and refrigerate overnight. Serve the vegetables garnished with cilantro leaves.

Serves 6.

PINEAPPLE & PAPAYA SALSA

CUCUMBER RAITA

1 pineapple
1 papaya
½ cucumber, peeled, seeded, and chopped
2–3 scallions, finely chopped
1–2 small red chilies, cored, seeded, and sliced
  diagonally
2–3 tablespoons lemon or lime juice
1 tablespoon honey
½ cup salted peanuts, coarsely chopped
2–3 tablespoons chopped fresh cilantro or mint

Trim pineapple, cut away skin and cut out
any remaining 'eyes'. Quarter pineapple and
remove core. Chop remaining flesh.

1 small cucumber
1 teaspoon salt
2½ cups plain yogurt
1 teaspoon finely chopped onion
1 teaspoon chopped cilantro leaves
freshly ground black pepper
cilantro leaves, to garnish

Peel cucumber and chop finely. Put into a
nylon sieve, resting on a thick fold of paper
towels. Sprinkle with salt and leave for
1 hour for moisture in cucumber to drain
away.

Peel papaya and cut in half lengthwise.
Scoop out dark seeds. Chop flesh into ¼-in.
pieces. Put into a bowl.

Line another sieve with muslin, place over a
bowl, and pour in yogurt. Leave in a cool
place for 2 hours.

Add pineapple, cucumber, scallions, chilies,
lemon or lime juice, honey, peanuts, and
cilantro or mint to bowl. Stir well to
combine and spoon into a serving dish.
Cover and refrigerate for about 30 minutes.

Serves 8–10.

Discard the whey and mix drained yogurt,
cucumber, onion, and chopped cilantro
leaves together. Season with pepper. Transfer
to a bowl and garnish with cilantro leaves.

Makes 2 cups.

CUCUMBER-BELL PEPPER SALSA

2 large cucumbers
salt
1 red bell pepper, seeded and finely chopped
2 shallots, finely chopped
1 clove garlic, finely chopped
1 fresh red chili, cored, seeded, and finely chopped
2 tablespoons lime juice
2–3 tablespoons extra-virgin olive oil
1–2 teaspoons sugar
4–5 tablespoons chopped fresh dill or mint

Peel and quarter cucumbers lengthwise; discard seeds. Put cucumbers into a colander, sprinkle with about 2 teaspoons salt, and leave to drain for about 40 minutes.

Rinse cucumber pieces and spread on paper towels to dry. Transfer to a large bowl. Add red bell pepper, shallots, garlic, and chili, and toss to combine.

In a small bowl, stir lime juice, olive oil, and sugar to dissolve sugar. Pour over cucumber mixture, cover, and refrigerate for about 1 hour. Stir in dill or mint, then spoon into a serving dish.

Serves 6–8.

Tip: Thin-skinned cucumbers do not need peeling, but varieties with a thick skin, which is often waxed for a shiny presentation, do need to be peeled.

EGGPLANT PICKLE

1½ lb. baby eggplants
½ teaspoon ground turmeric
salt
2 cups vegetable oil
6 cloves garlic, crushed
1-in. piece fresh ginger, grated
1 tablespoon garam marsala
1 teaspoon red pepper

Cut eggplants in half lengthwise; sprinkle with turmeric and salt.

Heat 5 tablespoons of the oil in a large skillet and fry eggplants about 5 minutes, until golden brown, stirring frequently. Stir in garlic and ginger and fry 2 minutes. Stir in garam masala, red pepper, and remaining oil and cook, uncovered, 10–15 minutes, or until eggplants are soft, stirring occasionally.

Cool, then spoon into sterilized jars. Cover jars with a dry cloth 3 days, stirring gently every day. Seal jars and store in a cool, dark place. Serve at room temperature.

Makes about 4 cups.

Note: If baby eggplants are unavailable, use extra large eggplants and quarter lengthwise, then slice and prepare as above.

WATERMELON & ONION SALSA

2-lb. watermelon wedge
1 sweet onion, finely chopped
1 cup canned black beans, drained and rinsed
2 jalapeño chilies, cored, seeded, and finely chopped
1 clove garlic, finely chopped
1–2 tablespoons soft brown sugar
2 tablespoons lemon juice
3–4 tablespoons chopped fresh cilantro or mint

Using a large knife, peel, seed, and chop watermelon.

In a large bowl, combine watermelon, onion, black beans, chilies, and garlic.

In a small bowl, stir sugar and lemon juice to dissolve sugar. Pour over watermelon mixture, add cilantro or mint, and toss together. Spoon into a serving dish, cover, and refrigerate for about 1 hour.

Serves 10–12.

MANGO-PASSION FRUIT SALSA

⅓ cup sultanas
1 large ripe mango
2–4 passion fruit, halved
1 sweet onion or red onion, finely chopped
grated peel and juice 1 lime
2 tablespoons chopped fresh mint
salt
2–3 dashes hot pepper sauce

Put sultanas in a small bowl and cover with boiling water. Leave for 5 minutes to plump. Drain and dry well on paper towels.

Using a large sharp knife, slice down along large center pit of mango removing flesh from both sides. Cut each half vertically in half again. Remove skin by sliding knife between skin and flesh, trimming any stray pieces of skin. Chop into ½-in. pieces. Trim skin from side of pit. Cut away any flesh still clinging to pit, and chop. Put chopped mango and any juices into a large bowl.

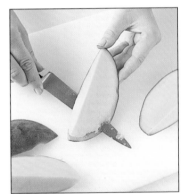

Using a spoon, scoop pulp and seeds from passion fruit. Put into bowl with mango, raisins, onion, lime peel and juice, mint, and salt. Sprinkle over a few dashes of hot pepper sauce. Toss and stir gently to blend. Spoon into a serving dish, cover, and refrigerate for about 30 minutes.

Serves 8–10.

Tip: Look for the most shrivelled and wrinkled passion fruit because this is a sign of ripeness.

APPLE, RAISIN, & MINT SALSA

½ cup raisins
2 large crisp, green apples, such as Granny Smith
1–2 tablespoons lemon juice
1 small mild onion or 4 scallions, finely chopped
leaves from 1 large bunch fresh mint
1 tablespoon honey

In a small bowl, put raisins, cover with boiling water, and leave for 5 minutes to plump. Drain, then dry well on paper towels.

Peel apples, if liked, remove cores, and chop. In a medium bowl, toss apples, lemon juice, and onion or scallions together.

Set aside a few mint leaves for garnish. Chop remaining mint very finely. Stir into apple mixture with raisins and honey, and stir well. Spoon into a serving bowl and garnish with reserved mint leaves. Serve within 30 minutes.

Serves 6–8.

PEAR SALSA

2 large, ripe dessert pears, about 1 lb., cored and cut
  into ½-in. cubes
2 dried pear halves, cut into ¼-in. pieces
½ cucumber, peeled, seeded, and chopped
½ small red onion, chopped
grated rind and juice 1 lime
1-in. piece fresh ginger, finely chopped
1 piece stem ginger in syrup, finely chopped
1 tablespoon ginger syrup
1 jalapeño chili, cored, seeded, and finely chopped
2 tablespoons chopped fresh mint
salt

In a large bowl, combine pears, dried pears, cucumber, red onion, and lime peel and juice.

Stir in fresh ginger, stem ginger and syrup, chili, mint, and a little salt. Spoon into a serving bowl, cover, and refrigerate for no longer than 1 hour.

Serves 8–10.

SPICY CITRUS SALSA

1 pink grapefruit
1 large orange
1 lime
1 plum tomato, seeded and chopped
1 clove garlic, finely chopped
1 green chili, cored, seeded, and finely chopped
2 tablespoons virgin olive oil
1–2 tablespoons raspberry or other fruit vinegar
salt
4 tablespoons chopped fresh chives

Using a sharp knife, slice top and bottom off grapefruit, orange, and lemon. Starting at one end, peel the skin and pith from fruit.

Holding grapefruit in one hand, and working over a large bowl to catch the juice, slice down between membranes of fruit, twisting to remove segment. Repeat to remove all segments. Squeeze juice from remaining segments and center core. Add to bowl. Prepare orange and lime in the same way. If liked, cut any large grapefruit and orange segments into smaller pieces.

Add tomato, garlic, chili, oil, vinegar, salt, and chives. Stir to blend. Cover and refrigerate until required, preferably no longer than 3–4 hours.

Serves 6–8.

CHERRY TOMATO & FETA SALSA

¼ small white, green, or red cabbage
1 cup Kalamata or other black olives
2–3 tablespoons red wine vinegar
1 lb. cherry tomatoes, halved
1 small cucumber, lightly peeled
8 oz. feta cheese, diced
1–2 pickled hot peppers or fresh chilies, cored, seeded, and chopped
⅓–½ cup virgin olive oil
4–6 tablespoons chopped fresh cilantro or flat-leaf parsley

Using a large, sharp knife, quarter cabbage and remove core. Finely shred cabbage.

With a cherry pitter, remove pits from olives.

In a large bowl, toss cabbage with vinegar, cherry tomatoes, and olives. Cut cucumber lengthwise into quarters and remove seeds. Chop into ½-in. pieces and add to the cabbage mixture. Stir in cheese, pickled peppers or chilies, olive oil, and cilantro or parsley. Cover and refrigerate for 3–4 hours.

Serves 10–12.

Tip: Pickled hot peppers are available from supermarkets and Greek specialty stores.

CHILI-LOVERS' SALSA

4–5 habanero chilies, or other hot chili
2 jalapeño chilies, cored and seeded
2 ripe plum or beefsteak tomatoes, peeled and seeded
2 cloves garlic, finely chopped
1 tablespoon finely chopped onion
2–3 tablespoons olive oil
2 tablespoons red wine vinegar
1 tablespoon light brown sugar
3–4 tablespoons chopped fresh cilantro or parsley

SPICY ALMONDS

1½ cups unskinned almonds
¼ teaspoon ground allspice
¼ teaspoon ground cumin
2 teaspoons salt
3 tablespoons butter

Put almonds into a saucepan of hot water. Bring to a boil and simmer for 30 seconds. Drain, leave for 1 minute, then rub off skins. Mix allspice, cumin, and salt together and set aside.

Preheat broiler. Arrange habanero chilies on a foil-lined broiler pan and broil for about 5 minutes until charred and blistered, turning frequently. Transfer to a large plastic bag, seal top, and leave until cool enough to handle. (See top left.) Peel off charred skin and remove stem, core, and seeds. Chop flesh.

Melt butter in a heavy-based saucepan or skillet. Add almonds and fry gently until nuts turn golden brown.

Chop both types of chilies and the tomatoes. Put into a medium bowl. Add garlic, onion, olive oil, vinegar, brown sugar, and cilantro or parsley. Stir together. Spoon salsa into a serving bowl, cover, and refrigerate until required.

Serves 8–10.

Drain almonds on paper towels. While still hot, sprinkle almonds with spiced salt, and toss to coat all over. When cooled, put into a strainer and shake to remove surplus salt.

Makes 1½ cups.

SPICED OLIVES

DUKKAH

1 lb. green or ripe olives
1 oregano sprig
1 thyme sprig
1 teaspoon finely chopped fresh rosemary
2 bay leaves
1 teaspoon fennel seeds, bruised
1 teaspoon finely crushed cumin seeds
1 fresh red chili, cored, seeded, and chopped
4 cloves garlic, crushed
olive oil

4 oz. sesame seeds
⅓ cup shelled, skinned hazelnuts
2 oz. coriander seeds
1 oz. ground cumin
1 teaspoon dried thyme
1 teaspoon salt
½ teaspoon freshly ground black pepper
bread and olive oil, to serve

Heat a large heavy skillet over a medium heat. Add sesame seeds and roast, stirring, until they are a light golden brown. Set aside to cool.

Using a sharp knife, make a lengthwise slit through to pit of each olive. Put olives into a bowl. Stir in oregano, thyme, rosemary, bay leaves, fennel seeds, cumin seeds, chili, and garlic.

Add hazelnuts to pan and roast, stirring until lightly and evenly browned. Set aside to cool. Add coriander seeds to pan and roast until they begin to pop. Set aside to cool. Place sesame seeds, hazelnuts, coriander seeds, cumin, thyme, salt, and pepper in a food processor or blender and process to a coarse powder.

Into a jar with a tight-fitting lid, pack olive mixture. Add enough oil to cover olives, seal, and leave at least 3 days before using, shaking jar occasionally.

Serves 6.

Transfer the dukkah to a serving bowl. To serve, dip a piece of bread into the olive oil and then into the dukkah mixture.

Serves 6.

Note: Take care not to over-grind the nuts and seeds otherwise they will release their oils and form a paste. Dukkah can be made in large quantities and stored in an airtight container.

MUSHROOM BRIOCHES

6 small brioches
⅓ cup olive oil
1 clove garlic, crushed
2 shallots, finely chopped
12 oz. mixed mushrooms, sliced
1 teaspoon Dijon mustard
2 tablespoons dry sherry
1 tablespoon chopped fresh tarragon
⅔ cup heavy cream
salt and freshly ground black pepper
watercress, to garnish

Pull tops off brioches and scoop out insides of each brioche to make a hollow case.

Brush insides of brioches with 3 tablespoons of the olive oil. Put on a baking tray and cook in for 10–12 minutes, until crisp. Meanwhile, heat remaining oil in a saucepan, add garlic and shallots, and cook, stirring occasionally, for 3 minutes, until soft. Add mushrooms and cook gently, stirring occasionally, for 5 minutes.

Stir in mustard, sherry, tarragon, cream, and salt and pepper. Cook for a few minutes until cream reduces and thickens slightly. Fill brioche cases with mushroom mixture, garnish with watercress, and serve at once.

Serves 6.

BRUSCHETTA

1 lb. ripe tomatoes, peeled
4 scallions, sliced
3 sun-dried tomatoes, chopped
6 black olives, pitted and chopped
1 tablespoon chopped fresh basil
salt and freshly ground black pepper
8 thick slices ciabatta
4 teaspoons pesto
2 tablespoons extra-virgin olive oil
basil sprigs, to garnish

Cut tomatoes into quarters, remove seeds, and cut flesh into small dice.

In a bowl, mix together tomatoes, scallions, sun-dried tomatoes, olives, basil, and salt and pepper. Toast slices of bread on both sides then spread a little pesto on one side of each slice.

Spoon tomato mixture on top of each slice of toast then drizzle with olive oil. Garnish with basil sprigs and serve.

Serves 4.

MARINATED CREAM CHEESE

¾ cup ricotta cheese
¾ cup cream cheese
8 Italian parsley sprigs, roughly chopped
8 basil sprigs
1 tablespoon chopped fresh oregano
2 cloves garlic, chopped
¼ teaspoon hot red pepper flakes
juice ½ lemon
10 black peppercorns, lightly crushed
⅔ cup extra-virgin olive oil
herb sprigs, to garnish
fresh vine leaves, to serve (optional)

TUNA & CAPER PÂTÉ

7 oz. canned tuna in brine or water, drained
4 tablespoons low-fat ricotta or curd cheese
grated rind 1 lemon
2 tablespoons freshly squeezed lemon juice
2 tablespoons olive oil
1 tablespoon capers in brine, drained and rinsed
1 clove garlic, finely chopped
1 teaspoon chopped fresh thyme
salt and freshly ground black pepper
toasted bead or prepared raw vegetables, to serve
thyme sprigs, to garnish (optional)

In a mixing bowl, beat cheeses together with a wooden spoon. Divide into 6 and shape into balls or round patties. Arrange in one layer in an oiled, shallow dish. Using a blender or food processor, process remaining ingredients until fairly smooth.

Place tuna in a bowl and mash with a fork. Beat in ricotta, lemon rind, lemon juice, olive oil, capers, garlic, and thyme until creamy. Taste, and season with salt and pepper.

Pour herb dressing over cheeses. Cover dish with foil and put in refrigerator for 3 hours, basting cheeses occasionally. Remove from refrigerator 30 minutes before garnishing with herb sprigs and serving on a bed of fresh vine leaves, if desired.

Serves 6.

Note: If available, 12 oz. stracchino or robiola can replace the cheeses in the recipe.

To serve, spread the pâté on slices of toasted bread. Alternatively, serve it as a dip with a selection of raw vegetables. Garnish with thyme sprigs, if desired.

Serves 4.

FAVA BEAN FALAFEL

1 lb. frozen fava beans
2 teaspoons coriander seeds
2 teaspoons cumin seeds
2 teaspoons sesame seeds
leaves from 1 large bunch cilantro
leaves from 1 bunch flat-leaf parsley
1 red onion, chopped
2 cloves garlic, crushed
3 eggs
salt and freshly ground black pepper
flour, for dusting
vegetable oil, for deep-frying
DIP:
¼ cup Greek-style yogurt
3 tablespoons chopped fresh cilantro

Boil beans until tender. Drain well and put in a blender. Heat a small, dry pan, add seeds and fry for 2–3 minutes until fragrant. Add to beans, with herbs, red onion, and garlic. Purée bean mixture, adding eggs one at a time, to make a smooth paste. Season with salt and pepper. Chill for 45 minutes.

To make dip, stir together yogurt, cilantro, and salt and pepper. Cover and chill. With floured hands, shape tablespoons of bean mixture into balls, then flatten them slightly. Heat oil in a deep pan to 350°F. Deep-fry falafel until crisp and brown, turning once. Drain on paper towels and keep warm. Serve with the dip.

Makes about 16.

RATATOUILLE TERRINE

1 plump clove garlic, finely crushed
¼ cup oil from jar of sun-dried tomatoes, or virgin olive oil
2 teaspoons pesto
6 large plum tomatoes, cored and halved lengthwise
salt and freshly ground black pepper
3 large yellow bell peppers, seeded and cut into quarters
3 large red bell peppers, seeded and cut into quarters
1 long eggplant, thinly sliced lengthwise
2 long zucchini, thinly sliced lengthwise

Preheat oven to 225°F. Mix garlic with 2 tablespoons of the oil and mix pesto with remaining oil; set aside. Arrange tomatoes on a baking tray in a single layer and sprinkle with salt. Bake for 4 hours. Cool. Meanwhile, preheat broiler. Broil bell peppers until skins char and blister. When cool enough to handle, peel off skins. Brush pesto oil over eggplant slices, and garlic oil over zucchini slices. Broil in batches in a single layer until tender and lightly browned.

Line a 4½-cup terrine with plastic wrap leaving excess to cover top. Layer vegetables alternately in terrine, adding salt and pepper between each layer. Fold excess plastic wrap over vegetables. Put weights on top and chill for about 8 hours. To serve, remove weights and top covering. Invert terrine on to a board. Using a large, sharp knife, cut into slices, then halve slices. Pierce pieces with small skewers and arrange on a serving dish.

Makes about 52.

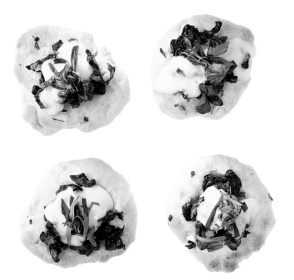

MINI PIZZAS

4 cups bread flour, plus extra for dusting
1 sachet fast rising yeast
salt and freshly ground black pepper
2 tablespoons virgin olive oil, plus extra for brushing
virgin olive oil for greasing
TOPPING:
2 tablespoons virgin olive oil
2 shallots, finely chopped
2 cloves garlic, finely crushed
1 lb. mixed brown, shiitake, and oyster mushrooms, diced
1 tablespoon chopped fresh tarragon
9-oz. jar hollandaise sauce

To make topping, heat oil in a skillet, add shallots, and cook until tender and lightly browned. Stir in garlic and mushrooms, and cook for an additional 5 minutes or until all the liquid has evaporated. Add tarragon, and season with salt and pepper. Set aside.

In a large mixing bowl, stir together flour, yeast, and salt and pepper. Gradually stir in scant 1 cup warm water, the oil, and beat to a soft but not wet dough. Turn on to a lightly floured surface and knead for 10 minutes, until smooth and elastic.

Preheat oven to 450°F. Oil 2 baking trays. Punch down dough and knead briefly. Divide into 16 pieces. Roll each piece to ¼-in.-thick circle.

Put into an oiled bowl, cover with plastic wrap, and leave until doubled in volume.

Transfer dough circles to baking trays. Brush with virgin olive oil. Spoon on mushroom mixture. Bake for about 10 minutes or until bases are crisp and browned. Preheat broiler. Spoon hollandaise sauce on to pizzas and put briefly under broiler until glazed.

Makes 16.

PEPPERED PECORINO CHEESE

1 lb. pecorino cheese
3 tablespoons black peppercorns, lightly crushed
1 teaspoon finely grated lemon rind (optional)
⅔ cup extra-virgin olive oil
Italian parsley sprigs, to garnish

Remove rind from cheese and discard. Cut cheese into 1-in. cubes. Put into a shallow dish.

Sprinkle peppercorns, and lemon rind, if using, over cheese. Pour oil over.

Cover dish with foil and put in refrigerator for 2 hours, basting cheese occasionally. Remove from refrigerator 30 minutes before serving. Garnish with Italian parsley sprigs.

Serves 6–8.

Note: This dish can be kept covered in the refrigerator for up to 4 days but it is important to return it to room temperature 30 minutes before serving.

ROASTED BELL PEPPER SALAD

4 red bell peppers, broiled or roasted until charred
4 canned anchovy fillets, drained and cut lengthwise into slivers
1 tablespoon capers, drained (optional)
½ cup extra-virgin olive oil
1 tablespoon finely chopped fresh parsley
salt and freshly ground black pepper

Peel bell peppers and remove and discard cores and seeds. Cut bell peppers into strips.

Place bell peppers in a shallow dish. Arrange anchovy fillets on top, and sprinkle with capers, if using.

In a small bowl, beat together oil, parsley, black pepper, and just a little salt, if needed. Drizzle the dressing over bell peppers, anchovies, and capers.

Serves 4.

LEEK SALAD

8 long, slim leeks
1 small red bell pepper, seeded and cut into strips
½ cup extra-virgin olive oil
¼ cup white wine vinegar
pinch sugar
generous pinch paprika
salt and freshly ground black pepper
chopped parsley, capers (optional), and pitted oil-
    cured ripe olives, to garnish

In a saucepan of boiling salted water, cook leeks about 6 minutes or until tender but still firm.

Meanwhile, in a bowl, mix together red bell pepper strips, oil, vinegar, sugar, paprika, salt, and pepper. Drain leeks well, pat dry with paper towels to absorb excess moisture, then place in a warm, shallow dish.

Pour vinegar mixture over leeks, turn leeks to coat well, then cover and leave in a cool place for 2 hours, turning leeks occasionally. Garnish with chopped fresh parsley, capers, if using, and ripe olives.

Serves 4.

VEGETABLES WITH TWO OILS

½ cup virgin olive oil
2 cloves garlic, peeled
½ teaspoon coriander seeds, bruised
½ teaspoon fennel seeds, bruised
2 strips lemon rind
2 thyme sprigs, bruised
⅓ cup peanut oil
½ teaspoon sesame oil
2 slices fresh ginger, bruised
1 small shallot, sliced
1 teaspoon crushed dried red chilies
½ teaspoon Szechuan peppers, bruised
1½ lb. selection of baby vegetables, to serve

In a pan, heat 1 tablespoon of the olive oil and fry whole garlic cloves, coriander, and fennel seeds for 5 minutes until golden. Cool and transfer to a screw-top jar. Add remaining olive oil, lemon rind, and thyme, seal the jar and set aside. In a second jar, mix together peanut oil, sesame oil, and all remaining ingredients, except the vegetables for crudités. Leave both the oils to infuse for 1–2 days.

When ready to serve, transfer the two oils to small bowls. Wash and trim the vegetables as necessary and serve as crudités with the oils and slices of fresh Italian bread.

Serves 6.

Note: Choose from a selection of your favorite vegetables, such as small radishes, asparagus, broccoli, cauliflower, carrots, bell peppers, celery, and fennel. Lightly cooked vegetables can also be used as crudités.

CHEESE & TOMATO SKEWERS

FRESH HERB FRITTATA

8 oz. pecorino cheese, cut into about ½-in. cubes
24 small cherry tomatoes
3 tablespoons extra-virgin olive oil
1½ tablespoons lemon juice
1 tablespoon chopped fresh parsley
1 tablespoon chopped fresh oregano
freshly ground black pepper

6 eggs
2 egg whites
2 scallions, trimmed and chopped
½ cup cottage cheese
½ cup chopped fresh mixed herbs
1 cup arugula
salt and freshly ground black pepper
olive oil

Whisk eggs and egg whites together until thoroughly mixed and stir in scallions, cheese, and herbs. Roughly chop arugula and add to mixture together with salt and pepper. Preheat broiler. Heat about 4 teaspoons oil

Thread cheese and cherry tomatoes alternately on to wooden toothpicks. Put in a shallow, nonmetallic dish.

in a nonstick skillet and pour in egg mixture, swirling to reach the edges of the pan. Cook, stirring, over a medium-low heat for about 3 minutes until eggs are beginning to set.

Whisk together olive oil, lemon juice, fresh herbs, and plenty of coarsely ground black pepper. Pour dressing over skewers, and turn them to coat; cover and marinate in the refrigerator for 2 hours.

Makes 24.

Place pan under the hot broiler and cook for an additional 2–3 minutes until set and lightly golden. Turn out on to a plate, cut into wedges, and serve warm or cold with a tomato and olive salad.

Serves 2–4.

ARTICHOKE & HAM TORTILLA

SALMON MOUSSE

3 artichokes
¼ cup olive oil
⅔ cup finely diced serrano ham
salt and freshly ground black pepper
6 eggs, lightly beaten
fresh parsley, to garnish

sunflower oil, for greasing
12 oz. skinless salmon fillet
½ cup curd cheese
½ cup plain yogurt
2 eggs, beaten
salt and freshly ground black pepper
2 teaspoons lemon juice
1 tablespoon chopped fresh dill
dill sprigs, to garnish
SORREL SAUCE:
1 tablespoon butter
2 cups sorrel, washed, dried, and very finely chopped
⅔ cup heavy cream

Trim artichoke stems. Tear off and discard outer leaves starting at the bottom until pale yellow leaves are reached. Cut top two-thirds off artichokes. Pare off any dark green leaves that remain. Cut bottoms into 4, trim away any purple leaves, and remove hairy choke. Cut each quarter in half.

In a large skillet, heat oil. Add artichoke pieces, ham, and a little salt. Fry over low heat about 15 minutes, stirring occasionally, until artichoke pieces are just soft. Add pepper. Stir in eggs, spreading mixture evenly in pan. Cook over medium heat, shaking pan occasionally or until underside is set and beginning to brown.

Preheat oven to 325°F. Lightly oil six ½-cup molds. Cut salmon into cubes and put in a blender or food processor with curd cheese, yogurt, eggs, and salt and pepper. Process until smooth. Add lemon juice and dill, and process briefly. Spoon mixture into prepared molds then place in a roasting pan. Pour in boiling water to come one-third of the way up sides of molds. Cover each one with foil and bake for about 20 minutes, until a skewer inserted in center comes out clean.

Cover pan with a large plate and hold in place with one hand. Quickly turn pan upside down so omelet falls on to plate. Return pan to heat, add a little more oil, then slide omelet into pan, cooked side up. Cook until lightly browned underneath. Slide on to a serving plate. Serve warm or at room temperature. Garnish with parsley.

Serves 4 as a main course, or 8 as an appetizer.

Meanwhile, make sorrel sauce. Heat butter in a saucepan, add sorrel, and cook, stirring, for 2–3 minutes, until softened. Stir in cream and salt and pepper, bring to a boil and simmer for 2–3 minutes, to thicken slightly. Turn each mousse on to a warmed serving plate, pour a little sorrel sauce around the mousse, garnish with dill sprigs, and serve.

Serves 6.

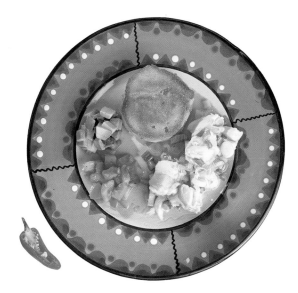

MEXICAN SEVICHE

1 lb. skinless cod fillets
1 bunch of scallions, thinly sliced
juice 1 orange and 5 limes
3 tablespoons olive oil
1 fresh green chili, cored, seeded, and chopped
salt
1 avocado
2 tomatoes
CORNMEAL PANCAKES:
½ cup self rising flour
⅓ cup cornmeal
1 teaspoon baking powder
½ fresh red chili, cored, seeded, and chopped
1 egg, beaten
½ cup milk
sunflower oil, for frying

To make the seviche, cut fish into bite-size pieces and put in a nonmetallic dish with scallions, and orange and lime juice. Mix well, cover, and chill for 3 hours, until fish becomes opaque and looks cooked. Stir in olive oil, chili, and ½ teaspoon salt, cover and chill for 1 hour. To make cornmeal pancakes, put flour, cornmeal, baking powder, ½ teaspoon salt, and chili into a bowl. Mix together egg and milk, add to dry ingredients, and mix to form a smooth batter.

Heat a little oil in a skillet. Drop spoonfuls of batter on to pan to make 6 small pancakes and cook for 2–3 minutes on each side, until cooked through and golden brown. Remove and keep warm. Halve avocado lengthwise, remove pit and peel. Dice avocado flesh and tomatoes. Serve seviche with cornmeal pancakes, avocado, and tomatoes.

Serves 6.

TUNA, BEAN, & ONION SALAD

1 cup dried white haricot or cannellini beans, soaked overnight
2 tablespoons olive oil
1 tablespoon sunflower oil
1 teaspoon balsamic vinegar
salt and freshly ground black pepper
1 small red onion, finely sliced
1 leek, white and light green parts finely sliced
1 tablespoon chopped fresh parsley
7 oz. canned tuna fish in brine, drained
1 tablespoon chopped fresh chives

Drain and rinse beans. Place in a saucepan and cover with cold water.

Bring to a boil, reduce the heat, cover and simmer for 1–1½ hours or until beans are tender but not falling apart. Drain and transfer to a large bowl. Whisk together oils, vinegar, salt and pepper, and mix into hot beans.

Stir in onion, leek, parsley, and then tuna fish, being careful not to break up fish too much. Allow to cool, then transfer mixture to a serving dish, sprinkle with chopped chives, and serve.

Serves 4.

SHRIMP & LETTUCE POCKETS

TUNA-STUFFED TOMATOES

2 crisp lettuces
1 tablespoon olive oil
1 bunch of scallions, chopped
1 clove garlic, crushed
1 red bell pepper, seeded and diced
8 oz. large cooked, peeled shrimp
4 teaspoons chopped fresh chives
salt and freshly ground black pepper
1¼ cups dry white wine
1¼ cups fish stock
½ cup butter, diced
1 teaspoon pink peppercorns
chives and red bell pepper strips, to garnish

8 firm but ripe tomatoes
1 red onion, finely chopped
1 clove garlic, crushed
2 tablespoons chopped fresh Italian parsley
2 tablespoons chopped basil
3 tablespoons extra-virgin olive oil
2 teaspoons red wine vinegar
7 oz. canned tuna in olive oil, drained and flaked
salt and freshly ground black pepper
basil leaves, to garnish
mixed salad leaves, to serve

Separate 12 large leaves from lettuces and wash thoroughly. Bring a large pan of water to a boil, add lettuce leaves, and blanch for 30 seconds. Drain and plunge into a bowl of cold water. Spread on a dish towel and leave to drain. Heat oil in a saucepan, add scallions, garlic, and red bell pepper and cook, stirring occasionally, for 3 minutes. Add shrimp, half the chives, and salt and pepper.

Slice tops off tomatoes and discard. Using a teaspoon, carefully scoop out seeds from tomatoes. Set tomatoes aside and discard seeds.

Divide filling among lettuce leaves and wrap up to form pockets. Put wine and stock in a saucepan. Bring to a boil and boil rapidly until reduced by half. Add pockets and heat gently to warm through. Remove with a slotted spoon, transfer to warmed serving plates and keep warm. Whisk butter into sauce, a little at a time, until thickened. Stir in remaining chives and pink peppercorns. Pour around pockets, garnish with chives and red bell pepper strips, and serve.

In a bowl mix together onion, garlic, parsley, basil, olive oil, and vinegar. Add tuna and season with salt and pepper; stir lightly to mix. With a spoon, fill each tomato with an equal amount of tuna mixture. Chill in refrigerator for at least 1 hour. Garnish with basil and serve with mixed salad leaves.

Serves 4.

Serves 6.

SESAME SHRIMP SALAD

8 oz. snow peas
2 oz. oyster mushrooms, thinly sliced
4 oz. canned water chestnuts, rinsed and sliced
8 oz. cooked, peeled large shrimp, thawed and dried,
 if frozen
2 tablespoons sesame seeds
DRESSING:
1 tablespoon sesame oil
1 tablespoon light soy sauce
2 teaspoons white rice vinegar
1 teaspoon brown sugar
salt and freshly ground black pepper

SHRIMP-STUFFED EGGS

4 hard-boiled eggs
¼ cup mayonnaise
2 oz. shelled cooked shrimp, chopped
salt, red pepper, and lemon juice
lettuce leaves, to serve
whole shrimp, paprika and parsley sprigs, to garnish

With a sharp knife, slice eggs in half lengthwise. Using a teaspoon, scoop yolks into a bowl, reserving whites.

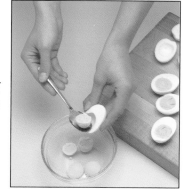

Remove ends from snow snow peas and string if necessary. Bring a saucepan of water to a boil and cook 2 minutes or until just softened. Drain and rinse under cold water. Drain and leave to cool completely.

Add mayonnaise to yolks and, using a fork, mash with yolks and chopped shrimp. Add salt, red pepper, and lemon juice to taste.

Mix together the sliced mushrooms, water chestnuts, shrimp, and sesame seeds. Stir in the snow peas. Mix together the dressing ingredients and pour over the salad just before serving.

Serves 4.

With a small spoon, fill each egg white with an equal amount of shrimp mixture. Arrange stuffed eggs on lettuce leaves and garnish with whole shrimp, paprika, and parsley sprigs.

Serves 4.

SHRIMP CRYSTAL ROLLS

8 oz. cooked peeled shrimp
1¼ cups coarsley chopped cooked pork
1¼ cups coarsley chopped cooked chicken
2 tablespoons grated carrot
2 tablespoons chopped water chestnuts
1 tablespoon chopped Chinese preserved vegetable
1 teaspoon finely chopped garlic
2 scallions, finely chopped
1 teaspoon sugar
2 tablespoons fish sauce
salt and freshly ground black pepper
10–12 sheets dried rice paper
flour and water paste
mint and cilantro leaves
iceberg or leaf lettuce leaves
Spicy Fish Sauce (see page 128)

Cut any large shrimp in half. In a bowl, mix shrimp, pork, chicken, grated carrot, water chestnuts, preserved vegetable, garlic, onions, sugar, fish sauce, salt, and pepper. Fill a bowl with warm water, then dip sheets of rice paper in water one at a time. If using large sheets of rice paper, fold in half then place about 2 tablespoons of the filling on to the long end of the rice paper, fold sides over to enclose filling, and roll up, then seal the end with a little of the flour paste. (The roll with be transparent, hence the name crystal.)

To serve, place some mint and cilantro in a piece of lettuce leaf with a crystal roll and make into a neat wrap, then dip the wrap into the Spicy Fish Sauce before eating.

Serves 4.

SZECHUAN SHRIMP SALAD

1 teaspoon chili oil
1 teaspoon Szechuan peppercorns, toasted and ground
pinch salt
1 tablespoon white rice vinegar
1 teaspoon sugar
12 oz. cooked, peeled large shrimp, thawed and dried if frozen
½ large cucumber
1 tablespoon sesame seeds
½ head Chinese cabbage, shredded
fresh red chili strips and lemon wedges, to garnish

In a large bowl, mix together oil, peppercorns, salt, vinegar, and sugar.

Add shrimp and mix well. Cover and chill 30 minutes. Thinly slice cucumber and slice each piece into thin strips. Pat dry with paper towels and mix into shrimp with sesame seeds.

Arrange Chinese cabbage on 4 serving plates and top with shrimp mixture. Garnish with chili strips and lemon wedges, and serve immediately.

Serves 4.

BRESAOLA & PEAR SALAD

CHICKEN & APRICOT TERRINE

2 ripe pears
8 slices bresaola
½ head lettuce
Italian parsley sprigs, to garnish
DRESSING:
2 oz. dolcelatte cheese
½ teaspoon Dijon mustard
2 tablespoons peanut oil
1 tablespoon lemon juice
½-1 teaspoon granulated sugar
3 tablespoons light cream
salt and freshly ground black pepper

1 lb. ground chicken
8 oz. ground pork
¾ cup coarsely chopped ready-to-eat dried apricots
1 clove garlic, crushed
⅔ cup dry white wine
2 tablespoons chopped fresh mint
½ teaspoon ground cinnamon
salt and freshly ground black pepper
mint leaves, to garnish
APRICOT VINAIGRETTE:
3 tablespoons ready-to-eat dried apricots
2 teaspoons chopped fresh mint
4 teaspoons white wine vinegar
⅓ cup olive oil

To make dressing, put dolcelatte in a small bowl. Using a fork, mash cheese then gradually beat in oil and lemon juice until smooth. Beat in remaining ingredients.

Preheat oven to 350°F. In a bowl, mix together ground chicken and ground pork. Add chopped apricots, garlic, wine, mint, cinnamon, and salt and pepper, and mix well. Spoon into a 3¾-cup terrine or loaf pan. Cover tightly with foil and place in a roasting pan. Pour boiling water into roasting pan to come halfway up sides of terrine. Bake for 1 hour, or until juices run clear. Leave to cool. Remove from pan, wrap in foil, and chill overnight.

Peel and core pears, and cut lengthwise into thin slices. Arrange on a serving plate or 4 individual plates with bresaola and lettuce. Garnish with Italian parsley sprigs. Serve immediately with dressing.

Serves 4.

Note: Bresaola is dried, salted beef fillet available from supermarkets and Italian delicatessens.

To make apricot vinaigrette, put apricots in a small saucepan and cover with water. Bring to a boil and simmer for 10–15 minutes, until soft. Drain apricots and put in a blender or food processor with mint, vinegar, oil, and salt and pepper. Process until smooth. Allow terrine to come to room temperature before serving. Slice terrine, garnish with mint leaves, and serve with apricot vinaigrette.

Serves 6.

EGGS & ANCHOVY MAYONNAISE

3 cups arugula or other lettuce leaves
4 hard-boiled eggs, halved
1 teaspoon finely chopped fresh Italian parsley
1 teaspoon snipped fresh chives
DRESSING:
5 anchovy fillets canned in oil, drained
⅓ cup prepared mayonnaise
3–4 tablespoons milk
freshly ground black pepper

To make the dressing, put anchovy fillets in a small bowl, mash with a fork, then blend in mayonnaise, adding milk to give a smooth creamy consistency. Season with pepper.

Arrange salad leaves and eggs on a serving plate. Spoon anchovy mayonnaise over and around eggs, and sprinkle with the herbs.

Serves 4.

WATERCRESS CUSTARDS

2 red bell peppers
2 tablespoons olive oil
½ cup vegetable stock
1 tablespoon butter
4 cups watercress leaves
3 eggs
¾ cup heavy cream
¼ cup finely grated cheddar cheese
1 teaspoon Dijon mustard
salt and freshly ground black pepper

Preheat oven to 400°F and roast the bell peppers for 20–25 minutes until skins are lightly charred. Transfer to a plastic bag and leave to cool for 30 minutes. Peel bell peppers, discard seeds, reserving any juices. Purée bell peppers and juices with oil and stock to form a smooth sauce. Pass through a sieve into a small pan. Reduce oven temperature to 350°F and grease 6 dariole molds.

Melt butter and fry watercress leaves for 1 minute until just wilted. Purée in a blender or food processor and gradually add eggs, cream, cheese, mustard, and salt and pepper until smooth. Pour into the molds. Place in a roasting pan and pour in enough boiling water to come two-thirds the way up the sides of the molds. Bake custards for 25 minutes until firm in the center. Leave to rest for 5 minutes, then unmold and serve warm with the reheated pepper sauce.

Serves 6.

EGG & WALNUT SALAD

1 head lettuce
6 tomatoes, roughly chopped
½ red onion, thinly sliced
16 pitted black olives, halved
⅓ cup walnut pieces
4 hard-boiled eggs, cut into quarters
1 tablespoon chopped fresh fennel
1 tablespoon snipped fresh chives
DRESSING:
3 tablespoons extra-virgin olive oil
2 tablespoons walnut oil
2 tablespoons red wine vinegar
1 teaspoon whole-grain mustard
pinch granulated sugar
salt and freshly ground black pepper

Tear lettuce into bite-size pieces and put in a salad bowl with tomatoes, onion, olives, walnuts, eggs, and herbs. Toss gently to mix.

To make dressing, mix ingredients together in a small bowl until evenly blended, or shake together in a screw-top jar. Pour over salad and serve at once.

Serves 4–6.

RICOTTA MOLDS

1½ cups ricotta cheese
1 tablespoon finely chopped fresh Italian parsley
1 tablespoon chopped fresh fennel
1 tablespoon snipped fresh chives
1 tablespoon unflavored gelatin
⅔ cups prepared mayonnaise
salt and freshly ground black pepper
fresh chives, fennel, and Italian parsley sprigs, to
  garnish
PEPPER SAUCE:
2 large red bell peppers, broiled, seeded and chopped
3 tablespoons extra-virgin olive oil
few drops balsamic vinegar
salt and freshly ground black pepper

In a bowl, mix together ricotta and herbs. Oil six ½-cup molds. In a small bowl, soak gelatin in 3 tablespoons cold water for 2 minutes. Place bowl over a saucepan of simmering water, stirring until dissolved. Cool slightly then stir into cheese mixture with mayonnaise and salt and pepper. Divide between molds and chill until set.

To make sauce, put bell peppers and oil in a food processor or blender and process until smooth. Add a few drops of balsamic vinegar, and season with salt and pepper. Chill until required. To serve, turn out molds on to individual plates; spoon pepper sauce around ricotta molds and garnish with fresh herbs.

Serves 6.

LETTUCE & EGG SALAD

12 quail eggs or 3 hen eggs
6 Little Gem lettuces
3 cups watercress
3 scallions, trimmed
1 oz. Parmesan or cheddar cheese
½ cup roughly shredded chervil
DRESSING:
3 tablespoons virgin olive oil
2 teaspoons Champagne vinegar
salt and freshly ground black pepper

Boil quail eggs for 3 minutes or hen eggs for 12 minutes, then plunge immediately into cold water. Peel and then cut into halves or quarters.

Trim and discard outer leaves of lettuces, and cut each lettuce into quarters. Discard any thick stalks from watercress, then wash and pat dry. Thinly slice scallions. Divide lettuce quarters, watercress, and onions between 4 serving plates and, using a potato peeler, shave a little Parmesan or cheddar over each. Sprinkle with chervil and garnish each salad with the hard-boiled eggs.

Blend dressing ingredients together until combined, pour dressing over the salads, and serve at once.

Serves 4.

ASPARAGUS & EGG SALAD

2 lb. asparagus
7 hard-boiled eggs
6 tablespoons olive oil
2 tablespoons white wine vinegar
2 small pickled gherkins, finely chopped
salt and freshly ground black pepper
chopped fresh Italian parsley and sprigs, to garnish

Snap off and discard woody ends of asparagus stems. Using a small, sharp knife, scrape stems, rinse, then tie into small bundles with string.

Stand bundles upright in a deep pan of boiling salted water so tips are above water. Cover, making a dome of foil, if necessary. Boil for 15 minutes until tips are just tender. Drain, refresh under cold running water, drain, untie bundles, and leave to cool.

Finely chop 4 of the hard-boiled eggs and place in a bowl. Using a wooden spoon, stir in oil, vinegar, and gherkins. Season with salt and pepper. Set aside. Quarter remaining eggs and arrange with asparagus around edge of a serving plate. Pour egg sauce into center and sprinkle with chopped Italian parsley. Garnish with Italian parsley sprigs.

Serves 4–6.

BEAN CURD SALAD

8 oz. firm bean curd
3 large carrots, cut into thin 3-in.-long sticks
3 oz. French beans, cut into 2-in. pieces
1 cucumber, peeled, halved, seeded, and cut into
  matchsticks
4 cups bean sprouts
PEANUT DRESSING:
2 cloves garlic, smashed
6 shallots, chopped
2 fresh red chilies, cored, seeded, and chopped
⅔ cup roasted unsalted peanuts
3 tablespoons peanut oil
2 tablespoons light brown sugar
¼ cup rice vinegar
1 tablespoon soy sauce
juice 1 lime

VEGETARIAN CAESAR SALAD

2 tablespoons mayonnaise
1 tablespoon vodka
1 tablespoon lime juice
1 teaspoon Worcestershire sauce or 2 drops Tabasco
⅔ cup light olive oil
1 tablespoon chopped fresh mint
1 tablespoon chopped fresh parsley
½ teaspoon ground cumin
¼ teaspoon chili powder
1 small clove garlic, crushed
2 slices day-old bread, ½ in. thick
2 romaine lettuces
¾ cup grated Cheshire cheese

Half-fill a saucepan with water. Bring to a boil. Add bean curd and simmer, turning once, for 10 minutes. Drain, cool on paper towels then cut into ½-in. cubes. Bring a large saucepan of water to a boil. Add carrots and beans. Simmer for 2 minutes until tender but still crisp. Add cucumber and simmer 1 minute more. Drain, rinse under cold running water, and drain thoroughly. To make dressing, put garlic, shallots, chilies, and nuts in a blender. Mix to a paste.

Preheat oven to 375°F. Blend the mayonnaise, vodka, lime juice, Worcestershire sauce or Tabasco together and whisk in ⅓ cup oil, a little at a time, until thickened slightly. Stir in half the herbs and set aside. Mix remaining oil and herbs, the spices, and garlic together and brush over both sides of the bread. Place on a wire rack or trivet and bake for 10–12 minutes. Turn bread and continue cooking for an additional 10–12 minutes until crisp and golden on both sides. Cool slightly and cut into cubes.

Heat oil in a wok or skillet over medium heat. Add spice paste and cook, stirring, for 3–5 minutes until slightly thickened and fragrant. Add sugar, vinegar, soy sauce, lime juice, and ¼ cup water. Bring to a boil. Remove pan from heat. Arrange bean sprouts on a serving plate. Top with other vegetables and bean curd. Spoon some dressing over. Cover and chill for 1 hour. Serve remaining dressing separately.

Just before serving, wash lettuce, discarding outer leaves, and dry well. Place in a large bowl, stir in the croûtons and cheese, add dressing, and toss well until evenly coated.

Serves 4.

Serves 4.

FAVA BEANS WITH FETA

12 oz. podded fava beans
2 oz. sun-dried tomatoes
4 oz. feta cheese
1 tablespoon olive oil
grated rind ½ lemon
freshly ground black pepper
chopped fresh chives, to garnish
salad leaves, to serve

Bring a saucepan of salted water to a boil. Add beans and cook for 3–5 minutes until just tender. Drain well and transfer beans to a bowl.

Cut sun-dried tomatoes into small pieces. Roughly crumble feta cheese.

Quickly toss together beans, sun-dried tomatoes, feta cheese, olive oil, lemon rind, and pepper. Transfer to a serving dish lined with salad leaves, garnish with chives, and serve immediately.

Serves 4.

WATERCRESS & CHEESE SALAD

3 cups watercress
3 cups arugula
1 ripe pear, cut into quarters and sliced
1 tablespoon pumpkin seeds, toasted
3 oz. Gorgonzola cheese, crumbled
DRESSING:
3 tablespoons olive oil
1 teaspoon whole-grain mustard
1 tablespoon chopped fresh mint
salt and freshly ground black pepper

Trim and discard any thick stalks from watercress. Wash and dry watercress and arugula. Shake off excess water, transfer to a large bowl, and stir in sliced pear, pumpkin seeds, and cheese.

Whisk all the dressing ingredients together until blended, pour over salad, toss well, and serve at once.

Serves 4.

SALADE NIÇOISE

8 oz. small green beans
1 crisp lettuce
4 ripe beefsteak tomatoes, cut into wedges
1 red bell pepper, seeded and chopped
3 hard-boiled eggs, cut into quarters
7 oz. canned tuna in olive oil, drained
leaves from small bunch of flat-leaf parsley, coarsely
   chopped
16 pitted black olives
6–8 anchovy fillets, halved lengthwise
DRESSING:
8 tablespoons olive oil
2 teaspoons wine vinegar
1–2 cloves garlic, crushed
salt and freshly ground black pepper

Halve beans and cook in a saucepan of boiling salted water for 10 minutes, until tender. Drain, rinse in cold water, and drain again. Leave to cool. Tear lettuce leaves and arrange on a serving plate with beans, tomatoes, pepper, eggs, and tuna.

Sprinkle with parsley and olives. Arrange anchovies on top in a lattice pattern. To make dressing, whisk together olive oil, vinegar, garlic, and salt and pepper. Pour over salad and serve.

Serves 4.

FRUITY CHEESE COLE SLAW

1 red apple
1 tablespoon lemon juice
1½ cups finely shredded white cabbage
2 sticks celery, finely sliced
¾ cup green grapes
¾ cup black grapes
2 oz. cheddar cheese
2 oz. Gouda cheese
2 tablespoons sunflower oil
2 tablespoons fromage frais or plain yogurt
1 teaspoon honey

Core the apple, cut into small chunks, and toss apple pieces in lemon juice.

Lift apple from juice (reserving juice) and add to cabbage and celery in a bowl. Cut grapes in half, remove pits, and add to the salad. Cut cheeses into small cubes and add to other ingredients.

Mixed reserved lemon juice with oil, fromage frais, and honey, and whisk until smooth, then fold into the salad.

Serves 4–6.

STUFFED VEGETABLES

¾ cup couscous
6 sun-dried tomatoes in oil, drained and chopped
¼ cup chopped ready-to-eat dried apricots
1 tablespoon chopped fresh mint
1 tablespoon pine nuts
4 scallions, chopped
½ teaspoon ground ginger
salt and freshly ground black pepper
4 baby eggplants
4 zucchini
4 baby red bell peppers
2 tablespoons olive oil
Greek-style yogurt, to serve

Place couscous in a bowl and pour ⅔ cup boiling water over.

Place sun-dried tomatoes in a bowl with apricots, mint, pine nuts, scallions, ginger, and salt and pepper. Fluff up couscous with a fork and add to bowl. Mix together. Bring a saucepan of salted water to a boil. Add eggplants, zucchini, and bell peppers, and cook for 3 minutes. Drain. Preheat oven to 400°F. Cut the tops off the eggplants and bell peppers. Cut a strip from one side of each zucchini.

Hollow out eggplants and zucchini, leaving a shell about ¼ in. thick. Roughly chop the flesh and add to couscous mixture. Core and seed bell peppers. Stuff vegetables with couscous mixture. Place in a baking dish and drizzle with olive oil. Cover dish with foil and bake for 15 minutes. Remove foil and bake for an additional 10 minutes or until vegetables are soft. Serve with Greek-style yogurt.

Serves 4.

STUFFED ZUCCHINI RINGS

½ cup bulgar wheat
6 zucchini, about 6 in. long
1 tablespoon olive oil
1 small onion, finely chopped
2 teaspoons tomato paste
1 teaspoon chopped fresh mint
salt and freshly ground black pepper
6 tablespoons lemon juice
fresh vine leaves, to serve
fresh herbs, to garnish

Put bulgar wheat in a bowl. Pour in enough boiling water to come well above wheat. Leave to soak for 1 hour. Drain thoroughly.

Preheat oven to 350°F. Cut rounded ends off zucchini. With a small corer, carefully remove centers from zucchini. In a skillet, heat oil. Cook onion until soft. Remove from heat. Stir in bulgar wheat, tomato paste, mint, salt, and pepper. Press stuffing firmly into hollowed out zucchini.

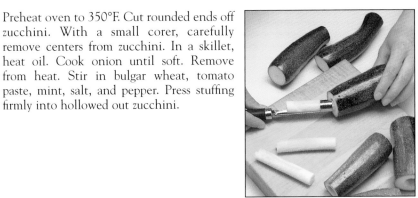

Place zucchini in an ovenproof dish. Pour lemon juice and ¼ cup water over. Cover dish and bake for 45 minutes or until zucchini are cooked but still firm enough to slice neatly. With a sharp knife, cut zucchini into ⅛-in. slices. Serve on a plate lined with vine leaves, garnished with fresh herbs.

Serves 6.

BELL PEPPERS WITH ARTICHOKES

6 red, orange, or yellow bell peppers
12 frozen artichoke hearts, thawed or 12 artichokes
   in brine, drained
24 anchovy fillets, drained
6 tablespoons extra-virgin olive oil
salt and freshly ground black pepper
4 cloves garlic, sliced
2 tablespoons chopped fresh oregano

Preheat broiler. Arrange whole bell peppers in a broiler pan and roast under broiler until skins begin to char. Turn bell peppers until they are evenly charred. Slip off the skins while still warm.

Cut bell peppers in half lengthwise and scrape out seeds. Place bell peppers cut side up in a shallow serving dish. Cut artichoke hearts in half and place 2 halves in each bell pepper. Arrange 2 anchovy fillets over each bell pepper half. Spoon a little olive oil over each artichoke.

Season with salt and pepper, then sprinkle with sliced garlic and oregano. Cover and refrigerate overnight for flavors to develop. Allow to come to room temperature before serving with crusty Italian bread.

Serves 6.

MARINATED MUSHROOMS

1 oz. dried Chinese mushrooms, soaked in hot water
   for 20 minutes
4 oz. oyster mushrooms
4 oz. button mushrooms
1 tablespoon sunflower oil
2 tablespoons light soy sauce
2 sticks celery, chopped
2 cloves garlic, thinly sliced
1 whole cinnamon stick, broken
chopped celery leaves, to garnish
MARINADE:
3 tablespoons light soy sauce
3 tablespoons dry sherry
freshly ground black pepper

Drain Chinese mushrooms and squeeze out excess water. Discard stems and thinly slice caps. Slice oyster and button mushrooms. Heat oil in a nonstick or well-seasoned wok and stir-fry all the mushrooms for 2 minutes.

Add remaining ingredients (except marinade and garnish) and stir-fry for 2 or 3 minutes or until just cooked. Transfer to a shallow dish and allow to cool. Mix together marinade ingredients and pour over cooled mushroom mixture. Cover and chill for 1 hour. Discard cinnamon stick, garnish, and serve on a bed of bean sprouts and shredded Chinese cabbage.

Serves 4.

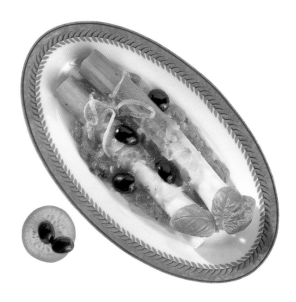

EGGPLANT & OLIVE SALAD

1 lb. eggplants, diced
salt
10 tablespoons light olive oil
2 onions, chopped
1 clove garlic, chopped
4 sticks celery, sliced
2 small zucchini, sliced
1 tablespoon chopped fresh rosemary
14 oz. canned chopped plum tomatoes
1 tablespoon sun-dried tomato paste
2 teaspoons sugar
⅓ cup red wine vinegar
1¼ cups pitted mixed olives, halved
2 tablespoons capers in wine vinegar, drained
salt and freshly ground black pepper
Italian parsley sprigs, to garnish

Put eggplants in a colander; sprinkle with plenty of salt, and leave to drain for 30–40 minutes. Rinse thoroughly to remove salt, drain, and pat dry on paper towels. Heat 4 tablespoons of the oil in a skillet over a high heat. Add eggplants and fry for 4–5 minutes until evenly browned. Transfer eggplants to paper towels. Heat remaining oil in a large skillet. Stir in onions and garlic, and fry gently for 5 minutes to soften.

Add celery, zucchini, and rosemary, and cook for an additional 5 minutes. Stir in tomatoes, sun-dried tomato paste, sugar, and vinegar, and cook, stirring frequently, for 10 minutes until vinegar has evaporated. Transfer to a serving dish. Set aside to cool, then add reserved eggplants, olives, and capers. Season with salt and pepper and toss well. Chill. Serve garnished with Italian parsley sprigs.

Serves 4–6.

LEEKS NIÇOISE

¼ cup olive oil
1 onion, thinly sliced
8 small leeks
3 tomatoes, peeled and cut into eighths
1 clove garlic, crushed
1 tablespoon chopped fresh basil
1 tablespoon chopped fresh parsley
8 black olives, pitted and halved
salt and freshly ground black pepper
basil sprigs, to garnish

Heat oil in a large skillet. Add onion and cook for 5 minutes until soft. Add leeks and cook, turning, until just beginning to brown.

Add tomatoes. Stir in garlic, basil, parsley, olives, and salt and pepper. Cover and cook gently for 15–20 minutes until leeks are tender, turning occasionally.

Remove leeks with a slotted spoon and transfer to a warmed serving dish. Boil the sauce for 1–2 minutes until reduced and thickened. Pour over leeks. Garnish with basil, and serve hot or at room temperature.

Serves 4.

MUSHROOMS WITH ANCHOVIES

½ cup crumbled fresh bread without crusts
¼ cup milk
1 lb. flat button mushrooms
4 bacon slices, finely chopped
4 canned anchovy fillets, finely chopped
1 clove garlic, finely chopped
1 egg, beaten
3 tablespoons finely chopped fresh parsley
pinch chopped fresh oregano
salt and freshly ground black pepper
¼ cup dry bread crumbs
¼ cup olive oil
fresh oregano, to garnish

Preheat oven to 400°F. Oil a large baking tray. Put bread in a small bowl. Add milk and allow to soak. Remove stems from mushrooms and chop stems finely. Put into a bowl with bacon, anchovy fillets, garlic, egg, parsley, oregano, salt, and pepper. Squeeze soaked bread dry, add to bacon mixture, and mix together well.

Divide bread mixture among mushrooms, piling mixture into small mounds. Place on baking tray and sprinkle with dry bread crumbs. Drizzle oil over mushrooms. Bake on top shelf of oven 20–30 minutes or until top of stuffing is crisp. Let stand a few minutes before serving; garnish with oregano.

Serves 4–6.

PARTY POTATO SKINS

2 lb. potatoes
3 tablespoons olive oil
salt
CHEESE AND HAM SAUCE:
1 tablespoon butter
¼ cup all-purpose flour
1¼ cups milk
½ cup grated cheddar cheese
2 oz. ham, finely diced
pinch red pepper (optional)

Cut unpeeled potatoes lengthwise into even, wedge-shaped pieces. Cook in boiling water for 5 minutes, then drain.

Preheat oven to 425°F. Leave potato wedges until cool enough to handle, then cut out flesh, leaving about ¼ in. potato attached to skin. Place skins on a baking tray and brush with oil, then sprinkle with salt and bake for about 20 minutes until crisp.

Meanwhile, make the sauce. Melt butter in a small saucepan, stir in flour, then gradually add milk. Cook, stirring constantly, until thickened. Stir in cheese and ham, reheat gently, and season with red pepper, if desired. Serve warm with the potato skins.

Serves 6–8.

CHILI CUCUMBER SALAD

1 lb. cucumber
2 teaspoons
1 green bell pepper
2 tablespoons sesame seeds
strips of fresh red chili, to garnish
DRESSING:
2 shallots, finely chopped
1 fresh red chili, cored, seeded, and chopped
3 tablespoons white rice vinegar
1 tablespoon rice wine
2 teaspoons sugar
2 teaspoons light soy sauce
1 teaspoon sesame oil

TUNISIAN ORANGE SALAD

4 small oranges
1 mooli
mint sprigs, to garnish
DRESSING:
1 tablespoon lemon juice
2 teaspoons orange-flower water
1 teaspoon superfine sugar
¼ cup olive oil
salt and freshly ground black pepper
1 tablespoon chopped fresh mint

Peel the oranges, removing all the pith. Thinly slice oranges.

Peel cucumber and slice very thinly. Place in a bowl, sprinkle with salt, and set aside for 15 minutes. Halve bell pepper and remove core and seeds; thinly slice lengthwise.

Peel mooli and thinly slice. Arrange orange and mooli slices on a large serving plate. To make the dressing, whisk together lemon juice, orange-flower water, sugar, olive oil, and salt and pepper.

Mix dressing ingredients together. Rinse cucumber slices, drain well, and pat dry with paper towels. Place in a bowl and carefully mix in green bell pepper. Add dressing, cover, and chill 1 hour. Mix well, sprinkle with sesame seeds, garnish with chili strips, and serve.

Serves 4.

Pour dressing over orange and mooli slices. Sprinkle with chopped mint and chill. Garnish with mint sprigs and serve.

Serves 4.

Note: A mooli is a large white radish. If it is unavailable, this salad is also delicious made with sliced fennel.

FAVA BEANS WITH DILL

2 lb. fresh fava beans
¼ cup olive oil
1 onion, finely chopped
1 clove garlic, crushed
2 tablespoons chopped fresh dill
salt and freshly ground black pepper
dill sprigs, to garnish
yogurt, to serve

VIETNAMESE SALAD

4–6 lettuce leaves
½ cucumber, cut into thin strips lengthwise
1–2 carrots, peeled and cut into thin strips
1 small onion, thinly shredded
2 firm tomatoes, cut into wedges
2–3 small red chilies, cored, seeded, and chopped
mint leaves
cilantro leaves
Spicy Fish Sauce (see page 128), to serve

Shell fava beans. In a saucepan, heat oil. Add onion and garlic, and cook gently until just beginning to color.

Line a serving platter with lettuce leaves.

Add beans and cook gently for 2–3 minutes. Add enough hot water to just cover beans, stir in chopped dill, and season with salt and pepper. Cook, covered, for 10 minutes or until beans are tender.

Arrange separate sections of cucumber and carrot strips, shredded onion, and tomato wedges on the bed of lettuce leaves.

When beans are tender, remove lid, and cook briskly until liquid has almost evaporated. Garnish with sprigs of dill and serve with yogurt.

Serves 6.

Arrange separate mounds of chopped red chilies, mint and cilantro leaves on top of the vegetables. Serve with the Spicy Fish Sauce poured over the salad at the table.

Serves 4.

Note: At Vietnamese meals this vegetable platter is served either as an appetizer or as a side dish, and the vegetables can be varied according to seasonal availability.

MOROCCAN BEET SALAD

2 lb. raw beets
1 red onion, finely chopped
2 cloves garlic, finely chopped
4 ripe tomatoes
1 tablespoon chopped fresh cilantro
1 tablespoon chopped fresh parsley
black olives, to garnish
DRESSING:
2 tablespoons balsamic vinegar
½ cup olive oil
½ teaspoon harissa
salt and freshly ground black pepper

Trim the ends off beets. Cook in boiling salted water for 1 hour until tender.

Drain and remove skins under cold running water. Thinly slice beets and put in a bowl. Sprinkle with onion and garlic. To make the dressing, whisk together vinegar, olive oil, harissa, and salt and pepper. Pour half the dressing over warm beet mixture and mix gently.

Thinly slice tomatoes and put in a bowl. Pour remaining dressing over and mix gently. Arrange tomatoes around outside of a shallow serving dish and arrange beets in center. Sprinkle with chopped cilantro and parsley, garnish with black olives, and serve.

Serves 4–6.

TOMATO & PEACH SALAD

¼ cup basil leaves, coarsely chopped
1 clove garlic, chopped
1 tablespoon pine nuts, toasted
3 tablespoons virgin olive oil
1 tablespoon freshly grated Parmesan or cheddar cheese
½ cup prepared mayonnaise
salt and freshly ground black pepper
2 large beefsteak tomatoes
2 large ripe peaches
½ small red onion (optional)
grated rind 1 lemon
basil leaves, to garnish

Put basil, garlic, and pine nuts into a spice grinder or food processor and purée until fairly smooth. Blend in 2 tablespoons of the oil and transfer to a small bowl. Stir in cheese, mayonnaise, and salt and pepper. Cover and chill until required.

Thinly slice tomatoes. Pit peaches and cut into thin wedges; thinly slice onion, if using. Arrange tomatoes and peaches in rings on a large plate, and sprinkle onion and grated lemon rind over. Spoon pesto dressing into center of salad. Drizzle remaining oil over tomatoes, and serve garnished with a few basil leaves.

Serves 4.

PICKLED CUCUMBER

1 cucumber
1 large or 2 small carrots, peeled and thinly sliced
2 shallots or 1 small onion, chopped
4–6 small dried red chilies
2 teaspoon salt
1 tablespoon sugar
2 tablespoons rice vinegar
1 tablespoon fish sauce
GARNISH:
1 tablespoon chopped fresh cilantro
1 tablespoon crushed roasted peanuts

Half the unpeeled cucumber lengthwise, then cut into thin slices.

Combine cucumber, carrots, shallots or onion, and chilies with salt, sugar, vinegar, and fish sauce in a sealed jar or container. Mix well and marinate in the refrigerator 4–6 hours.

Garnish the pickles with chopped cilantro and crushed peanuts, and serve either as a relish or as a side dish with main courses.

Serves 4–6 .

Variation: Other vegetables such as celery, cabbage, green beans, green and red bell peppers, and leeks can be cut into small pieces and pickled in the same way—allow a longer pickling time, 4–5 days in the refrigerator.

ASIAN CARROT SALAD

12 oz. carrots, scrubbed
3 tablespoons peanut oil
½ teaspoon sesame oil
1 teaspoon grated fresh ginger
1 small clove garlic, sliced
1 dried red chili, cored, seeded, and crushed
2 tablespoons lemon juice
1 teaspoon sugar
⅓ cup raw peanuts, toasted and chopped
salt and freshly ground black pepper
cilantro leaves, to garnish

Finely grate carrots and place in a large bowl.

Heat 1 tablespoon of the peanut oil with the sesame oil and fry ginger, garlic, and chili until just turning golden. Whisk in remaining oil, lemon juice, and sugar, and remove from heat.

Pour dressing over carrots, add nuts, and toss well until evenly combined. Cover and leave to marinate for 30 minutes. Stir again, season, and serve garnished with cilantro leaves.

Serves 4.

CUCUMBER & TOMATO SALAD

4 tomatoes
½ cucumber
1 bunch scallions
1 bunch watercress, washed
1 teaspoon chopped fresh mint
1 teaspoon chopped fresh fennel
⅓ cup olive oil
2 tablespoons lemon juice
salt and freshly ground black pepper
halved stuffed olives, to garnish

Put tomatoes in a bowl. Pour boiling water over. Leave for 1 minute, then put into cold water. Leave for 1 minute, peel, cut into small dice, and put in a bowl.

Peel cucumber, cut into small dice, and add to tomatoes. Trim and chop scallions and add to tomato and cucumber.

Break watercress into small sprigs. Mix with tomato and cucumber. In a bowl, whisk together mint, fennel, olive oil, lemon juice, salt, and pepper. Pour over salad. Serve garnished with halved stuffed olives.

Serves 4.

VEGETABLES IN SPICY SAUCE

2–3 tablespoons vegetable oil
8 oz. tofu, cut into small cubes
½ teaspoon very finely chopped garlic
2 shallots, sliced
1 tablespoon curry powder
2 tablespoons soy sauce
1 tablespoon chopped lemongrass
1 tablespoon chopped fresh ginger
1 teaspoon chili sauce (optional)
1 cup coconut milk
½ teaspoon salt
1 tablespoon sugar
2 small carrots and 1 onion, sliced
4–6 oz. cauliflower flowerets
8 oz. green beans, trimmed and cut in half
2 firm tomatoes, cut in wedges

Heat oil in a wok or large skillet and fry tofu until browned on all sides. Remove and drain. Stir-fry garlic and shallots in the same pan about 1 minute, then add curry powder, soy sauce, lemongrass, ginger, and chili sauce, if using, and cook 1 minute. Add coconut milk, salt, and sugar, and bring to a boil.

Add carrots, onion, cauliflower, beans, and tofu and stir-fry 3–4 minutes, then add tomatoes. Blend well and cook 2 minutes. Serve at once.

Serves 4–6.

Variation: If you prefer, either fish sauce or oyster sauce can be used instead of soy sauce this dish.

SZECHUAN EGGPLANT

1 lb. small eggplants, cut into 1-in. cubes or thin
   slices
salt
2 tablespoons peanut oil
2 cloves garlic, finely chopped
1-in. piece fresh ginger, peeled and finely chopped
3–4 scallions, finely sliced
2 tablespoons dark soy sauce
1–2 tablespoons chili bean paste or sauce or
   1 teaspoon crushed dried chilies
1 tablespoon yellow bean paste (optional)
2 tablespoons dry sherry or rice wine
1 tablespoon cider vinegar
1 tablespoon sugar
chopped fresh parsley, to garnish

Place eggplant cubes in a plastic or stainless
steel colander or sieve, placed on a plate or
baking tray. Sprinkle with salt and leave to
stand 30 minutes. Rinse eggplant under cold
running water and turn out on to layers of
paper towels; pat dry thoroughly. Heat a wok
until very hot. Add oil and swirl to coat wok.
Add garlic, ginger, and scallions, and stir-fry
for 1–2 minutes until scallions begin to
soften. Add eggplant and stir-fry for 2–3
minutes until softened and beginning to
brown.

Stir in remaining ingredients and
⅔ cup water and bring to a boil. Reduce heat
and simmer for 5–7 minutes until eggplant is
very tender, stirring frequently. Increase heat
to high and stir-fry mixture until liquid is
almost completely reduced. Spoon into
serving dish and garnish with parsley.

Serves 4–6.

MOROCCAN CASSEROLE

2 tablespoons olive oil
1 large onion, chopped
1 large eggplant, cut into chunks
2 cloves garlic, crushed
1 teaspoon ground cumin
1 teaspoon turmeric
1 teaspoon ground ginger
1 teaspoon paprika
1 teaspoon ground allspice
3 14-oz. cans chopped tomatoes
1 lb. canned chickpeas, drained
½ cup raisins
1 tablespoon chopped fresh cilantro
3 tablespoons chopped fresh parsley
salt and freshly ground black pepper

Heat oil in a flameproof casserole. Add
onion and cook, stirring occasionally, for
5 minutes, until soft. Add eggplant, cover,
and cook for 5 minutes. Add garlic, ground
cumin, turmeric, ground ginger, paprika, and
allspice, and cook, stirring, for 1 minute.

Stir in tomatoes, chickpeas, raisins, and
chopped cilantro and parsley. Season with
salt and pepper. Bring to a boil and simmer
for 45 minutes. Serve.

Serves 4–6.

SWEET & SOUR VEGETABLES

BELL PEPPERS & CAULIFLOWER

5 teaspoons cornstarch
15½ oz. canned pineapple chunks in natural juice,
   drained, juice reserved
3–4 tablespoons light brown sugar, or to taste
⅓ cup cider vinegar
2 tablespoons soy sauce
2 tablespoons dry sherry or rice wine
¼ cup tomato sauce
2 tablespoons vegetable oil
2 carrots, thinly sliced
1 red bell pepper, seeded, cut lengthwise in half and
   thinly sliced
1 fennel bulb, trimmed, thinly sliced
6 oz. baby corn, trimmed
6 oz. snow peas or sugar snap peas
6 oz. zucchini, thinly sliced

¼ cup vegetable oil
1 large onion, sliced
2 cloves garlic, crushed
2 fresh green chilies, cored, seeded, and chopped
1 cauliflower, cut into small flowerets
½ teaspoon ground turmeric
1 teaspoon garam masala
1 green bell pepper, seeded and thinly sliced
1 red bell pepper, seeded and thinly sliced
1 orange or yellow bell pepper, seeded and thinly
   sliced
salt and freshly ground black pepper
1 tablespoon chopped fresh cilantro, to garnish

In a small bowl, dissolve cornstarch in reserved pineapple juice. Stir in brown sugar, vinegar, soy sauce, dry sherry or rice wine, and tomato sauce until well blended. Set aside.

Heat oil in a large saucepan, add onion and cook over medium heat 8 minutes, or until soft and golden brown. Stir in garlic, chilies, and cauliflower, and cook 5 minutes, stirring occasionally. Stir in turmeric and garam masala; cook 1 minute.

Heat a wok until very hot. Add vegetable oil and swirl to coat wok. Add carrots, bell pepper slices, and fennel, and stir-fry for 3–4 minutes until carrots just begin to soften. Stir cornstarch mixture and stir into wok. Bring to a boil and stir until sauce bubbles and thickens. Add baby corn, snow peas or sugar snap peas, and zucchini, and simmer for 1–2 minutes. Stir in pineapple chunks and toss for 30 seconds. Spoon into serving dish.

Serves 4.

Reduce heat and add ¼ cup water. Cover and cook 10–15 minutes, until cauliflower is almost tender. Add bell peppers to pan and cook an additional 3–5 minutes, until softened. Season with salt and pepper. Serve hot, garnished with chopped cilantro.

Serves 4.

SPICY CAULIFLOWER

¼ cup whole almonds
1 large cauliflower, cut into flowerets
¼ cup butter
1 onion, finely chopped
½ teaspoon chili powder
½ teaspoon turmeric
3–4 tablespoons lemon juice
½ cup dried bread crumbs
salt and freshly ground black pepper
lime wedges and parsley sprigs, to garnish

MIXED VEGETABLES

2–3 tablespoons vegetable oil
12 oz. bok choy, cut into large pieces
4–6 dried Chinese mushrooms, soaked and sliced
2 oz. bean thread vermicelli, soaked and cut into
    short lengths
2 oz. dried bean curd sticks, soaked and cut into
    short sections
2 oz. dried lily buds, soaked
4 oz. sliced bamboo shoots, drained
4 oz. broccoli flowerets
salt and freshly ground black pepper
2 tablespoons soy sauce
½ teaspoon sesame oil

Heat a wok until hot. Add almonds and stir-fry over a moderate heat until browned on all sides. Remove to a plate. When cool, chop almonds coarsely.

Heat oil in a casserole over high heat and stir-fry bok choy 2–3 minutes.

Half-fill the wok with water and bring to a boil over high heat. Add cauliflower flowerets and simmer for 2 minutes. Drain and rinse; set aside. Wipe wok dry and return to heat. Add butter to wok and swirl until melted. Add onion, chili powder, and turmeric, and stir-fry for 2–3 minutes until softened.

Add blanched cauliflower pieces and lemon juice, and stir-fry for 3–4 minutes until tender but still crisp. Add bread crumbs and chopped almonds, and toss until cauliflower pieces are well coated. Season with salt and pepper. Transfer to a serving dish and serve hot, garnished with lime wedges and parsley.

Serves 4–6.

Add soaked mushrooms, vermicelli, bean curd sticks, lily buds, bamboo shoots, and broccoli, and stir-fry 2 minutes, then add salt, pepper, soy sauce, and some of the mushroom soaking water. Bring to a boil, cover, and simmer 2–3 minutes. Blend in sesame oil. Serve hot straight from the pot.

Serves 4–6.

MUSHROOM CURRY

1 lb. button mushrooms
2 fresh green chilies, cored and seeded
2 teaspoons ground coriander
1 teaspoon ground cumin
½ teaspoon chili powder
2 cloves garlic, crushed
1 onion, cut into wedges
⅔ cup coconut milk
salt
2 tablespoons butter
bay leaves, to garnish (optional)

Wipe mushrooms and trim stalks. Set aside.

Put chilies, coriander, cumin, chili powder, garlic, onion, and coconut milk in a blender or food processor fitted with a metal blade and blend until smooth. Season with salt.

Melt butter in a saucepan, add mushrooms and cook 3–4 minutes until golden brown. Add spice mixture, reduce heat, and simmer, uncovered, for 10 minutes, or until mushrooms are tender. Serve hot, garnished with bay leaves, if desired.

Serves 4.

VEGETABLE STIR-FRY

2 tablespoons peanut oil
2 fresh red chilies, cored, seeded, and finely chopped
1-in. piece fresh ginger, grated
2 cloves garlic, crushed
4 oz. each carrots, cut into matchsticks, French beans, broccoli flowerets, and baby corn, halved
1 red bell pepper, seeded and cut into fine strips
2 small bok choy, very coarsely chopped
4 scallions, including some green, sliced
1 tablespoon hot curry paste
1¼ cups coconut milk
2 tablespoons Satay Sauce (see page 125)
2 tablespoons soy sauce
1 teaspoon soft light brown sugar
4 tablespoons chopped fresh cilantro
whole roasted peanuts, to garnish

In a wok or sauté pan, heat oil. Add chilies, ginger, and garlic. Stir-fry for 1 minute. Add carrot, French beans, broccoli, corn, and red bell pepper strips. Over high heat, stir-fry for 3–4 minutes. Stir in bok choy, scallions, and curry paste, and stir-fry for an additional 1–2 minutes.

Stir in coconut milk, satay sauce, soy sauce, and sugar. Bring to a boil then simmer 1–2 minutes until vegetables are just tender. Add cilantro and serve garnished with peanuts.

Serves 4–6.

CHILLED SUMMER VEGETABLES

8 oz. baby new potatoes, scrubbed
1 small fennel bulb, trimmed
4 oz. baby carrots
2 oz. baby corn
2 oz. asparagus tips
2 baby leeks, trimmed
4 scallions, trimmed
2 tablespoons olive oil
1 cup vegetable stock
grated rind and juice 1 lime
½ teaspoon coriander seeds, bruised
2 bay leaves
2 parsley sprigs and 2 cilantro sprigs
2 tablespoons each sherry and wine vinegar
1½ teaspoons superfine sugar
4 ripe tomatoes, cut into wedges

Cook potatoes in boiling water for 5 minutes, drain, and set aside. Thickly slice fennel, trim carrots, corn, and asparagus. Thickly slice leeks and onions. Heat oil in a large pan, add fennel, carrots, and corn, and fry over a low heat for 5 minutes. Add asparagus, leeks, onions, and potatoes, and fry for 2 minutes. Add all remaining ingredients to the pan except tomatoes, bring to a boil, cover, and simmer gently for 6–8 minutes until all the vegetables are just cooked.

Strain stock into a clean pan and transfer the vegetables to a large dish. Bring stock to a boil, stir in tomatoes, and simmer gently for 3 minutes. Pour mixture over vegetables and leave to cool, then chill for several hours or overnight. Allow to return to room temperature and discard herbs before serving.

Serves 4.

Note: Garnish with fresh herbs, if desired.

FRICASSÉE OF GREENS

1 tablespoon olive oil
1 leek, trimmed and sliced
4 oz. French beans, trimmed
4 oz. sugar snap peas, trimmed
3 tablespoons vegetable stock
½ teaspoon sugar
4 oz. snow peas, trimmed
1 cup podded peas, thawed if frozen
grated rind and juice ½ lemon
1 tablespoon chopped fresh mint
1 tablespoon chopped fresh chives
3 teaspoons butter
salt and freshly ground black pepper

In a large pan, heat oil and fry leek for 2 minutes. Add the French beans and sugar snap peas, and stir-fry for 1 minute. Add stock and sugar, cover, and simmer gently for 2 minutes.

Add snow peas and peas to the pan, cover, and cook for an additional 2 minutes. Remove from the heat and stir in the lemon rind and juice, herbs, butter, and salt and pepper, and serve immediately.

Serves 4.

MIXED VEGETABLE SALAD

3 large carrots, cut into thin 3-in.-long sticks
3 oz. French beans, cut into 2-in. pieces
½ small cauliflower, cut into flowerets
1 cucumber, peeled, halved, seeded, and cut into
  matchsticks
8 oz. wedge green cabbage, cored and shredded
2 cloves garlic, smashed
6 candlenuts nuts or cashew nuts, chopped
2 fresh red chilies, cored, seeded, and chopped
6 shallots, chopped
1½ teaspoons ground turmeric
¼ cup vegetable oil
scant ¾ cup soft light brown sugar
½ cup rice vinegar
salt
3 tablespoons roasted unsalted peanuts

Bring a large saucepan of water to a boil. Add carrots, beans, and cauliflower. Simmer for 2–3 minutes until tender but still crisp. Add cucumber and cabbage, and simmer 1 minute longer. Drain, rinse under cold running water, and drain thoroughly. Put garlic, nuts, chilies, shallots, and turmeric in a blender. Mix to a paste.

Heat oil in a wok or skillet over medium heat. Add spice paste and cook, stirring, for 3–5 minutes until slightly thickened and spices are fragrant. Add sugar and vinegar, and season with salt. Bring to a boil. Add vegetables to pan. Stir and toss to coat thoroughly. Transfer to a bowl. Cover tightly and leave at room temperature for about 1 hour. To serve, mound vegetables in a serving dish and sprinkle peanuts on top.

Serves 8–10.

HERBED PEAS

2 tablespoons olive oil
1 onion, finely chopped
2 cloves garlic, chopped
1½ cups podded fresh green peas
½ cup dry white wine
bouquet garni of 2 parsley sprigs, 1 thyme sprig, and
  1 bay leaf
8 saffron strands
salt and freshly ground black pepper
strips of red bell pepper and mint sprigs, to garnish

In a large pan, heat oil. Add onion, and cook about 5 minutes, stirring occasionally, until soft, but not colored. Add 1 garlic clove and cook 1 minute, then stir in peas, wine, and bouquet garni. Heat until simmering, then cover, and simmer about 15 minutes or until peas are tender. Discard bouquet garni.

Using a mortar and pestle, crush together remaining garlic, the saffron, and a pinch of salt to make a smooth paste. Stir in a little of the cooking liquid, then stir mixture into peas. Season with pepper and cook a few more minutes. Serve garnished with strips of red bell pepper and mint sprigs.

Serves 4.

BEAN SALAD

2 tablespoons lime juice
2 tablespoons fish sauce
½ teaspoon crushed palm sugar
1½ tablespoons Nam Prik
2 tablespoons ground roasted peanuts
2 tablespoons vegetable oil
3 cloves garlic, chopped
3 shallots, thinly sliced
¼ dried red chili, cored, seeded, and finely chopped
2 tablespoons coconut cream
8 oz. French beans, very thinly sliced

In a small bowl, mix together lime juice, fish sauce, sugar, nam prik, peanuts, and 2 tablespoons water; set aside. In a small saucepan, heat oil, add garlic and shallots, and cook, stirring occasionally, until beginning to brown. Stir in chili and cook until garlic and shallots are browned. Using a slotted spoon, transfer to paper towels; set aside.

In a small saucepan over a low heat, warm coconut cream, stirring occasionally. Bring a saucepan of water to a boil, add beans, return to a boil, and cook for about 30 seconds. Drain and refresh under cold running water. Drain well. Transfer to a serving bowl, and toss with shallot mixture and contents of small bowl. Spoon warm coconut cream over.

Serves 3–4.

Note: Nam Prik is available from Thai shops.

GREEN BEANS IN SPICED SAUCE

2 cloves garlic, chopped
1 stalk lemongrass, chopped
6 shallots, chopped
3 tablespoons vegetable oil
2 strips lime rind
2 fresh red chilies, cored, seeded, and finely chopped
2 scallions, thickly sliced diagonally
1½ lb. green beans, cut into 1½-in. lengths
1 cup coconut milk
salt

Put garlic, lemongrass, and shallots in a food processor or blender. Add 2 tablespoons water and mix to a paste.

In a large skillet, heat oil over medium-high heat. Add spice paste from blender and fry, stirring, for 5 minutes until paste is lightly browned. Add lime rind, chilies, and scallions. Stir for an additional minute, then add beans and coconut milk.

Add 1 cup water. Bring to a boil. Reduce heat, cover and simmer gently for about 20 minutes until beans are tender. Season with salt.

Serves 4–6 as a side dish.

FRIED GREEN BEANS

2 tablespoons vegetable oil
1 clove garlic, chopped
1 small onion, sliced
1 lb. green beans, trimmed and cut in half
about 2 tablespoons stock or water
2–3 small fresh red chilies, cored, seeded, and
    shredded
2 firm tomatoes, cut into wedges
salt and freshly ground black pepper
½ teaspoon sugar

Heat oil in a wok or skillet and stir-fry garlic
and onion about 1 minute.

Add green beans and stir-fry 2–3 minutes,
adding a little stock or water if the beans
seem to be too dry.

Add chilies and tomatoes, and stir-fry
1 minute, then add salt, pepper, and sugar,
and blend well. Serve the beans hot or cold.

Serves 4.

SNOW PEA SALAD

1 lb. snow peas
¼ cup olive oil
juice ½ lemon
salt and freshly ground black pepper
1 clove garlic
1 tablespoon chopped fresh cilantro
1 tablespoon chopped fresh mint
lemon rind strips, to garnish

Top and tail snow peas. In a large saucepan,
heat 1 tablespoon oil, add snow peas, and stir
to coat with oil.

Add enough water to cover snow peas. Bring
to a boil, cover, and cook for about 5 minutes
until snow peas are just cooked and still have
a slight crunch. Drain and return to pan.

Pour lemon juice and remaining oil over
snow peas. Add salt and pepper, and mix
well. Transfer to a serving dish and leave to
cool. Before serving, chop garlic finely and
sprinkle over snow peas with cilantro and
mint; garnish with lemon rind.

Serves 4–6.

BROCCOLI & CHILI DRESSING

2 lb. ripe tomatoes
3 tablespoons olive oil
1 clove garlic, crushed
2 teaspoons lemon juice
1 teaspoon hot chili sauce
1 teaspoon balsamic vinegar
1 lb. broccoli
¼ cup pitted black olives, sliced
¼ cup pine nuts, toasted
1 tablespoon chopped fresh parsley
¼ cup Parmesan shavings

Place tomatoes in a large heatproof bowl and pour boiling water over to cover.

Leave for 1 minute, then drain and refresh under cold water. Skin, and discard skins and seeds, and finely chop the flesh. Heat oil in a large saucepan, add tomatoes, garlic, lemon juice, chili sauce, and vinegar. Bring to a boil, cover, and cook for 10 minutes. Uncover, increase the heat, and cook until slightly reduced and thickened.

Meanwhile, trim broccoli and steam for 5 minutes. Add to tomato sauce with the olives, pine nuts, and parsley, and stir well until combined. Transfer to a warmed serving dish, sprinkle Parmesan shavings over, and serve at once.

Serves 4.

BEANS IN TOMATO SAUCE

6 tablespoons olive oil
2 cloves garlic, chopped
1 small onion, finely chopped
2 sage sprigs
2 lb. fava beans, podded
14 oz. canned chopped plum tomatoes
1 tablespoon sun-dried tomato paste
salt and freshly ground black pepper
fresh sage, to garnish·

Heat oil in large, heavy-based saucepan. Add garlic, onion, and sage, and cook gently for 4–5 minutes to soften.

Stir in beans, tomatoes, and sun-dried tomato paste, and bring to a boil. Reduce the heat, cover, and cook for 20 minutes, stirring frequently, until beans are tender. Discard sage sprigs and season with salt and pepper. Serve hot, garnished with sage leaves.

Serves 4–6.

SWEET & SOUR ZUCCHINI

1 lb. small zucchini
3 tablespoons olive oil
2 cloves garlic, crushed
juice 1 lemon
2 teaspoons soft brown sugar
3 tablespoons chopped almonds
¼ cup raisins
salt and freshly ground black pepper
lemon slices, to garnish

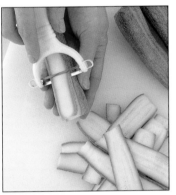

Trim zucchini and cut into long thin slices or ribbons, using a potato peeler.

Heat oil in a large skillet. Add garlic and cook for 2 minutes. Add zucchini and stir until coated with oil. Stir in lemon juice, brown sugar, almonds, raisins, and salt and pepper.

Simmer, stirring, for 5–10 minutes, until zucchini are cooked. If there is too much liquid in the pan, increase the heat for 1–2 minutes to allow it to evaporate. Serve, garnished with lemon slices.

Serves 4.

Variation: Other vegetables such as leeks and baby onions are suitable for cooking in this way.

ZUCCHINI WITH GINGER

2 tablespoons vegetable oil
small piece fresh ginger, peeled and sliced
1 teaspoon very finely chopped garlic
1 lb. zucchini, peeled and cut into small wedges
1 small carrot, sliced
2–3 tablespoons stock or water
2 oz. straw mushrooms, halved lengthwise
1 tomato, sliced
2 scallions, cut into short lengths
salt and freshly ground black pepper
½ teaspoon sugar
1 tablespoons fish sauce

Heat oil in a wok or skillet over high heat, and stir-fry ginger and garlic about 30 seconds until fragrant. Add zucchini and carrot, and stir-fry about 2 minutes, then add stock or water to create steam, and cook, stirring, 1–2 minutes.

Add straw mushrooms, tomato, and scallions with salt, pepper, and sugar; blend well and cook 1–2 minutes. Sprinkle with fish sauce and serve at once.

Serves 4.

Variation: Other fresh delicate vegetables, such as asparagus, snow peas, green bell peppers, or cucumber can all be cooked in the same way.

OKRA & TOMATOES

1 lb. fresh young okra
3 tablespoons olive oil
1 small onion, chopped
1 stick celery, chopped
1 fresh red chili, cored, seeded, and finely chopped
1 clove garlic, crushed
1 lb. tomatoes, peeled and chopped
1 tablespoon lime juice
salt and freshly ground black pepper
1 teaspoon sugar
chopped fresh parsley, to garnish

ZUCCHINI WITH GARLIC

6 zucchini
1 cup corn or peanut oil
1 cup olive oil
2 cloves garlic, chopped
⅓ cup red wine vinegar
1–2 tablespoons chopped fresh dill
salt and freshly ground black pepper
12 mint leaves

Preheat oven to 375°F. Using a potato peeler and pressing fairly firmly, peel along the lengths of zucchini to make long, thick ribbons. Divide between 2 baking trays and bake for 20 minutes until just tender.

Cut stalks off okra, taking care not to pierce pods. In a large skillet, heat oil. Add onion and celery, and cook gently for 10 minutes until soft. Add okra, chili, and garlic, and turn carefully in the oil. Cook for 5 minutes.

Transfer zucchini to paper towels to drain for 30 minutes. Half-fill a saucepan or deep-fat fryer with both oils and heat to 375°F. Line a baking tray with paper towels. Fry zucchini slices in batches in hot oil for 2–3 minutes until a light golden brown. Using a slotted spoon, transfer to prepared baking tray to drain. When all zucchini are cooked and drained, transfer to a serving dish.

Add tomatoes, lime juice, salt, pepper, and sugar. Cover and simmer gently for 10 minutes. Remove the lid and cook for an additional 10 minutes until okra are tender and the sauce reduced. If sauce becomes too dry, add a little water. Serve hot or cold, garnished with chopped parsley.

Serves 4–6.

Add garlic, red wine vinegar, chopped dill, and salt and pepper to zucchini. Toss gently to mix. Cover and leave in refrigerator for at least 2 hours. Serve sprinkled with mint leaves.

Serves 6.

FUNGHETTO

8 oz. eggplant, diced
8 oz. zucchini, thinly sliced
½ oz. dried ceps
2 tablespoons butter
¼ cup olive oil
2 cloves garlic, crushed
8 oz. button or oyster mushrooms, or a mixture,
  sliced
2 tablespoons rosemary leaves
2 tablespoons chopped fresh Italian parsley
salt and freshly ground black pepper
rosemary sprigs, to garnish

Put eggplant and zucchini in a colander and sprinkle with plenty of salt.

Leave to drain for 30 minutes. Rinse thoroughly to remove salt, and drain on paper towels. Put dried ceps in a small bowl. Cover with warm water and set aside for 20 minutes. Strain, reserving 3 tablespoons soaking liquor. Rinse ceps thoroughly and chop.

Heat butter and oil in a large, heavy skillet. Add garlic and sauté for 1 minute. Add eggplant and zucchini, mushrooms, ceps, and rosemary. Sauté for 3–4 minutes. Stir in reserved soaking liquor and parsley, reduce heat, and soak for 20–25 minutes until vegetables are soft and liquid evaporated. Season with salt and pepper, and garnish with rosemary sprigs.

Serves 4–6.

ARUGULA & PINE NUT SALAD

⅓ cup pine nuts
3 cups arugula
4 scallions, thinly sliced
8 chervil sprigs, roughly torn
2 thin slices Parma ham, cut into strips
DRESSING:
juice 1 lemon
3 tablespoons extra-virgin olive oil
1 tablespoon walnut oil
½ teaspoon Dijon mustard
salt and freshly ground black pepper

In a small saucepan heat pine nuts, without oil, over a medium heat, stirring continuously for about 3 minutes until golden brown.

Remove pine nuts to a plate and set aside to cool. Place arugula, scallions, chervil, and ham in a serving bowl. Toss gently to mix.

To make dressing, mix ingredients together in a small bowl until evenly blended, or shake together in a screw-top jar. Pour over salad and toss. Sprinkle reserved pine nuts over salad.

Serves 4–6.

CAPONATA

½ cup olive oil
1 onion, chopped
4 sticks celery, sliced
12 oz. tomatoes, peeled and chopped
3 tablespoons balsamic vinegar
1 tablespoon sugar
2 eggplants, diced
1 tablespoon capers, drained
12 green olives, pitted and roughly chopped
1 tablespoon pine nuts, lightly toasted
salt and freshly ground black pepper
2 tablespoons chopped fresh basil
red bell pepper strips and basil sprigs, to garnish

Heat 2 tablespoons of the oil in a saucepan. Add onion and cook for 5 minutes.

Add celery and cook for 3 minutes. Stir in tomatoes and simmer, uncovered, for 5 minutes. Add vinegar and sugar, and simmer for 15 minutes. Heat remaining oil in a large skillet and cook eggplants until tender and golden.

Remove eggplants with a slotted spoon and add to tomato sauce. Add capers, olives, and pine nuts, and season with salt and pepper. Simmer for 2–3 minutes. Stir in basil, transfer to a serving dish, and leave to cool. Garnish with pepper strips and basil sprigs, and serve.

Serves 4–6.

BROCCOLI CAPONATA

2 tablespoons olive oil
1 red onion, chopped
1 red bell pepper, seeded and chopped
1 clove garlic, chopped
1 teaspoon chopped fresh thyme
⅓ cup red wine
1 lb. tomatoes, skinned, seeded and chopped
⅔ cup vegetable stock
1 tablespoon red wine vinegar
1 tablespoon brown sugar
1 lb. broccoli, trimmed and chopped
2 tablespoons tomato paste
½ cup pitted green olives
¼ cup capers, drained
1 tablespoon shredded fresh basil

In a large pan, heat oil and fry onion, pepper, garlic, and thyme for 6–8 minutes until lightly browned. Add wine and boil rapidly for 3 minutes. Add tomatoes, stock, vinegar, and sugar. Stir well, then cover and simmer gently for 20 minutes.

Steam broccoli for 5 minutes until almost cooked, add to tomato mixture with tomato paste, olives, capers, and basil. Cook for an additional 3–4 minutes, remove from the heat, and leave to cool. Serve at room temperature.

Serves 4.

PEPERONATA

2 green bell peppers
1 red bell pepper
1½ lb. tomatoes, peeled, seeded, and roughly
   chopped
⅓ cup olive oil
1 onion, roughly chopped
1 clove garlic, crushed
pinch granulated sugar
salt and freshly ground black pepper
1 tablespoon chopped fresh Italian parsley

Preheat broiler. Put bell peppers under the hot broiler and cook for about 10 minutes, turning occasionally, until skins are evenly blistered and charred.

Transfer to a plastic bag for a few minutes then peel away and discard skins. Cut bell peppers in half, discard seeds, and cut into strips. Heat oil in a large skillet. Add onion and garlic, and cook gently for 3 minutes to soften.

Stir in tomatoes and sugar, and cook gently for 10–12 minutes until thickened. Increase heat if necessary. Add bell peppers strips, and simmer gently for 5 minutes until bell peppers are soft. Season with salt and pepper, and serve hot, sprinkled with chopped Italian parsley.

Serves 4.

MUSHROOM RATATOUILLE

¼ cup dried ceps
3 tablespoons olive oil
1 clove garlic, crushed
1 tablespoon chopped fresh basil
14 oz. canned chopped tomatoes
1 large onion, chopped
2 teaspoons chopped fresh thyme
1 lb. 2 oz. mixed mushrooms, wiped
salt and freshly ground black pepper

Place ceps in a small bowl and pour ⅔ cup boiling water over. Set aside for 20 minutes to soak. Strain, reserving liquid, then chop ceps and set aside.

Heat 1 tablespoon of the oil in a pan and add garlic and basil; add the tomatoes. Bring to a boil and simmer for 20 minutes.

Heat remaining oil in a large skillet and fry onion and thyme for 5 minutes. Add ceps and fresh mushrooms, and stir-fry over a high heat for 3–4 minutes until golden. Add cep soaking liquid and simmer for 3 minutes; stir in tomato sauce and simmer gently for an additional 5 minutes. Season and serve hot, warm or cold with crisp French bread.

Serves 4–6.

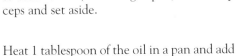

EGGPLANT IN SPICY SAUCE

1 lb. eggplant, cut in small strips
2–3 tablespoons vegetable oil
1 clove garlic, chopped
2 shallots, finely chopped
salt and freshly ground black pepper
½ teaspoon sugar
2–3 small fresh red chilies, cored, seeded, and
    chopped
2 tomatoes, cut into wedges
1 tablespoon soy sauce
1 teaspoon chili sauce
1 tablespoon rice vinegar
about ½ cup vegetable or chicken stock
2 teaspoons cornstarch
½ teaspoon sesame oil
cilantro leaves, to garnish

Stir-fry eggplant in a dry wok or skillet 3–4 minutes or until soft and a small amount of natural juice has appeared. Remove eggplant and its juice and set aside. Add oil to the pan and heat. Stir-fry garlic and shallots about 30 seconds. Add eggplant and its juice, salt, pepper, sugar, and chilies, and stir-fry 2–3 minutes.

Add tomatoes, soy sauce, chili sauce, vinegar, and stock, blend well and bring to a boil. Reduce heat and simmer 3–4 minutes. Mix cornstarch with 1 tablespoon water and stir into sauce. Cook, stirring, until thickened. Blend in sesame oil, garnish, and serve.

Serves 4.

Variation: Fish sauce or shrimp paste can be used instead of soy sauce.

SPANISH VEGETABLE SALAD

2 Spanish onions, unpeeled
1 lb. baby eggplants
2 red bell peppers
3 firm but ripe beefsteak tomatoes
8 cloves garlic
1½ teaspoons cumin seeds
juice 1 lemon
¼ cup extra-virgin olive oil
3 tablespoons white wine vinegar
salt
2 tablespoons finely chopped fresh parsley (optional)

Preheat oven to 350°F. Place onions on a baking tray and bake 10 minutes. Add eggplants.

Bake an additional 10 minutes, then add bell peppers. Bake 10 minutes before adding tomatoes and 6 of the garlic cloves, then bake 15 minutes or until all vegetables are tender. If necessary, remove vegetables from oven as they are done. When vegetables are cool enough to handle, peel them with your fingers.

Remove and discard cores and seeds from bell peppers, then cut into strips. Halve tomatoes and discard seeds, then slice. Slice eggplants into strips and onions into rings. Arrange in a serving dish. Using a mortar and pestle, pound roasted and raw garlic and cumin seeds to a paste. Beat in lemon juice, oil and vinegar. Season with salt. Pour over vegetables, and sprinkle with parsley, if desired. Serve warm or cold.

Serves 4.

RATATOUILLE

2 eggplants, sliced
3 zucchini, sliced
salt and freshly ground black pepper
3–4 tablespoons olive oil
1 Spanish onion, very thinly sliced
3 cloves garlic, crushed
2 large red bell peppers, seeded and thinly sliced
4 beefsteak tomatoes, peeled, seeded, and chopped
leaves from a few sprigs of thyme, marjoram, and
   oregano
2 tablespoons each chopped fresh parsley and basil

Put eggplants and zucchini in a colander, sprinkle generously with salt, and leave for 1 hour.

Rinse eggplant and zucchini well, drain and dry thoroughly with paper towels. Heat 2 tablespoons of the oil in a heavy flameproof casserole, add eggplant and cook, stirring occasionally, for a few minutes. Add 1 tablespoon oil, the onions and garlic, and cook, stirring occasionally, for 2–3 minutes. Add bell peppers and cook, stirring occasionally, for 1–2 minutes.

Add zucchini to casserole with more oil if necessary. Cook, stirring occasionally, for 2–3 minutes, then add tomatoes, thyme, marjoram, and oregano. Season lightly with salt and pepper, cover, and cook very gently for 30–40 minutes, stirring occasionally. Stir in parsley and basil, and cook, uncovered, for 5–10 minutes, until liquid had evaporated. Serve warm or cold.

Serves 4.

BOMBAY POTATOES WITH PEAS

¼ cup vegetable oil
1 onion, finely chopped
2 cloves garlic, finely chopped
1 teaspoon whole cumin seeds
1 teaspoon black mustard seeds
1 tablespoon medium curry powder
½ teaspoon ground cardamom
1 lb. potatoes, cut into ½-in. pieces and boiled until
   just tender
6 oz. fresh or frozen peas
1–2 tablespoons lemon juice
2 tablespoons chopped fresh cilantro
cilantro sprigs, to garnish

Heat a wok over high heat. Add oil and swirl to coat. Add onion and garlic, and reduce heat to medium. Stir-fry for 4–6 minutes until onion is tender and golden. Add cumin seeds and black mustard seeds, and stir-fry for 2 minutes until seeds begin to pop. Stir in curry powder and ground cardamom, and stir-fry for an additional 2–3 minutes.

Add potatoes and peas, and stir-fry, tossing to coat with spice mixture, for 2–3 minutes. Add lemon juice and chopped cilantro, and toss gently until potatoes and peas are well coated and heated through, adding a little water if potatoes begin to stick. Serve hot, garnished with cilantro sprigs.

Serves 4–6.

MEDITERRANEAN POTATO SALAD

1 lb. new potatoes
4 oz. French beans, trimmed
4 oz. trimmed fennel
¼ cup pitted olives
2 tablespoons capers, drained
2 tablespoons chopped fresh chives
2 teaspoons chopped fresh tarragon
¼ cup virgin olive oil
juice ½ lemon
2 eggs
14 oz. canned artichoke hearts, drained and halved

POTATO SALAD

1½ lb. new potatoes
4–5 mint leaves, chopped
1 tablespoon chopped fresh chives
½ shallot, finely chopped
mint sprigs, to garnish
DRESSING:
1 tablespoon wine vinegar
2 teaspoons Dijon mustard
salt and freshly ground black pepper
3 tablespoons olive oil

Cook potatoes in a saucepan of lightly salted boiling water for 15 minutes, until tender.

Cook potatoes in a pan of lightly salted boiling water for 10–12 minutes until just cooked. Drain and place in a large bowl. Blanch beans in boiling water for 1–2 minutes until just tender, drain, and refresh under cold water; pat dry. Very thinly slice fennel and halve olives. Add to potatoes with beans, capers, and herbs. Stir in oil and lemon juice, and set aside until potatoes are cold.

Meanwhile, make dressing. Whisk together vinegar, mustard, and salt and pepper. Slowly pour in oil, whisking constantly.

Hard-boil the eggs, plunge into cold water and peel. Roughly chop and add to salad with artichoke hearts. Toss well and serve at once.

Serves 4–6.

Drain potatoes thoroughly, cut into halves or quarters, if necessary, then immediately toss with dressing, herbs, and shallot. Leave to cool. Garnish with mint sprigs and serve.

Serves 4.

PEA TABBOULEH

COUSCOUS SALAD

1¼ cups bulgar wheat
⅔ cup olive oil
1 clove garlic, crushed
1 tablespoon red wine vinegar
1 tablespoon chopped fresh cilantro
1 tablespoon chopped fresh mint
1 teaspoon ground coriander
½ teaspoon ground cumin
4 oz. sugar snap peas, trimmed
1 cup frozen peas, thawed
1 large ripe peach, pit removed and flesh chopped
1 red onion, finely chopped
salt and freshly ground black pepper

⅔ cup quick-cook couscous
1 fresh red chili
8 oz. cherry tomatoes
1 bunch scallions
¼ cup extra-virgin olive oil
2 tablespoons lemon juice
4 tablespoons chopped fresh parsley
4 tablespoons chopped fresh cilantro
salt and freshly ground black pepper
salad leaves, to serve

Put the couscous in a bowl and pour ⅔ cup cold water over. Leave for 30–60 minutes until the water has been completely absorbed.

Cover bulgar wheat with plenty of cold water and leave to soak for 30 minutes. Drain well and squeeze out excess liquid. Mix together oil, garlic, vinegar, herbs, and spices, and pour over bulgar; stir well, cover and set aside for 30 minutes.

Meanwhile, cut chili in half and remove core and seeds. Finely chop chili. Cut cherry tomatoes in half, and slice scallions. Gently fluff up couscous with a fork.

Cook sugar snap peas in boiling water for 2 minutes and peas for 1 minute. Drain both and refresh under cold water. Pat all the peas dry. Stir into bulgar wheat with chopped peaches, onion, and salt and pepper.

Serves 4–6.

Add olive oil, lemon juice, parsley, cilantro, and salt and pepper to the couscous. Gently stir in the chili, tomatoes, and scallions. Leave for 1 hour. Line a serving dish with salad leaves, pile couscous in center, and serve.

Serves 4.

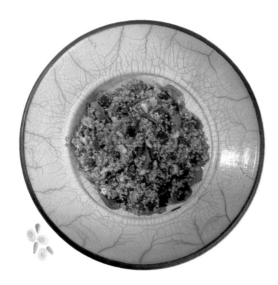

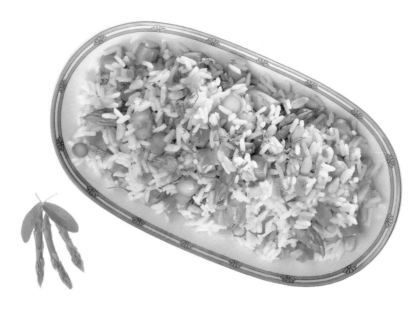

COUSCOUS & BEET SALAD

RICE WITH ASPARAGUS & NUTS

1 lb. couscous
chicken or vegetable stock
juice 1 lemon
3 tablespoons olive oil, plus extra for drizzling
salt and freshly ground black pepper
10 oz. cooked beets, cut into ½-in. cubes
4 scallions, chopped
2½ cups baby arugula leaves
2½ oz. toasted pine nuts
1 teaspoon toasted cumin seeds
1 tablespoon chopped fresh mint

Place couscous in a bowl and pour enough stock over to cover. Set aside for 10 minutes until liquid is absorbed.

Fluff up grains of couscous with a fork. Stir in lemon juice and olive oil, and season generously with salt and pepper.

Just before serving, stir beets into couscous. Add scallions, arugula leaves, pine nuts, cumin seeds, and mint. Transfer to a salad bowl and drizzle a little olive oil over.

Serves 6.

8 oz. asparagus spears
¼ cup butter or ¼ cup olive oil
1 small onion, finely chopped
1 clove garlic, crushed
1¼ cups long-grain rice, washed well in cold water
2 cups vegetable stock
9 teaspoons pine nuts
2 tablespoons chopped fresh sage
salt and freshly ground black pepper

Trim off and discard woody ends of asparagus stems. Set aside.

Heat 1 tablespoon of the butter or olive oil in a saucepan, and fry onion and garlic for 5 minutes. Add rice and stir-fry for 1 minute until transparent and glossy, and pour in stock. Bring to a boil, stir once, cover, and cook gently for 12 minutes.

Steam asparagus for 3 minutes, refresh under cold water, drain, and dry well, then coarsely chop. Heat remaining butter or olive oil in a large pan and stir-fry pine nuts over a medium heat for 3–4 minutes until golden. Add sage and asparagus, and stir in cooked rice. Season and heat through, stirring, for 2 minutes and serve at once.

Serves 6.

JAMAICAN RICE SALAD

1⅓ cups long-grain rice
salt and freshly ground black pepper
1 red bell pepper
1 yellow bell pepper
1 fresh green chili, cored, seeded, and finely chopped
¾ cup roasted, salted cashew nuts
½ coconut, flesh coarsely grated
⅓ cup seedless raisins
grated rind and juice ½ orange
⅔ cup mayonnaise
1 banana, sliced
chopped fresh chives, to garnish

In a pan of boiling salted water, cook rice for 10–15 minutes until tender. Drain, then rinse under cold running water. Drain again and set aside. Preheat broiler. Broil bell peppers, skin side up, and cook until skins have blackened. Place in a plastic bag until cool enough to handle, then peel off skins and cut flesh into strips.

In a bowl, stir together rice, bell peppers, chili, cashew nuts, coconut, and raisins. In another bowl, mix orange rind and juice with mayonnaise. Stir mayonnaise into rice mixture, then carefully stir in banana. Transfer to a serving dish, sprinkle with chives, and serve immediately.

Serves 6.

WARM PASTA SALAD

8 oz. mixed mushrooms
¼ cup drained sun-dried tomatoes in oil, sliced
½ cup olive oil
2 cloves garlic, chopped
grated rind 1 lemon
1 tablespoon lemon juice
2 tablespoons chopped fresh mint
2½ cups dried penne
2 ripe tomatoes, skinned, seeded, and chopped
salt and freshly ground black pepper

Thinly slice mushrooms and place in a large bowl with sun-dried tomatoes.

Heat 1 tablespoon oil and sauté garlic for 1 minute until starting to turn golden. Remove pan from heat and stir in remaining oil, lemon rind and juice, and mint; pour half over mushrooms and set aside remainder. Stir mushrooms until well coated, cover, and set aside to soften for several hours.

Cook pasta in lightly salted, boiling water for 10 minutes until al dente. Drain well, toss with remaining dressing, and stir into marinated mushrooms with the fresh tomatoes. Season with salt and pepper.

Serves 4.

Note: Use a selection of button, field, oyster, and shiitake mushrooms.

GREEN RICE

1¼ cups long-grain white rice, rinsed
3½ cups vegetable stock
8 oz. small broccoli flowerets
8 oz. fresh spinach, tough ribs removed
1 tablespoon peanut oil
2 cloves garlic, finely chopped
1 fresh green chili, cored, seeded, and chopped
1 bunch scallions, finely chopped
8 oz. frozen green peas
2 tablespoons light soy sauce
salt and freshly ground black pepper
4 tablespoons chopped fresh chives
fresh chives, to garnish

SPICY COLD NOODLES

3 tablespoons vegetable oil
2 eggs, beaten
1 clove garlic and 2 shallots, chopped
4 oz. pork, shredded
4 oz. peeled raw shrimp
1 tablespoon dried shrimp, soaked
1–2 tablespoons Chinese preserved vegetable, chopped
1 cup bean sprouts
2 small fresh red chilies, cored, seeded, and chopped
salt and freshly ground black pepper
2 tablespoons fish sauce
8 oz. rice vermicelli, cooked in boiling water 5 minutes, drained and rinsed
3 tablespoons crushed peanuts
2–3 scallions, shredded

Place rice and stock in a large saucepan, bring to a boil, reduce heat, and simmer 25 minutes or until rice is cooked and liquid has been absorbed. Cook broccoli in a saucepan of boiling water 2 minutes. Drain and set aside. Blanch spinach in a saucepan of boiling water a few seconds or until just wilted. Drain well, shred, and set aside.

Heat about 1 tablespoon oil in a wok or pan and scramble eggs until just set, then break up into small pieces, remove, and set aside. Heat remaining oil, and stir-fry garlic and shallots about 30 seconds. Add pork and raw shrimp and stir-fry 1–2 minutes. Add dried shrimp, preserved vegetable, bean sprouts, scrambled eggs, chilies, salt, pepper, and fish sauce. Blend well and stir-fry 2–3 minutes. Set aside.

Heat oil in a nonstick or well-seasoned wok and stir-fry garlic, chili, scallions, and broccoli 1 minute. Add cooked rice, spinach, frozen peas, and soy sauce. Season with salt and pepper, and simmer 5 minutes. Stir in chopped chives. Garnish with chives and serve.

Serves 4.

Place vermicelli on a large serving dish or plate, add shrimp mixture, and a mound of crushed peanuts and scallions on top.

Serves 4.

Notes: Chinese preserved vegetable is sold in cans or jars in specialist shops. Serve with chili sauce and/or Spicy Fish Sauce (see page 128), if desired.

WILD & BROWN RICE SALAD

NOODLES & THAI HERB SAUCE

1 cup wild rice
salt
1¼ cups brown rice
⅔ cup pecan nuts
6 scallions, trimmed
⅓ cup dried cherries, cranberries, or raisins
2 tablespoons chopped fresh cilantro
1 tablespoon chopped fresh parsley
DRESSING:
⅓ cup olive oil
2 teaspoons raspberry vinegar
¼ teaspoon honey or sugar
salt and freshly ground black pepper

⅓ cup vegetable oil
2 tablespoons raw shelled peanuts
1 small fresh green chili, cored, seeded, and sliced
¾-in. piece galangal, chopped
2 large cloves garlic, chopped
leaves from bunch Thai holy basil
leaves from small bunch Thai mint
leaves from small bunch cilantro
2 tablespoons lime juice
1 teaspoons fish sauce
12–16 oz. egg noodles, soaked for 5–10 minutes

Cook wild rice in a pan of lightly salted boiling water for 35–40 minutes until just tender. Cook brown rice in a pan of lightly salted boiling water for 25 minutes or until just tender. Drain well and place both in a large bowl. Meanwhile, preheat oven to 400°F.

Over a high heat, heat oil in a wok, add peanuts, and cook, stirring, for about 2 minutes, until browned. Using a slotted spoon, transfer nuts to paper towels to drain; set aside oil.

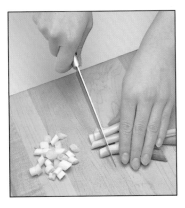

Roast nuts on a baking tray for 5–6 minutes until browned; allow to cool and coarsely chop. Set aside. Chop scallions and add to rice with dried fruit and herbs, and stir well. Blend dressing ingredients well together and pour over the salad, stir once, cover, and leave rice to cool. Just before serving, toss in roasted nuts, and season with salt and pepper.

Serves 4–6.

Using a small blender, roughly grind nuts. Add chili, galangal, and garlic. Mix briefly. Add herbs, lime juice, fish sauce, and reserved oil. Drain noodles, shake loose, then cook in a pan of boiling salted water for 2 minutes until soft. Drain well, transfer to a warmed dish, and toss with the sauce.

Serves 4.

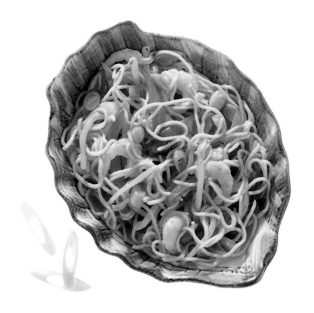

VEGETARIAN FRIED NOODLES

2 tablespoons vegetable oil
1 clove garlic, chopped
1 onion, sliced
2–3 small fresh red chilies, cored, seeded, and
    shredded
1 carrot, thinly shredded
4 cups bean sprouts
salt and freshly ground black pepper
8 oz. rice vermicelli, soaked in hot water 5 minutes,
    drained, and cut into short lengths
2 tablespoons soy sauce
shredded scallion, to garnish

Heat oil in a wok or skillet and stir-fry garlic
and onion 1 minute or until softened.

Add chilies and carrot shreds and cook,
stirring, 2 minutes, then add bean sprouts,
and salt and pepper. Blend well and stir-fry
2 minutes.

Add rice vermicelli and soy sauce, mix and
toss well, then cook 2–3 minutes. Garnish
with shredded scallion and serve at once.

Serves 4.

Note: Serve this dish with chili sauce or
Spicy Fish Sauce (see page 128), if desired.

SINGAPORE NOODLES

8 oz. thin round egg noodles
¼ cup vegetable oil
2 cloves garlic, chopped
1-in. piece fresh ginger, peeled and finely chopped
1 fresh chili, cored, seeded, and chopped
1 red bell pepper, seeded and thinly sliced
4 oz. snow peas, sliced if large
4–6 scallions, finely sliced
6 oz. peeled cooked shrimp, defrosted if frozen
2 cups bean sprouts, trimmed, rinsed, and dried
⅓ cup tomato sauce
1 teaspoon chili powder
1–2 teaspoons chili sauce

In a large saucepan of boiling water, cook
noodles according to package directions.
Drain and toss with 1 tablespoon of the oil.
Set aside. Heat a wok until hot. Add
remaining oil and swirl to coat wok. Add
garlic, ginger, and chili, and stir-fry for
1 minute. Add red bell pepper and snow
peas, and stir-fry for 1 minute.

Add scallions, shrimp, and bean sprouts, and
stir in tomato sauce, chili powder, chili
sauce, and ½ cup water. Bring to a boil. Add
noodles and toss. Stir-fry for 1–2 minutes
until coated with sauce and heated through.
Transfer to a large shallow serving bowl and
serve at once.

Serves 4.

SUMMER NOODLE SALAD

6 oz. egg noodles
1 teaspoon sesame oil
2 tablespoons crunchy peanut butter
2 tablespoons light soy sauce
2 teaspoons sugar
pinch chili powder
1 lb. tomatoes, thinly sliced
1 bunch scallions, finely chopped
2 cups bean sprouts
1 large carrot, grated
8 pitted dates, finely chopped

SAUCY BEANS

1 cup dried lima beans or pinto beans, soaked
   overnight in cold water to cover
1 bay leaf
¼ cup virgin olive oil
1 red onion, chopped
2 cloves garlic, chopped
1 tablespoon chopped fresh sage
1 lb. ripe tomatoes, peeled, seeded, and chopped
1 teaspoon balsamic vinegar
salt and freshly ground black pepper
1 tablespoon chopped fresh parsley
virgin olive oil, to serve

Cook noodles in boiling water 4–5 minutes or until tender but firm. Drain well and rinse in cold water. Leave in cold water until required.

Mix together oil, peanut butter, soy sauce, sugar, and chili powder. Drain noodles well, place in a large bowl, and mix in peanut sauce. Arrange tomato slices on a serving plate.

Drain the beans. Place in a pan with bay leaf and cold water to cover. Bring to a boil, then simmer, covered, for 40–45 minutes. In a large pan, heat oil and fry onion, garlic, and sage for 10 minutes until golden. Add chopped tomatoes and vinegar to pan. Cover and cook for 5 minutes until softened.

Using chopsticks or 2 forks, toss scallions, bean sprouts, grated carrot, and dates into noodles and mix well. Pile on top of sliced tomato and serve.

Serves 4.

Drain cooked beans, rinse well, and shake off excess water. Stir them into onion mixture in pan, cover, and cook for 4–5 minutes until heated through. Season with salt and pepper and sprinkle chopped parsley over. Serve with extra olive oil drizzled over beans.

Serves 4.

Note: This dish is delicious served warm or cold. Pass round plenty of crusty bread to mop up the juices.

PASTA PRIMAVERA

1 lb. tagliatelle, linguine, or thin spaghetti
2–4 tablespoons olive oil
8 oz. asparagus, cut into 2-in. pieces
8 oz. broccoli, cut into small flowerets
2 yellow or green zucchini, sliced
4 oz. snow peas, cut in half if large
2–4 cloves garlic, finely chopped
14 oz. canned chopped tomatoes
2 tablespoons butter
¾ cup frozen peas
4–6 tablespoons shredded fresh basil or chopped
    fresh dill
grated Parmesan, to serve

In a wok or a large saucepan, cook pasta according to package directions.

Drain, transfer to a large bowl, toss with 1 tablespoon olive oil, and set aside. Heat the wok until hot. Add remaining oil and swirl to coat wok. Add asparagus and broccoli, and stir-fry for 4–5 minutes until tender but still crisp. Remove to a bowl. Add zucchini and snow peas, and stir-fry for 1–2 minutes until tender but still crisp. Remove to the bowl. Add garlic to oil remaining in wok and stir-fry for 1 minute. Stir in chopped tomatoes and their juice, and simmer for 4–6 minutes until slightly thickened.

Stir butter into tomato sauce and add reserved vegetables, frozen peas, basil or dill, and reserved pasta. Toss to coat well. Stir and toss for 2–3 minutes to heat through. Serve with grated Parmesan cheese.

Serves 4–6.

LENTIL SALAD

1¼ cups green lentils
¼ cup olive oil
1 onion, finely chopped
3 tomatoes, peeled and chopped
salt and freshly ground black pepper
1 tablespoon chopped fresh parsley
2 tablespoons lemon juice
onion rings, chopped fresh parsley, and lemon slices,
    to garnish

Put lentils in a bowl, cover with cold water, and leave to soak for 3–4 hours. Drain well.

In a large saucepan, heat half the oil, add onion, and cook until soft. Add tomatoes, cook for 1 minute, then add lentils. Cover with water, cover pan, and simmer gently for 30 minutes, adding water if necessary, until lentils are tender and all water has been absorbed. The lentils should still be holding their shape.

Add salt, pepper, parsley, lemon juice, and remaining oil to lentils. Mix carefully, then transfer to a serving dish and leave to cool. Serve garnished with onion rings, chopped parsley, and lemon slices

Serves 4–6.

COCONUT NOODLES

8 oz. whole-wheat tagliatelle or spaghetti
¼ cup peanut oil
4 oz. shiitake or oyster mushrooms
1 red bell pepper, seeded and thinly sliced
½ small Chinese cabbage, thinly shredded
4 oz. snow peas, thinly sliced
4–6 scallions, thinly sliced
¾ cup unsweetened coconut milk
2 tablespoons rice wine or dry sherry
1 tablespoon soy sauce
1 tablespoon oyster sauce
1 teaspoon Chinese chili sauce
1 tablespoon cornstarch dissolved in 2 tablespoons
　water
8 tablespoons chopped fresh mint or cilantro
mint or cilantro sprigs, to garnish

In a large saucepan of boiling water, cook the noodles according to package directions. Drain and toss with 1 tablespoon of peanut oil. Heat a wok until hot. Add the remaining oil and swirl to coat wok. Add mushrooms, bell pepper, and Chinese cabbage, and stir-fry for 2–3 minutes until vegetables begin to soften. Stir in reserved noodles, snow peas, and scallions, and stir-fry for 1 minute to combine.

Slowly pour in coconut milk, rice wine or sherry, soy sauce, oyster sauce, and chili sauce and bring to simmering point. Stir cornstarch mixture and, pushing ingredients to one side, stir into the wok. Stir to combine liquid ingredients well, then stir in chopped mint or cilantro and toss to coat well. Stir-fry for 2–3 minutes until heated through. Serve hot, garnished with sprigs of mint or cilantro.

Serves 4.

CARIBBEAN BEAN SALAD

1¼ cups red kidney beans, soaked overnight
sprig thyme
4 sticks celery, chopped
1 green bell pepper, chopped
1 small red onion, finely chopped
salad leaves, to serve
celery leaves, to garnish
DRESSING:
¼ cup olive oil
1 tablespoon lime juice
½-1 teaspoon hot pepper sauce
1 teaspoon sugar
1 tablespoon chopped fresh cilantro
salt

Drain beans and put in a large saucepan with thyme sprig and plenty of cold water. Bring to a boil and boil vigorously for 10 minutes. Reduce heat, cover pan, and simmer for 45–60 minutes until beans are tender. Drain beans, and remove and discard thyme.

To make dressing, in a bowl whisk together olive oil, lime juice, hot pepper sauce, sugar, cilantro, and salt. Pour over warm beans, mix together thoroughly, and leave to cool. Gently stir in celery, green bell pepper, and onion. Arrange salad leaves in a serving bowl and pile beans on top. Garnish with celery leaves.

Serves 4.

CURRIED CHICKPEAS

1 cup dried chickpeas
salt
2 tablespoons vegetable oil
1 small onion, finely chopped
1-in. piece fresh ginger, grated
2 cloves garlic, crushed
½ teaspoons ground turmeric
1 teaspoon ground cumin
1 teaspoon garam masala
½ teaspoon chili powder
2 tablespoons chopped fresh cilantro

Rinse chickpeas, put them in a bowl, cover with cold water, and soak overnight.

Drain chickpeas, add 2 cups cold water, and salt. Boil 10 minutes, then reduce heat, and simmer, partially covered 1 hour. In a separate pan, heat oil, add onion; cook about 8 minutes, until soft and golden brown.

Add ginger, garlic, turmeric, cumin, garam masala, and chili powder; cook 1 minute. Stir in chickpeas and their cooking water and bring to a boil. Cover and simmer 20 minutes, until beans are very tender, but still whole. Serve hot, sprinkled with chopped cilantro.

Serves 4.

CHICKPEA SALAD

1½ cups chickpeas, soaked overnight
1 tablespoon finely chopped fresh parsley
1½ teaspoons finely chopped tarragon
4 scallions, finely chopped
sliced scallion and flat-leaf parsley, to garnish
DRESSING:
2 cloves garlic, finely chopped
1 tablespoon red wine vinegar
2–3 tablespoons Dijon mustard
salt and freshly ground black pepper
¼ cup olive oil

Drain and rinse chickpeas. Put in a saucepan and cover with cold water.

Bring to a boil. Cover pan and simmer for 1–1½ hours, until chickpeas are tender. Meanwhile, make dressing. Mix together garlic, vinegar, mustard, and salt and pepper. Slowly pour in the oil, whisking constantly.

Drain chickpeas and immediately toss with dressing, parsley, tarragon, and scallions. Garnish with scallion slices and flat-leaf parsley, and serve warm.

Serves 4.

BLACK-EYED PEA SALAD

BEET & BEAN SALAD

12 oz. black-eyed peas, soaked overnight
salt
1 red onion, chopped
red bell pepper strips, to garnish
DRESSING:
½ cup olive oil
juice 1 lemon
1 clove garlic, crushed
4 tablespoons chopped fresh flat leaf parsley
1 teaspoon cumin
½–1 teaspoon harissa

¼ cup hazelnuts
1 lb. cooked beets, skinned
4 oz. green beans, trimmed
2 small leeks, trimmed
1 pear
1 cup cooked flageolet or navy beans
DRESSING:
2 tablespoons chopped fresh dill
1 clove garlic, crushed
1 teaspoon whole-grain mustard
1 teaspoon sherry vinegar
⅓ cup olive oil

Drain peas and place in a large saucepan. Cover with water and bring to a boil.

Preheat oven to 400°F and roast hazelnuts for 6–8 minutes until golden. Cool slightly, chop, and set aside. Cut beets into bite-size pieces and place in a large bowl. Blanch beans in boiling water for 1–2 minutes until tender. Drain, refresh under cold water, and pat dry. Wash and thinly slice leeks, then quarter, core, and slice pear. Add to beets with green beans and flageolet or navy beans.

Boil peas briskly for 10 minutes then simmer, covered, for 20 minutes, or until tender. Add salt toward the end of cooking time. Drain peas and place in a large bowl. To make the dressing, place oil, lemon juice, garlic, parsley, cumin, and harissa in a bowl, and whisk together. Pour dressing over warm peas.

Add chopped onion and mix well. Leave until cold, then transfer to a serving dish. Serve pea salad garnished with strips of red bell pepper.

Serves 6.

Variation: Other legumes, such as flageolet or red kidney beans may be used instead of, or combined with, black-eyed peas.

Mix dill, garlic, mustard, and vinegar together, and whisk in oil. Pour over salad, toss well, and set aside for 1 hour for flavors to develop. Sprinkle nuts over and serve at once.

Serves 4–6.

Note: Use canned flageolet or haricot beans and drain well before use. Replace flageolet with cannellini beans, if preferred.

CHICKPEA & ARUGULA SALAD

1 cup chickpeas, soaked overnight
¼ cup olive oil
1 clove garlic, crushed
1 tablespoon ground cumin
2 teaspoons balsamic vinegar
1 small red onion, chopped
salt and freshly ground black pepper
1½ oz. arugula
red onion rings and arugula leaves, to garnish

Drain chickpeas, put in a saucepan and cover with cold water. Bring to a boil and boil rapidly for 10 minutes. Reduce heat, cover and simmer gently for 1–1½ hours until tender.

Heat oil in a skillet. Add garlic and cumin and cook gently, stirring for 2–3 minutes. Drain chickpeas and transfer to a bowl. Add oil, garlic and cumin mixture. Add balsamic vinegar, onion and salt and pepper. Mix gently and leave to cool.

Roughly chop arugula and stir gently into chickpeas. Garnish with red onion rings and arugula leaves and serve.

Serves 4.

POTATO & BEAN SALAD

1 lb. small new potatoes
2 tablespoons olive oil
1 onion, sliced
2 cloves garlic, sliced
1 teaspoon cumin seeds
1 lb. plum tomatoes, peeled
14 oz. canned chickpeas, drained
salt and freshly ground black pepper
2 tablespoons roughly chopped fresh mint

Either scrub or peel potatoes, according to preference. Cut in half unless they are very small. Boil in salted water for 10 minutes or until soft. Drain.

Meanwhile, heat oil in a large saucepan. Add onion and cook for 10 minutes until soft and golden brown. Add garlic and cumin seeds and cook for 3 or 4 minutes. Cut tomatoes into eighths and add to the pan. Cook for a few minutes until tomatoes begin to soften.

Add drained chickpeas and potatoes. Cook for a few minutes until warmed through. Season with salt and pepper and stir in mint. Serve hot or cold.

Serves 4–6.

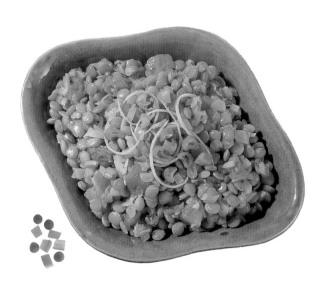

LENTIL & TOMATO SALAD

1¼ cups green lentils
¼ cup olive oil
1 onion, finely chopped
2 cloves garlic, crushed
4 plum tomatoes, peeled and chopped
salt and freshly ground black pepper
1 tablespoon chopped fresh parsley
2 tablespoons lemon juice
strips of lemon rind and chopped scallions, to garnish

Place lentils in a bowl, cover with cold water, and leave to soak for 3–4 hours. Drain well.

Heat half the oil in a large saucepan, add onion and garlic, and cook for 10 minutes or until soft. Add tomatoes, cook for 1 minute, then add lentils. Cover with water. Cover the pan and simmer gently for 30 minutes, adding water if necessary, until lentils are tender and all the water has been absorbed. The lentils should still be holding their shape.

Add salt, pepper, parsley, lemon juice, and remaining oil. Mix carefully, then transfer to a serving dish and leave to cool. Serve, garnished with strips of lemon rind and chopped scallions.

Serves 4–6.

MUSHROOMS & LIMA BEANS

8 oz. dried lima beans, soaked overnight and drained
8 oz. button mushrooms, thinly sliced
2 oz. piece Parmesan cheese
1 tablespoon finely chopped fresh Italian parsley
lettuce leaves, to garnish (optional)
DRESSING:
5 tablespoons extra-virgin olive oil
finely grated rind ½ lemon
½ teaspoon whole-grain mustard
pinch granulated sugar
salt and freshly ground black pepper

Put beans in a large saucepan with plenty of water to cover. Bring to a boil and boil briskly for 10 minutes then reduce heat, cover, and simmer for about 40–45 minutes or until beans are tender. Drain and rinse under cold running water. Drain well and leave until cold. To make the dressing, put all ingredients in a small bowl, or put into a screw-top jar and stir or shake together. Set aside.

Put beans and mushrooms in a large serving bowl. Pour dressing over and toss well to mix. Leave for up to 2 hours, if desired. Using a small, sharp knife, pare wafer-thin slices of Parmesan, add to salad, and toss lightly to mix. Sprinkle chopped Italian parsley over, garnish with lettuce leaves, if desired, and serve immediately.

Serves 6.

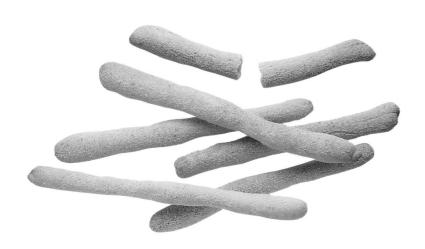

GRISSINI

4 cups strong all-purpose flour
½ teaspoon salt
1 oz. grated Parmesan or provolone cheese
¼ oz. dry yeast
1 teaspoon granulated sugar
**2 tablespoons extra-virgin olive oil, plus extra for
  oiling**
1 cup cornmeal

Preheat the oven to 450°F. Oil 2 more baking trays. Cut dough into 24 equal pieces. Sprinkle cornmeal on counter. Using your hands, roll each piece of dough to a thin stick about 9 in. long.

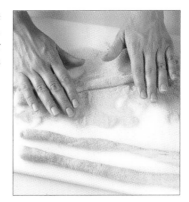

Sieve flour and salt into a large mixing bowl. Stir in cheese. In a small bowl mix yeast, sugar, and 1¼ cups warm water. Leave for 10–15 minutes until frothy.

Arrange slightly apart on the baking trays and bake for 15–20 minutes until golden and crisp. Cool on wire racks. Serve warm or cold.

Makes 24 .

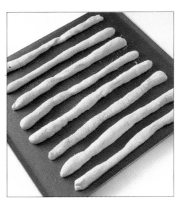

Stir olive oil into frothy yeast liquid then beat into flour using a wooden spoon to give a soft dough. Turn on to a floured surface and knead for 5 minutes until smooth and elastic. Lightly oil a baking tray. Roll out dough to a large rectangle and transfer to prepared baking tray. Brush the surface with a little oil, cover loosely, and leave in a warm place for 35–40 minutes until doubled in size.

Variation: Replace cornmeal with 3 oz. sesame seeds.

FOCACCIA

4 cups strong all-purpose flour
pinch salt
½ oz. sachet dried yeast
1 cup warm milk
1 teaspoon granulated sugar
¼ cup extra-virgin olive oil, plus extra for brushing
2 teaspoons rosemary leaves
coarse sea salt

Sieve flour and salt into a large mixing bowl. In a small bowl, mix together yeast, milk, and sugar. Leave for 10–15 minutes, until frothy.

Stir in oil then gradually beat into flour mixture using wooden spoon to give a soft, but not wet, dough; add a little more warm milk if necessary. Turn dough on to a floured surface; knead for 5 minutes until smooth and elastic. Place in an oiled bowl, cover, and leave in a warmed place for about 40 minutes until doubled in size. Turn on to a floured surface and knead for 5 minutes.

Preheat oven to 450°F. Oil a baking tray. Roll dough to a large circle about ½ in. thick and transfer to the baking tray. Brush with olive oil, and sprinkle rosemary and sea salt over, pressing in lightly. With a clean finger, make deep indentations over surface of dough. Leave to rise for 25 minutes. Bake for 20–25 minutes until golden. Brush again with olive oil. Serve warm.

Makes 1 loaf.

PITA BREAD

7 cups strong white flour
½ oz. sachet dried yeast
2 teaspoons salt
2 tablespoons olive oil

Sift flour into a large bowl. Stir in yeast and salt. Add oil and scant 2 cups warm water. Mix together, then turn dough out on to a floured surface.

Knead thoroughly for 10 minutes until smooth and elastic. Cut into 12 equal pieces. Roll each piece into a ball, then roll out to an oval shape 7 in. long. Place on floured trays; cover with a cloth and leave in a warm place for 1 hour or until puffed up and doubled in size.

Preheat oven to 475°F. Oil 2 baking trays and place in the oven until hot. Place 3 pita breads on each baking tray and sprinkle with water. Bake for 5 minutes until puffed up and lightly browned. Remove from baking trays and wrap in a cloth while baking remaining bread.

Makes 12.

WALNUT BREAD

½ oz. sachet dried yeast
⅔ cup warm milk
1 tablespoon honey
3 cups strong all-purpose flour
3 cups plain whole-wheat flour
1½ teaspoons salt
2 tablespoons butter, diced
1¼ cups walnuts, chopped
2 teaspoons fennel seeds, lightly crushed
½ teaspoon grated nutmeg
milk, to glaze

In a small bowl or jug, mix yeast with warm milk and honey. Leave for 10–15 minutes until frothy.

Sieve flours and salt into a large mixing bowl. Rub in butter until mixture resembles bread crumbs. Stir in walnuts, 1 teaspoon of the fennel seeds, and the grated nutmeg.

Using a wooden spoon, stir yeast liquid into flour mixture with sufficient warm water to form a soft, but not wet, dough.

Oil a mixing bowl. Turn dough out on to a lightly floured surface and knead for 5 minutes until elastic. Put into an oiled mixing bowl, cover, and leave in a warm place for 35–40 minutes until doubled in size. Turn on to a lightly floured surface and knead again for 5 minutes.

Preheat oven to 425°F. Oil a deep 6-in. round cake pan. Divide dough into 7 equal sized pieces and shape into balls. Arrange in the cake pan. Brush tops with milk, and sprinkle with remaining fennel seeds. Leave in a warm place for 25 minutes then bake for about 45 minutes until the top is well browned and the bottom sounds hollow when tapped.

Turn bread on to a wire rack and leave to cool.

Makes 1 large loaf.

Note: This bread is delicious served with cheese and fish dishes, for soaking up olive oil dressings, and is particularly good toasted.

WHOLE CORN BREAD

1⅔ cups coarse cornmeal
2 cups all-purpose flour
1 teaspoon fast action dried yeast
1 teaspoon sugar
½ teaspoon salt
7-oz. can corn kernels
⅔ cup milk
2 tablespoons butter, melted

Combine cornmeal, flour, yeast, sugar, and salt in a large bowl and make a well in the center.

Drain corn, set aside juices, and pour into a small pan. Add milk and heat gently until warm. Stir into cornmeal mixture with melted butter, and gradually work to form a soft dough. Knead on a lightly floured surface for 6–8 minutes until smooth, then carefully begin working in corn kernels, adding a little more flour if necessary. Place in an oiled bowl, cover, and leave to rise in a warm place for 45 minutes until doubled in size.

Preheat oven to 425°F. Knock back risen dough, form into a log shape, and press into an oiled 9 x 5-in. loaf pan. Cover and leave to rise for 30 minutes until dough reaches the top of the pan. Bake for 25 minutes until risen and golden, and the base sounds hollow when tapped. Leave to cool on a wire rack before serving.

Makes 1 large loaf.

SPANISH COUNTRY BREAD

2 cups strong white flour
2 teaspoons salt
½ oz. sachet dried yeast
olive oil, for brushing
cornmeal, for sprinkling

Into a large bowl, sift flour and salt. Stir in yeast and form a well in center. Slowly pour ¼ cup water into well, stirring with a wooden spoon, to make a dough. Beat well until dough comes away from sides of bowl.

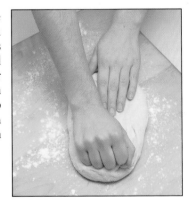

Turn dough out on to a lightly floured surface and knead 10–15 minutes or until smooth and elastic; add a little more flour if dough is sticky. Put dough in an oiled bowl, cover and leave in a warm place, about 2½ hours or until doubled in volume. Lightly sprinkle a baking tray with cornmeal. Turn dough on to lightly floured surface and punch down, then roll to a 6 x 16-in. rectangle. Roll up like a jelly roll and pinch seam to seal.

Place roll, seam-side down, on baking tray. Using a very sharp knife, make 3 diagonal slashes on roll at equal distances. Brush top lightly with water. Leave in a warm place about 1 hour or until doubled in size. Preheat oven to 450°F. Place a pan of water in the bottom of oven. Brush loaf again with water and bake 5 minutes. Remove pan of water. Brush loaf once more with water. Bake about 20 minutes or until loaf sounds hollow when tapped on base.

Makes 1 loaf.

OLIVE BREAD

6 cups strong all-purpose flour
pinch salt
1 tablespoon chopped fresh oregano
½ oz. sachet dried yeast
1 teaspoon granulated sugar
¼ cup extra-virgin olive oil, plus extra for brushing
30 pitted green olives

Sieve flour and salt into a large bowl; stir in oregano. In a small bowl mix together yeast, sugar and 1⅓ cups warm water. Leave 10–15 minutes until frothy.

Stir oil into yeast liquid then gradually add to flour mixture beating well with a wooden spoon, to give a soft, but not wet, dough; add a little more warm water if necessary.

Oil a bowl. Turn dough on to a lightly floured surface and knead for 5 minutes until elastic. Place dough in the bowl, cover, and leave in a warm place for about 40 minutes until doubled in size.

Oil 1 or 2 baking sheets. Turn dough on to a floured surface. To make one large loaf roll out to a large circle, 1 in. thick. Or cut the dough in half and roll out 2 ovals just over ½ in. thick. Place on the baking sheet or sheets.

With a clean floured finger make 30 deep indentations over surface of large loaf, or 15 for each small one. Press an olive into each indentation.

Preheat oven to 450°F. Brush loaves with olive oil and leave to rise for 25 minutes. Bake for 20–25 minutes for small loaves, 30–35 minutes for a large loaf, until a rich golden brown and undersides sound hollow when tapped. Cool on a wire rack. Serve warm or cold.

Makes 1 large or 2 small loaves.

CASABLANCA FRUIT SALAD

4 oranges
2 peaches
4 fresh figs
2 pomegranates
1 tablespoon orange flower water
confectioners' sugar

Carefully cut skins off oranges, removing any pith. Cut oranges into segments by cutting down between membranes with a sharp knife. Set aside any juice in a bowl. Place orange segments in a serving dish.

Place peaches in a bowl and cover with boiling water. Leave for 30 seconds, then plunge into cold water for 30 seconds. Peel off skins. Carefully cut peaches into wedge shaped slices down to pit; add peach slices to oranges. Cut figs, lengthwise, into wedges and add to prepared fruit.

Halve pomegranates and scoop out seeds. Place about two thirds of the seeds in a food processor and blend for 2–3 seconds to extract juice. Strain through a nylon sieve into the bowl of reserved orange juice. Stir in orange flower water and sugar, to taste, and pour over fruit. Sprinkle with remaining pomegranate seeds and serve.

Serves 4–6.

BLUSHING SUMMER FRUITS

1¼ cups red wine
⅓ cup superfine sugar
grated rind 1 lemon
2 red-skinned eating apples
4 dessert plums
1½ cups strawberries
1½ cups black grapes
¾ cup raspberries
lemon slices and rind and mint sprigs, to decorate

Put wine and sugar into a saucepan with grated lemon rind and 1¼ cups water. Bring to a boil slowly and boil rapidly for 5 minutes.

To prepare fruit, core apples, and cut flesh into chunks. Halve and pit plums, and halve strawberries. Halve and seed grapes.

Place all the fruit into a serving dish and pour the hot wine mixture over. Stir gently to mix. Leave to cool, and serve decorated with lemon slices and rind, and mint sprigs.

Serves 6.

Note: If the fruits are left to soak overnight, they absorb more of the liquor, producing an even more delicious dessert!

PEACHES IN CINNAMON SYRUP

⅓ cup blanched almonds
¾ cup shelled pistachio nuts
½ teaspoon ground cinnamon
5 teaspoons superfine sugar
1 egg yolk
6 ripe but firm peaches, halved and pit removed
Greek-style yogurt, to serve
CINNAMON SYRUP:
3 tablespoons honey
2 cinnamon sticks
2 tablespoons rosewater

Coarsely chop almonds and pistachio nuts in a food processor, then stir in cinnamon and superfine sugar.

Stir in egg yolk and mix to a paste. Preheat oven to 350°F. Spoon the mixture into peach halves and arrange fruit closely in a baking dish.

To make the cinnamon syrup, place honey in a saucepan with 1¼ cups water. Heat gently to dissolve honey. Add cinnamon sticks, and boil for 5–6 minutes until slightly thickened. Add rosewater, and pour syrup round peaches. Bake for 15–20 minutes until peaches are tender but not falling apart. Baste occasionally with syrup. Serve with Greek-style yogurt.

Serves 6.

CITRUS FRUIT COCKTAIL

6 oranges
2 pink grapefruit
1 grapefruit
8 kumquats
1¼ cups freshly squeezed orange juice
9 teaspoons honey
grated rind 1 lime
chopped fresh mint, or grated lemon or lime rind, to decorate (optional)

To prepare fruit, cut off peel and pith from oranges and grapefruit.

Cut out segments from between membranes of fruit holding them over a bowl to catch juice. Place fruit segments in the bowl. Squeeze membranes over bowl to extract juice. Wipe and thinly slice kumquats crosswise. Place in bowl.

In a measuring jug, mix together orange juice, honey, and lime rind. Pour over fruit in the bowl and mix gently to combine. Place in a serving dish and chill in the refrigerator before serving. Serve decorated with chopped fresh mint, or lemon or lime rind, if desired.

Serves 4.

BAKED MANGO CUSTARDS

2 large ripe mangoes
juice 1 lime
4 egg yolks
⅓ cup superfine sugar
1 teaspoon ground ginger
2½ cups heavy cream
toasted flaked almonds, to decorate

Preheat oven to 325°F. Peel mangoes, cut away and discard pit, and coarsely chop flesh. Place in a blender or food processor, add lime juice, and purée until smooth.

Beat egg yolks, sugar, and spices together until pale and thick, and stir in mango purée. Put 2 cups of the heavy cream into a pan and heat until gently simmering. Beat into mango mixture until evenly blended, and pour into 8 ramekin dishes. Place in a roasting pan, and pour in enough boiling water to come two-thirds up the sides of the dishes. Bake for 30 minutes, remove from the oven, and leave to cool, then chill for several hours.

Beat remaining cream until stiff, and spoon or pipe a swirl on to each custard; decorate with almonds.

Makes 8.

EXOTIC FRUIT BRÛLÉE

3 egg yolks
¼ cup vanilla sugar
⅔ cup crème fraîche
2 teaspoons kirsch or brandy
1 small ripe mango, peeled
1 small ripe pear, peeled, cut into quarters, and cored
1 large ripe fig
8 large ripe strawberries
freshly grated nutmeg
tuille cookies, to serve

Preheat broiler. Beat egg yolks and sugar together until pale and thick, and stir in crème fraîche and kirsch or brandy; set aside. Remove mango pit and cut flesh into thin slices; slice pear, fig, and strawberries thinly. Arrange all the fruit over the bases of 4 individual gratin dishes or flameproof plates.

Carefully spoon a quarter of the sauce over each dish, as evenly as possible, to cover the fruit, and grate a little fresh nutmeg on top. Place under a medium-hot broiler and cook for 3–4 minutes until the sauce is lightly caramelized. Cool slightly, and serve with tuille or other cookies.

Serves 4.

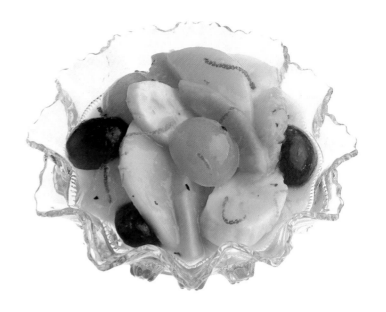

GREEN TEA FRUIT SALAD

4 teaspoons jasmine tea leaves
2 tablespoons dry sherry
2 tablespoons sugar
1 lime
2 kiwi fruit
8 oz. fresh lychees
¼ honeydew melon
¾ cup seedless green grapes
lime slices, to decorate

Place tea leaves in a small bowl and add 1¼ cups boiling water. Leave to steep 5 minutes. Strain through a strainer into a saucepan.

Stir in sherry and sugar. Using a vegetable peeler, pare rind from lime and add to the pan. Squeeze juice from lime, and add juice to pan. Bring to a boil, reduce heat, and simmer 5 minutes. Leave to cool, then discard lime rind.

Peel and thinly slice kiwi fruit. Peel, halve, and pit lychees. Peel melon and slice thinly. Arrange prepared fruits and grapes in small clusters on serving plates. Spoon cooled tea syrup over fruit, decorate, and serve.

Serves 4.

INDIAN FRUIT SALAD

2 mangoes
2 bananas
2 oranges
½ cup black grapes
½ cup green grapes
1 papaya
grated peel and juice 1 lime
¼ cup superfine sugar
freshly ground black pepper
plain yogurt, to serve

Peel and seed mangoes, and cut flesh into thin slices, reserving any scraps. Peel and diagonally slice bananas.

Peel and section oranges, working over a bowl to catch juice. Halve and seed both black and green grapes. Peel and halve papaya, scoop out seeds, and cut flesh into slices, reserving any scraps. Put fruit in a serving bowl and stir to combine.

Put orange juice, lime juice, sugar, and scraps of mango and papaya in blender or food processor fitted with a metal blade, and process until smooth. Add lime peel and pepper. Pour over fruit, and chill at least 1 hour before serving with yogurt.

Serves 4–6.

Note: Substitute other fruits, such as melon, guava, or pineapple, if preferred.

MELON & CHILLED BERRIES

2½ cups mixed fresh berries (raspberries,
    strawberries, blackberries, blueberries)
½ cup Muscat dessert wine
1 teaspoon chopped preserved stem ginger
2 teaspoons stem ginger syrup (from jar)
1 teaspoon shredded fresh mint
2 small Cantaloupe or Charentais melons
mint leaves, to decorate
crème fraîche or mascarpone cheese, to serve

PINEAPPLE WITH COCONUT

scant ½ cup superfine sugar
1½-in. piece fresh ginger, grated
scant ¼ cup light brown sugar
12 thin slices fresh pineapple
3–4 tablespoons toasted coconut flakes

Put superfine sugar, ginger, and light brown
sugar in a heavy based saucepan. Stir in
1⅔ cups water. Heat gently, stirring with a
wooden spoon, until sugars have melted.
Bring to a boil. Simmer until reduced by
about one-third.

Wash and dry the berries, and hull and halve
as necessary. Place in a bowl and add the
wine, ginger, ginger syrup, and mint. Stir
well, cover, and chill for 2 hours.

Remove cores from slices of pineapple using
a small sharp knife or a small cookie cutter.
Strain syrup over pineapple rings and leave
to cool. Cover and chill.

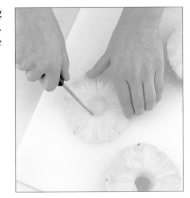

With a sharp knife, cut melons in half,
cutting into flesh in a zigzag pattern all the
way around each fruit to form attractive
edges. Carefully scoop out and discard seeds,
and fill each hollow with a large spoonful of
chilled berries. Pour in juices, decorate with
mint leaves, and serve with crème fraîche or
mascarpone cheese.

Serves 4.

To serve, place 2 pineapple rings on each
plate. Spoon some of the syrup over, and
sprinkle with the toasted coconut flakes.

Serves 6.

STUFFED RAMBUTANS

1 small banana, chopped
grated rind and juice 1 lime
16 rambutans
12 pitted dates, chopped
1 papaya, peeled, seeded, and chopped
strips of lime rind, to decorate

Mix banana with lime rind and juice and set aside. Slice top off rambutans, exposing tip of the pit. Using a sharp, small-bladed knife, carefully slice down around the pit, loosening flesh away from pit.

Peel away skin, and slice lengthwise through flesh at quarterly intervals. Gently pull down the flesh to expose pit, and carefully cut away pit. The flesh should now resemble a four-petalled flower.

In a food processor or blender, blend banana and dates until smooth. Place a teaspoon of filling in the center of each rambutan, and bring up the sides to enclose filling. Cover and chill 30 minutes. Blend papaya in a food processor or blender until smooth, pass through a strainer, and spoon on to serving plates. Top with rambutans, decorate with strips of lime rind, and serve.

Serves 4.

FLAMBÉED FRUIT

¼ cup butter
¼ cup superfine sugar
2 oranges, peeled and cut into segments
12 oz. canned pineapple pieces in natural juice
4 bananas, thickly sliced
1 tablespoon orange liqueur or brandy
mint sprigs, to decorate

Put butter and sugar in a flameproof dish and cook over a gentle heat until sugar dissolves in melted butter, and they turn a caramel color.

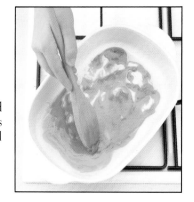

Add oranges, pineapple pieces and their juice, and bananas. Bring to a boil and boil for 5 minutes, until the sauce thickens.

Put the liqueur or brandy in a ladle and warm gently. Set alight and pour over the fruit. Cook for 1 minute, until the flames die down. Decorate with mint and serve warm.

Serves 4.

MALAYSIAN FRUIT SALAD

FRUIT PLATTER

⅓ cup light brown sugar
grated rind and juice 1 lime
1 small pineapple, peeled, cored, and cubed
1½ lb. lychees, peeled, halved, and pits removed
3 ripe mangoes, peeled, pitted, and chopped
1 papaya, peeled, seeded, and chopped

Put sugar, lime rind and juice, and ⅔ cup water in a saucepan. Heat gently, stirring with a wooden spoon, until sugar has dissolved.

Heat syrup to boiling point then simmer for 1 minute. Remove from heat and leave to cool.

Put pineapple, lychees, mangoes, and papaya in a serving dish. Pour cool syrup over. Cover dish with plastic wrap, and put in the refrigerator to chill.

Serves 4.

1 small melon
2 peaches
4 fresh figs
1¼ cups seedless green grapes
orange flower water
2 pomegranates

Halve melon and remove seeds. Cut into thin slices and remove skin. Arrange slices on 4 plates.

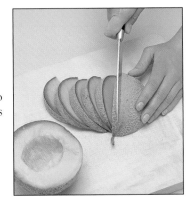

Put peaches in a bowl and pour boiling water over. Leave for 30 seconds, then plunge into cold water for 30 seconds. Peel off skins. Cut peaches in half and remove pits. Cut into slices and arrange on the plates. Cut figs into slices and add to the plates. Arrange grapes on the plates.

Sprinkle fruit with orange flower water. Cut pomegranates in half and scoop out seeds, removing any pith. Sprinkle with the seeds.

Serves 4.

RED FRUIT MEDLEY

½ cup superfine sugar
1½ cups strawberries
8 oz. cherries
8 red dessert plums
2 red-skinned eating apples
1½ cups raspberries
fresh mint, to decorate

Put 1¼ cups water into a saucepan with the sugar. Dissolve sugar over a low heat, stirring occasionally. Bring mixture to a boil and boil rapidly, uncovered, for 10 minutes. Set aside to cool.

To prepare fruit, cut strawberries in half and pit cherries. Halve and pit plums. Core apples and cut into chunks. Place all the fruit in a large serving dish.

Pour cooled sugar mixture over fruit, and stir gently to mix. Chill in the refrigerator before serving. To serve, decorate with mint, and serve chilled with Greek-style yogurt.

Serves 6.

ORANGES & WALNUTS

4 oranges
1 teaspoon orange flower water
¾ cup dates
⅔ cup walnuts
mint leaves, to decorate

Carefully cut skins off oranges, removing any pith. Cut oranges into segments by cutting down between the membranes. Set aside any juice in a bowl.

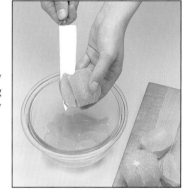

Arrange segments on a serving plate. Pour reserved juice over the top, and then sprinkle with orange flower water.

Remove pits from dates. Chop dates and walnuts. Sprinkle oranges with chopped dated and walnuts. Serve decorated with mint leaves.

Serves 4.

FIVE-FRUIT SALAD

½ melon
2 red-skinned eating apples
12 fresh dates
1¼ cups green seedless grapes
14 oz. canned apricot halves in fruit juice
1¾ cups tropical fruit juice
low-fat fromage frais, to serve

MANDARIN CRUSH

10 oz. canned mandarin oranges in fruit juice
¼ cup superfine sugar
1¾ cups Greek-style yogurt
fresh orange wedges and rind, to decorate

To prepare fruit, peel and remove seeds from melon, and cut flesh into chunks. Core apples and cut into chunks.

Place mandarin oranges and juice, sugar, and Greek-style yogurt in a blender of food processor and blend until smooth and well mixed.

Halve and pit dates. Halve grapes, if they are large in size. Drain apricots, reserving juice. Place all the fruit in a large glass serving dish.

Pour mandarin and yogurt mixture into a chilled, shallow plastic container. Cover and freeze for 1½–2 hours or until the mixture is mushy in consistency. Transfer to a chilled bowl, and beat with a fork or whisk until the mixture is smooth.

Mix reserved apricot juice with tropical fruit juice, pour over fruit, and stir gently to mix. Cover and leave in a cool place for 2–3 hours before serving. Serve with low-fat fromage frais.

Serves 6.

Return mixture to container, cover, and freeze until firm. Transfer to the refrigerator for 30 minutes before serving to soften. Serve in scoops, decorated with orange wedges and rind.

Serves 4.

PEACHES IN WHITE WINE

4 ripe peaches
4 raspberries, strawberries, or small pieces of almond paste
1–2 tablespoons confectioners' or superfine sugar, preferably vanilla flavored
1¼ cups fruity white wine, chilled
lemon twists, raspberries, and raspberry leaves, to decorate

Put peaches in a large bowl, cover with boiling water, and leave for 20 seconds. Remove peaches from water, peel, then cut in half and remove pits.

Put a raspberry, strawberry, or piece of almond paste in cavity of each peach and reassemble peaches. Put peaches in 4 serving dishes, sprinkle with sugar, and pour wine over. Cover and chill, turning peaches once. Decorate and serve.

Serves 4.

LEMON FRUIT KABOBS

1 small pineapple
3 kiwi fruit
½ small lemon
2 peaches
12 large strawberries
grated rind and juice 1 lemon
1 tablespoon cornstarch
2 tablespoons superfine sugar
lime slices, to decorate (optional)

To prepare fruit, cut pineapple into thick slices, then peel and discard core, and cut flesh into chunks.

Peel kiwi fruit and cut into quarters. Peel and remove seeds from melon, and cut flesh into chunks. Peel peaches and remove pits; cut flesh into chunks. Halve strawberries. Thread fruit on to 12 skewers, place on a serving dish, cover, and refrigerate.

To make sauce, in a measuring jug make lemon juice up to 1¼ cups with water. In a saucepan, blend cornstarch and sugar with lemon juice and water. Add grated lemon rind. Bring to a boil over a low heat, stirring continuously until mixture thickens. Cook for an additional 3 minutes. Serve hot lemon sauce immediately with fruit skewers. Serve 2 skewers per person and decorate with lime slices, if desired.

Serves 6.

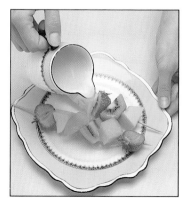

KISSEL

1½ lb. canned black currants in juice
8 oz. canned pitted dark sweet cherries in juice
1 tablespoon arrowroot
grated peel and juice 1 orange
1½ cups fresh raspberries
2 tablespoons crème de cassis
mint leaves, to decorate (optional)

Drain black currants and cherries, reserving 2 cups juice. In a saucepan, bring juice to a boil.

In a small bowl, mix arrowroot and orange juice, and add to juices in pan. Stir in orange peel. Stir over medium heat until juice is thick and clear; syrup should boil 1–2 minutes to cook arrowroot.

Place black currants, cherries, and raspberries in individual glass serving dishes. Pour thickened juice over fruit and cool. Stir in crème de cassis. Refrigerate until ready to serve. Decorate with mint leaves, if desired.

Serves 6.

Note: Add crème de cassis when the syrup is cold; the flavor of the liqueur remains unaltered.

SAFFRON NECTARINES

4 ripe nectarines
1 tablespoon butter
4 tablespoons blossom honey
pinch saffron strands
1 tablespoon rosewater
toasted flaked almonds, to decorate

Cut nectarines in half and remove pits. Put nectarine halves in a saucepan with the butter.

Spoon honey over nectarines and sprinkle with saffron. Add ½ cup water and the rosewater. Bring slowly to a boil and simmer gently for 8–12 minutes, until nectarines are tender.

Remove nectarines with a slotted spoon and arrange on serving plates. Decorate with toasted flaked almonds, and serve warm or cold.

Serves 4.

CHERRY YOGURT SYLLABUB

14 oz. canned cherries
2 cups low-fat cherry yogurt
⅔ cup dry white wine
⅔ cup reduced-fat heavy cream
ladyfingers, to serve

Drain and pit the cherries.

In a blender or food processor, blend yogurt, wine, and cherries together. In a large bowl, whip cream until thick. Gradually fold into the fruit mixture.

Spoon cherry and yogurt mixture into 6 individual glasses. Chill in the refrigerator for at least 2 hours before serving. Serve with ladyfingers.

Serves 6.

Variation: Set aside a few of the cherries for decoration, if desired.

POACHED NECTARINES

2½ cups unsweetened apple juice
⅓ cup superfine sugar
pared rind 1 lemon
1 cinnamon stick
8 cloves
4 nectarines
¼ cup flaked almonds, toasted

In a saucepan, mix together apple juice, sugar, lemon rind, cinnamon stick, and cloves. To peel nectarines, dip into boiling water for about 15 seconds, then plunge into a bowl of cold water. Lift nectarines out of the water and peel off skins with a sharp knife.

Add nectarines to juice mixture in the saucepan as soon as they are peeled to prevent discoloring. Over a high heat, bring mixture to a boil. Reduce heat to low, cover, and simmer for 5–10 minutes, shaking pan occasionally. Spoon nectarines and juice mixture into a bowl. Cool, cover, and refrigerate overnight.

Remove cinnamon stick, and rind and cloves if desired, from juice before serving. To serve, place nectarines and some juice in individual dishes, and sprinkle each with some flaked almonds.

Serves 4.

Variation: If nectarines are not available, peaches may be used instead.

NECTARINE MERINGUE NESTS

3 egg whites
¾ cup superfine sugar
½ cup low-fat cream cheese
⅔ cup low-fat fromage frais
3 nectarines
1 cup black currants
2 tablespoons reduced sugar apricot jam

Preheat oven to 300°F. Line a large baking tray with nonstick baking parchment. In a large bowl, whisk egg whites stiffly. Gradually add sugar, beating well after each addition, until mixture is stiff and glossy.

Spoon meringue into a pastry bag fitted with a star tube and pipe meringue in six 4-in. rounds on to the lined baking tray, leaving a gap between them. Pipe remaining meringue in stars around the edge of each round to form an attractive border. Bake meringue nests for 1–1½ hours until crisp on the outside. Cool on a wire rack. In a bowl, stir together cream cheese and fromage frais, mixing well. Peel and pit nectarines, and slice thinly. Top and tail black currants, wash, and drain.

In a saucepan, gently heat apricot jam with 1 tablespoon water until warm. To fill each meringue nest, place some cheese mixture in the nest. Top with sliced nectarines and black currants, then brush with warmed jam to glaze. Refrigerate until ready to serve.

Serves 6.

ORANGE-STRAWBERRY ROMANOFF

4½ cups fresh strawberries
grated rind 1 orange
1 tablespoon plus 1 teaspoon Grand Marnier
1¼ cups heavy cream
2 tablespoons crème fraîche
1–2 tablespoons confectioners' sugar
cookies, to serve

Set aside 4 strawberries and slice remainder into a bowl. Add orange rind and Grand Marnier. Gently mix, then let stand 15 minutes.

In a bowl, whip cream until quite stiff, then fold in crème fraîche. Sift confectioners' sugar over whipped cream and fold in. Place 1 spoonful of strawberries into each of 4 dessert dishes. Mash remainder gently and fold into whipped cream mixture.

Carefully spoon mixture over strawberries in glasses and chill until ready to serve. Decorate with reserved strawberries, cut in fan shapes. Serve with cookies.

Serves 4.

Note: Keep strawberries in a colander. The air circulating around them helps to keep them fresh. Do not hull strawberries until ready to use.

AMARETTI-STUFFED PEACHES

4 large peaches
2 oz. amaretti cookies
1 egg yolk
4 teaspoons superfine sugar
2 tablespoons softened butter
1 cup sweet white wine
toasted flaked almonds and vine leaves, to decorate

Preheat oven to 375°F. Butter an ovenproof dish. Cut peaches in half and remove pits.

Scoop out a little flesh from each peach half and place in a bowl. Crush amaretti cookies and add to the bowl. Stir in egg yolk, superfine sugar, and butter, and mix well. Put some filling in each peach half, forming it into a smooth round.

Put peaches in the prepared dish and pour in wine. Bake for 30–40 minutes until peaches are tender and filling is firm. Transfer to serving plates, sprinkle with toasted almonds, and decorate with vine leaves. Spoon baking juices around and serve.

Serves 4.

Note: Be careful not to bake the peaches for too long—they should retain their shape.

FRUIT & ELDERFLOWER CREAM

½ cup heavy cream
½ cup fromage frais
2 tablespoons elderflower syrup
1 small ripe mango
1 small ripe papaya
1 large ripe peach
1 large apple
¾ cup strawberries
¾ cup seedless grapes
freshly grated nutmeg, and fresh lemon balm or mint, to decorate

Whip heavy cream and gently fold in fromage frais and elderflower syrup, cover, and chill until required.

Peel mango, cut down either side of the pit, and cut the flesh into thin slices. Peel and halve papaya, scoop out and discard seeds, and cut flesh into thin strips. Halve and pit peach, and cut into thin wedges. Quarter and core apple, and cut into thin wedges. Hull and halve strawberries.

Arrange all prepared fruit and grapes on a large platter, and place bowl of elderflower dip in the center. Sprinkle a little nutmeg over, and serve the fruit decorated with lemon balm or mint.

Serves 8.

Note: Use any fruit liqueur such as crème de cassis or crème de pêche as an alternative to elderflower syrup, if desired. Sprinkle lemon juice over the fruit if not serving immediately.

LYCHEES & COCONUT CUSTARD

3 egg yolks
3–4 tablespoons superfine sugar
scant 1 cup coconut milk
⅓ cup coconut cream
about 1 tablespoon triple distilled rose water
red food coloring
about 16 fresh lychees, peeled, halved, and pits
    removed
rose petals, to decorate

In a bowl, whisk together egg yolks and sugar.

In a medium, preferably nonstick, saucepan, heat coconut milk to just below boiling point, then slowly stir into bowl. Return to pan and cook very gently, stirring with a wooden spoon, until custard coats the back of the spoon.

Remove from heat and stir in coconut cream, rose water to taste, and sufficient red food coloring to color pale pink. Leave until cold, stirring occasionally. Spoon a thin layer of rose-flavored custard into 4 small serving bowls. Arrange lychees on custard. Decorate with rose petals. Serve remaining custard separately to pour over lychees.

Serves 4.

RHUBARB & ORANGE FOOL

2 lb. rhubarb, cut into 1-in. lengths
6 tablespoons unsweetened orange juice
15 teaspoons strawberry jam
2 tablespoons honey
1¼ cups Greek-style yogurt
orange slices and mint sprigs, to decorate
ladyfingers, to serve

Put rhubarb into a saucepan with orange juice, jam, and honey. Bring to a boil, cover, and simmer gently until rhubarb is soft and pulpy.

Cool slightly, then purée in a blender or food processor. Transfer to a bowl and cool completely. In a separate bowl, whip cream lightly. Fold cream and yogurt into cooled rhubarb mixture.

Spoon mixture into 6 individual glasses and chill in the refrigerator until ready to serve. Decorate each dessert with orange slices and mint sprigs, and serve with ladyfingers.

Serves 6.

FEATHER-LIGHT TIRAMISU

3 tablespoons very strong cold espresso coffee
few drops vanilla extract
1 tablespoon brandy or rum
⅓ cup vanilla sugar
8 oz. reduced-fat cream cheese
½ cup reduced-fat crème fraîche
2 egg whites
18 ladyfingers
2 oz. dark chocolate, grated

In a bowl, mix together coffee, vanilla extract, and brandy. In another bowl, beat sugar and cream cheese together. Whisk crème fraîche until just holding its shape and fold into cream cheese mixture.

In a clean bowl, whisk egg whites until forming peaks, then fold into cheese and cream mixture.

Break half the ladyfingers into pieces and place in 6 individual dessert glasses. Drizzle with half the coffee mixture. Spoon on half the cream mixture and sprinkle with half the grated chocolate. Repeat with remaining ingredients, finishing with grated chocolate. Chill until firm and serve within 1 day.

Serves 6.

SUMMER PUDDINGS

2 cups red currants
2 cups black currants
juice ½ orange
½ cup superfine sugar
1⅔ cups fresh raspberries
12–16 thin slices white bread
additional red currants, to garnish (optional)

In a saucepan, combine red currants, black currants, orange juice, and sugar. Cook over low heat, stirring occasionally, until currants are juicy and just tender. Gently stir in raspberries; allow to cool.

Cut crusts from bread. From 6 slices, line 6 ramekin dishes or dariole molds, overlapping bread to line dishes completely. From remaining bread, cut circles same size as top of small ramekin dishes or dariole molds. Strain fruit, reserving juice, and spoon fruit into bread-lined dishes, pressing down quite firmly. Cover with bread circles. Pour some of reserved juice into dishes to soak bread. Place a small weight on top of each pudding.

Chill puddings and remaining juice several hours or overnight. To serve, turn puddings out on to individual plates and spoon a small amount of reserved juices over them. Garnish with additional red currants, if desired.

Serves 6.

Note: A dariole mold is a small cylindrical mold used for cooking pastries or vegetables.

LYCHEE & GINGER MOUSSE

COCONUT CUSTARD

12 oz. fresh lychees, peeled and pits removed
½ teaspoon ground ginger
3 tablespoons sweet sherry
2 pieces stem ginger in syrup, chopped
¼ cup ground almonds
2 teaspoons plain gelatin powder dissolved in
    2 tablespoons boiling water
2 egg whites
sliced stem ginger and mint leaves, to decorate

3 eggs
2 egg yolks
2 cups coconut milk
⅓ cup superfine sugar
few drops rosewater or jasmine extract

Preheat oven to 350°F. Place 4 individual heatproof dishes in a baking pan.

Place lychees in a food processor with ground ginger, sherry, and chopped ginger. Blend until smooth. Transfer to a small bowl and stir in ground almonds and gelatin mixture.

Chill 30 or 40 minutes or until beginning to set. In a large, grease-free bowl, whisk egg whites until very stiff. Using a large metal spoon, carefully fold in the lychee mixture.

In a bowl, stir together eggs, egg yolks, coconut milk, sugar, and rosewater or jasmine extract until sugar dissolves. Pass through a sieve into the dishes. Pour boiling water into baking pan to surround dishes.

Divide mixture among 4 sundae glasses or dishes and chill 1 hour or until set. Decorate with stem ginger and mint leaves, and serve.

Serves 4.

Cook in the oven for about 20 minutes until custards are lightly set in center. Remove from baking pan and allow to cool slightly before unmolding. Serve warm or cold. Decorate with coconut.

Serves 4.

GOOSEBERRY YOGURT SNOW

2½ cups gooseberries
⅓ cup superfine sugar
1¾ cups Greek-style yogurt
mint sprigs, to decorate

Place gooseberries in a saucepan with 2 tablespoons water. Cook gently until soft.

Stir sugar into gooseberries and leave to cool. Purée cooled gooseberries, juice, and yogurt in a blender or food processor until smooth.

Pour mixture into 6 serving dishes and chill in the refrigerator before serving. To serve, decorate with mint sprigs.

Serves 6.

Variation: Bottled gooseberries in syrup may be used instead of fresh gooseberries—omit ¼ cup of the superfine sugar and blend gooseberries with remaining sugar and yogurt.

SUMMER FRUIT GRATIN

2 large peaches, peeled, pits removed, and sliced
½ cup raspberries
¾ cup strawberries, sliced
½ cup red currants and blueberries or black currants
2 tablespoons kirsch or Cointreau (optional)
2 tablespoons superfine sugar
1¼ cups crème fraîche or heavy cream
½ cup soft brown sugar

Divide the fruit between 4 heatproof serving dishes. Sprinkle with kirsch or Cointreau, if using, and superfine sugar.

Whip crème fraîche or cream until it forms soft peaks. Spread over fruit and chill for at least 1 hour.

Preheat broiler to very hot. Sprinkle a thick even layer of brown sugar over crème fraîche or cream. Broil until sugar is bubbling and caramelized. Serve immediately.

Serves 4.

RASPBERRY BAVAROIS

14 oz. canned raspberries in fruit juice
4½ oz. raspberry jello tablet
1¾ cups reduced-fat evaporated milk
fresh raspberries and mint sprigs, to decorate

Drain raspberries over a bowl, reserving fruit juice. In a measuring jug, make juice up to 1¼ cups with water.

Put juice and jello tablet in a saucepan and place on a low heat. When jello has dissolved, remove from heat, and leave to cool. In a large bowl, whisk evaporated milk until thick. Add raspberries and jello and mix well.

Pour mixture into a serving bowl. Chill in the refrigerator until set. Decorate with raspberries and mint sprigs before serving.

Serves 6.

LOGANBERRY LAYER DESSERT

1½ cups loganberries
1 cup reduced-fat heavy cream
2½ cups very low-fat fromage frais
½ cup confectioners' sugar, sifted
fresh loganberries and herb sprigs, to decorate

Place loganberries in a saucepan with 2 tablespoons water. Cook gently until just softened. Cool slightly, then purée in a blender or food processor. Cool completely. In a bowl, whip cream until thick.

In a separate bowl, gently mix together puréed loganberries, half the cream, half the fromage frais and ¼ cup of the confectioners' sugar. In another bowl, gently mix together remaining cream, fromage frais, and confectioners' sugar.

Layer loganberry mixture and fromage frais mixture in 6 glasses, finishing with a loganberry layer. Chill in the refrigerator until ready to serve. Decorate desserts with fresh loganberries and herb sprigs before serving.

Serves 6.

ORANGE FLANS

grated rind 1 orange
1¼ cups fresh orange juice
3 whole eggs
3 egg yolks
2 tablespoons sugar
orange slices and fresh mint, to decorate
CARAMEL:
½ cup superfine sugar

In a small bowl, put orange rind and orange juice. Set aside to soak. Meanwhile, preheat oven to 350°F. Warm 4 ramekin dishes.

To make the caramel, in a small, heavy saucepan, gently heat sugar and 1 tablespoon of water, swirling pan until sugar has dissolved. Cook until golden-brown. Immediately pour one-quarter into each ramekin and swirl them around so caramel coats sides and bottoms of ramekins. Put ramekins in a baking pan. Gently heat orange juice and orange rind until just below a simmer.

Meanwhile, in a bowl, whisk whole eggs and egg yolks with sugar until thick. Slowly pour in orange juice and rind, whisking constantly. Divide among ramekins, then pour boiling water around them. Cover dishes with waxed paper and bake about 25 minutes or until lightly set. Remove dishes from pan and refrigerate until cold. Just before serving, unmold desserts on to cold plates. Decorate with orange slices and mint.

Serves 4.

BLACKBERRY JELLY RING

1½ cups blackberries
1½ cups raspberries
¼ cup superfine sugar
5 teaspoons powdered gelatin
1¼ cups unsweetened apple juice
fresh berries and herb sprigs, to decorate

Place blackberries and raspberries in a saucepan with 1¼ cups water and the sugar. Simmer over a low heat until soft. Allow to cool.

Purée fruit mixture in a blender or food processor, then press through sieve, until all the juice has been extracted. Discard pips. Sprinkle gelatin over 3 tablespoons water in a small bowl and leave for 2–3 minutes to soften. Stand bowl in a saucepan of hot water and stir until gelatin has dissolved. Cool slightly.

Stir gelatin into fruit juice mixture with apple juice. Mix well and pour into a wetted 3¾ cup ring mold. Chill in the refrigerator until set. To serve, turn out of mold, and decorate with fresh berries and herb sprigs.

Serves 4.

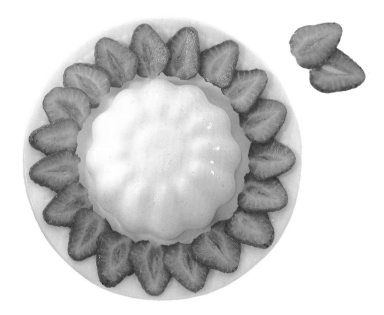

STRAWBERRY YOGURT MOLDS

2 cups strawberry-flavored yogurt
1 tablespoon unflavored gelatin
2 cups strawberries

Pour yogurt into a bowl and chill.

In a small bowl, sprinkle gelatin over water and let stand for 2 to 3 minutes, until softened. Set bowl of gelatin in a saucepan of hot water and stir until dissolved. Whisk into chilled yogurt, then pour into a wetted mold or 4 wetted individual molds. Chill until set.

To serve, slice strawberries. Turn out mold or molds on to a serving plate or plates and surround with sliced strawberries.

Serves 4.

Note: For a softer texture, increase quantity of yogurt slightly and set in a bowl rather than a mold.

PASSION-FRUIT MOUSSE

12 passion fruit
grated rind and juice 1 large orange
5 eggs
½ cup superfine sugar
1 tablespoon unflavored gelatin
1¼ cups heavy cream
additional passion fruit (optional)
mint leaves to decorate (optional)

Cut passion fruit in half and scoop out pulp. In a saucepan, combine pulp and orange juice. Heat gently 2 to 3 minutes, allow to cool, then chill.

In a large bowl, whisk orange rind, eggs, and sugar until thick and mousse-like. In a small bowl, sprinkle gelatin over 3 tablespoons water and let stand 2–3 minutes, until softened. Set bowl of gelatin in a saucepan of hot water and stir until dissolved. Add to egg mixture. Sieve chilled passion-fruit mixture and stir half of mixture into mousse. Chill remainder.

In a bowl, whip cream lightly and fold into mousse mixture. Spoon into a soufflé dish or glass serving bowl and chill. Serve with additional passion fruit, if desired, and garnish with mint leaves, if desired. Serve reserved passion-fruit mixture as a sauce.

Serves 6.

COEURS À LA CRÈME

2 cups fromage frais or curd cheese
1 cup heavy cream
3 egg whites
TO SERVE:
sugar or vanilla sugar
fresh fruit

Line 6 individual *coeurs à la crème* molds with pieces of muslin.

In a large bowl, beat fromage frais or curd cheese until smooth then whisk in cream. Whisk egg whites until stiff. Fold into the cheese mixture. Spoon into molds, put molds in a roasting pan or on a tray and leave in the refrigerator for 12–24 hours to drain: the longer the mixture is left, the firmer it becomes.

Turn molds out on to chilled serving plates. Decorate with mint sprigs, and serve with sugar or vanilla sugar and fresh fruit.

Serves 6.

Note: To make vanilla sugar, simply store a vanilla pod in a jar of sugar, so that it absorbs the flavor.

APRICOPITTA

5 cardamom pods
2 lb. fresh apricots
½ cup superfine sugar
¼ teaspoon vanilla extract
⅓ cup butter, melted
12 sheets phyllo pastry
3 egg whites
2 tablespoons soft brown sugar
1¼ cups ground almonds
confectioners' sugar, for dusting

Remove seeds from cardamom pods and discard pods. Put apricots in a bowl. Cover with boiling water. Leave for 2 minutes, then drain.

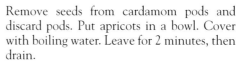

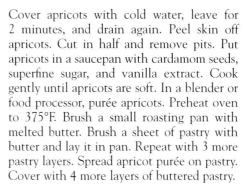

Cover apricots with cold water, leave for 2 minutes, and drain again. Peel skin off apricots. Cut in half and remove pits. Put apricots in a saucepan with cardamom seeds, superfine sugar, and vanilla extract. Cook gently until apricots are soft. In a blender or food processor, purée apricots. Preheat oven to 375°F. Brush a small roasting pan with melted butter. Brush a sheet of pastry with butter and lay it in pan. Repeat with 3 more pastry layers. Spread apricot purée on pastry. Cover with 4 more layers of buttered pastry.

In a bowl, whisk egg whites until stiff. Whisk in soft brown sugar. Fold in ground almonds. Spread meringue on pastry. Cover gently with 4 more sheets buttered pastry. Tuck top layer of pastry down sides. With a sharp knife, cut diamond shapes in pastry, down to meringue layer. Dust with confectioners' sugar, then bake for 40–50 minutes until browned and crisp. Serve warm or cold, cut into diamonds, and dusted with more sugar.

Serves 6–8.

ROSE CREAM

2½ cups heavy cream
1 tablespoon unflavored gelatin
2 tablespoons triple strength rose water
grated peel and juice 1 lemon
¼ cup superfine sugar
ROSE PETALS:
1 egg white
petals from 1 rose
superfine sugar

Prepare rose petals, preheat oven to 225°F. Line a baking tray with parchment paper. Whisk egg white until frothy and dip in rose petals to cover.

Toss dipped petals in sugar and place on prepared baking tray. Place on bottom shelf of oven and bake about 2½ hours, leaving oven door slightly ajar, until dry and hard. Store in an airtight container. Combine all ingredients for rose cream in a heavy-based saucepan and stir over very low heat until gelatin and sugar dissolve; do not boil.

Pour into 6 ramekin dishes and cool at room temperature. Refrigerate creams until ready to serve. Decorate with rose petals.

Serves 6.

Note: Triple strength rose water is available from specialty food stores. The delicate flavor of ordinary rose water would be completely lost in this pudding.

STRAWBERRY PROFITEROLES

½ cup all-purpose flour
¼ cup low-fat spread
2 eggs, beaten
⅔ cup reduced-fat heavy cream
1½ cups strawberries
2 tablespoons confectioners' sugar

Preheat oven to 400°F. Line 2 baking trays with baking parchment. Sift flour on to a plate. Put low-fat spread and ⅔ cup water into a saucepan, heat gently until fat has melted, then bring to a boil. Remove from heat, add flour, and heat until mixture leaves the side of the pan.

Gradually beat in eggs until mixture is smooth and shiny. Put mixture into a pastry bag fitted with a medium plain tube and pipe walnut-size balls on to prepared baking trays. Bake for 20–25 minutes until brown and crisp. Make a slit in side of each profiterole to allow steam to escape, then cool in a wire rack. In a bowl, whisk cream until stiff, and spoon into a pastry bag fitted with a medium plain tube. Pipe some cream into each profiterole.

Halve strawberries and place some strawberries into each profiterole. Pile profiteroles into a pyramid on a serving plate, and dust with sifted confectioners' sugar. Serve immediately.

Serves 8.

SAFFRON YOGURT

ROSE WATER PUDDING

2½ cups plain yogurt
pinch saffron strands
seeds from 6 cardamom pods
3 tablespoons superfine sugar
lemon rind and cardamom seeds, to decorate

1 tablespoon unflavored gelatin
2½ cups milk
3 tablespoons sugar
2 teaspoons rose water
few drops red food coloring
pink rose petals, to decorate

Pour yogurt into a nylon sieve lined with cheesecloth and refrigerate to drain overnight.

Sprinkle gelatin over 3 tablespoons water in a small bowl and soften 2–3 minutes. Put milk in a separate saucepan and heat until almost boiling, add gelatin, and stir until dissolved completely. Stir in sugar and rose water.

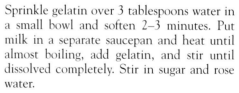

Put saffron and 2 tablespoons boiling water in a small bowl and soak 30 minutes. Turn drained yogurt into a bowl and stir in saffron and its soaking liquid.

Pour half the mixture into a bowl, add a few drops red food coloring to color it a delicate pink, and whisk until cool and frothy. Wet four ¾ cup molds and divide pink mixture among them. Refrigerate about 30 minutes until mixture is just set, but still sticky on top. Meanwhile, keep remaining white mixture in a warm place to prevent it from setting. Whisk white mixture until frothy and pour into molds on top of set pink mixture.

Put cardamom seeds in a mortar and crush lightly with a pestle. Stir into yogurt with sugar. Serve chilled, decorated with lemon rind and cardamom seeds.

Serves 4–6.

Chill until set completely, then dip molds in hot water 1–2 seconds, and turn out on to plates. Serve cold, decorated with rose petals.

Serves 4.

Note: Before turning puddings out, wet each serving plate with a very little cold water to prevent them from sticking to the plate, allowing you to center them, if necessary.

RASPBERRY & APPLE STRUDEL

8 oz. cooking apples
1½ cups raspberries
¼ cup superfine sugar
¼ cup chopped mixed nuts
1 teaspoon ground cinnamon
8 sheets phyllo pastry
¼ cup low-fat spread
1 tablespoon confectioners' sugar

Preheat oven to 375°F. Peel, core, and slice apples. Place in a saucepan with raspberries and 2 tablespoons water. Cover and cook gently until just soft. Stir in sugar and cool. Add nuts and cinnamon and mix well.

Place one sheet of pastry on a sheet of baking parchment and brush lightly with melted fat. Place another sheet of pastry on top and layer all 8 sheets of pastry on top of one another, brushing each one lightly with melted fat. Spoon fruit mixture over pastry leaving a 1-in. border uncovered all around edge. Fold these edges over fruit mixture.

With a long side toward you, using baking parchment, roll up strudel. Carefully place it on a greased baking tray, seam-side down. Brush it lightly with melted fat. Bake for about 40 minutes until golden brown. Dust with sifted confectioners' sugar.

Serves 8.

RASPBERRY & HAZELNUT ROLL

1⅔ cups hazelnuts
5 eggs, separated
⅔ cup superfine sugar
confectioners' sugar, for dusting
1¾ cups heavy cream
2¼ cups raspberries
additional raspberries and mint leaves, to decorate
  (optional)

Preheat oven to 350° F. Line a jelly roll pan with a double thickness of foil and oil thoroughly. In a food processor fitted with a metal blade, process hazelnuts until finely ground.

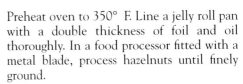

In a large bowl, whisk egg yolks and superfine sugar until thick and mousse-like. Fold in ground hazelnuts. In a separate bowl, whisk egg whites until stiff but not dry. Fold carefully into nut mixture, then pour into prepared pan and spread evenly. Bake 15–20 minutes, until risen and firm to touch. Cover immediately with a damp dish towel and let stand overnight. The next day, turn out cake on to a sheet of foil thickly dusted with confectioners' sugar. Peel off foil.

In a bowl, whip 1¼ cups of the cream to stiff peaks. In a separate bowl, lightly crush half the raspberries, then fold into whipped cream. Spread raspberry cream over cake. Dot remaining raspberries over raspberry cream, then roll up cake using foil to help. Transfer to a serving plate. Whip remaining cream until thick. Slice roll and serve with whipped cream. Decorate individual servings with additional raspberries and mint leaves, if desired.

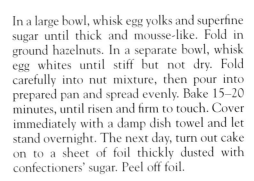

Serves 6.

RASPBERRY ÉCLAIRS

CHOUX PASTRY:
¼ cup unsalted butter or margarine
⅓ cup all-purpose flour, sifted
2 eggs, beaten
FILLING:
¾ cup heavy cream
1 tablespoon confectioners' sugar
1¼ cups raspberries
FROSTING:
¾ cup confectioners' sugar, sifted
2 teaspoons lemon juice
pink food coloring (optional)

Preheat oven to 425°F. In a saucepan, melt butter or margarine, add ⅔ cup water, and bring to a boil. Add flour, all at once, and beat thoroughly until mixture leaves the sides of the pan. Cool slightly, then vigorously beat in eggs, one at a time. Put mixture into a pastry bag fitted with a plain ½-in. tube and pipe twenty to twenty-four 3-in. lengths on to dampened baking trays. Bake for 10 minutes. Reduce temperature to 375°F and bake for 20 minutes until golden.

Slit the side of each éclair and leave on wire racks to cool. To make filling, whip cream and confectioners' sugar in a bowl until thick, put in a pastry bag fitted with a ⅛-in. plain tube and pipe into each éclair. Put a few raspberries in each éclair. Make frosting: mix confectioners' sugar with lemon juice and enough water to make a smooth paste. Add pink coloring, if desired. Spread frosting over éclairs and leave to set.

Makes 20–24.

PINK GRAPEFRUIT CHEESECAKE

8 oz. low-fat oatmeal cookies
½ cup butter, melted
2 pink grapefruits
1 tablespoon unflavored gelatin
1 cup cream cheese, softened
⅓ cup milk
⅓ cup light cream
2 tablespoons superfine sugar
grated peel and juice 1 lemon
4 egg whites

Crush cookies to crumbs and mix with melted butter.

Press two-thirds of crumb mixture over bottom of a 9-in. loose-bottom or springform pan, and chill. Cut off peel and pith from grapefruits, holding over a bowl to catch juice. Cut out sections from between membranes and set aside. Squeeze membranes into bowl to extract juice. Sprinkle gelatin over juice and let stand 2–3 minutes, until softened. Set bowl of gelatin in a pan of hot water and stir until dissolved. In a bowl, beat cream cheese, milk, cream, and sugar. Stir in gelatin, and lemon rind and juice.

In a large bowl, whisk egg whites until stiff. Fold into creamy mixture. Pour over crust and refrigerate until set. To serve, remove cheesecake from pan and decorate with reserved grapefruit sections. Press remaining crumbs evenly into sides of cheesecake.

Serves 6–8.

TROPICAL CHOUX RING

¼ cup butter
½ cup all-purpose flour, sifted
2 eggs, beaten
1¾ cups low-fat ready-made cold custard
8 oz. pineapple, peeled, cored, and chopped
1 papaya, peeled, seeds removed, and chopped
2 kiwi fruit, peeled and chopped
1 starfruit, sliced
2 tablespoons confectioners' sugar

Preheat oven to 400°F. Place butter in a saucepan with ⅔ cup water. Heat gently until fat has melted, then bring mixture to a boil.

Remove saucepan from heat. Add flour to hot mixture and beat thoroughly with a wooden spoon. Beat mixture until it is smooth and forms a ball in the center of the pan. Allow mixture to cool slightly, then gradually add eggs, beating well after each addition, until pastry dough is smooth and shiny. Drop tablespoons of dough on to a greased baking tray to form a ring. Bake for 40 minutes until risen and golden brown. Remove from oven carefully, transfer to a wire rack, and immediately slice ring horizontally in half to release steam inside.

Allow to cool completely. In a bowl, gently mix together custard and prepared fruit. Spoon fruit mixture on to bottom of pastry ring. Replace top of pastry ring. Sprinkle with sifted confectioners' sugar to serve.

Serves 8.

Note: Place the tablespoons of dough so that they are just touching on the baking tray.

FOREST FRUITS CHEESECAKE

3 tablespoons low-fat spread
4 oz. low-fat oatmeal cookies, crushed
1½ cups mixed berries, such as raspberries,
    strawberries, blackberries, black- and red currants
1 tablespoon unflavored gelatin
½ cup skimmed milk cream cheese
9 teaspoons superfine sugar
⅔ cup very low-fat fromage frais
⅔ cup reduced-fat heavy cream
1 tablespoon reduced sugar black currant jam
fresh mixed berries, to decorate

Melt low-fat spread in a saucepan over a low heat. Mix in biscuit crumbs.

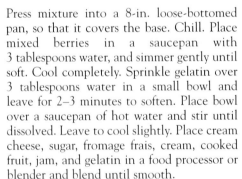

Press mixture into a 8-in. loose-bottomed pan, so that it covers the base. Chill. Place mixed berries in a saucepan with 3 tablespoons water, and simmer gently until soft. Cool completely. Sprinkle gelatin over 3 tablespoons water in a small bowl and leave for 2–3 minutes to soften. Place bowl over a saucepan of hot water and stir until dissolved. Leave to cool slightly. Place cream cheese, sugar, fromage frais, cream, cooked fruit, jam, and gelatin in a food processor or blender and blend until smooth.

Pour on to biscuit base and chill in the refrigerator until set. To serve, remove from pan, place on a serving plate, and decorate with mixed berries.

Serves 8.

Note: To crush cookies easily, place them in a large plastic bag and roll over the bag with a rolling pin until cookies are crushed.

LEMON CHEESE FLAN

5 oz. low-fat oatmeal cookies
1½ tablespoons low-fat spread, melted
1 tablespoon unflavored gelatin
⅔ cup reduced-fat heavy cream
1¼ cups very low-fat fromage frais
½ cup low-fat cream cheese
¼ cup superfine sugar
grated rind and juice 2 lemons
lemon slices and mint sprigs, to decorate

In a bowl, crush cookies to crumbs and mix with melted low-fat spread. Press mixture over base of a 8-in. loose-bottomed quiche pan. Chill in the refrigerator.

Sprinkle gelatin over 3 tablespoons water in a small bowl and leave for 2–3 minutes to soften. Stand bowl in a saucepan of hot water and stir until gelatin has dissolved. Cool slightly. Place cream, fromage frais, cream cheese, sugar, lemon rind and juice, and gelatin into a blender or food processor and blend until smooth and well mixed.

Pour over cookie crumb base, level surface, and chill in the refrigerator until set. To serve, remove carefully from quiche pan and place on a serving plate. Decorate with lemon slices and mint sprigs before serving.

Serves 8.

VINE FRUITS GÂTEAU

4 eggs
½ cup superfine sugar
1 cup all-purpose flour
1 cup reduced-fat heavy cream
¾ cup black grapes, halved and seeded
½ small cantaloupe melon, seeded and diced
2 kiwi fruit, sliced
1 tablespoon confectioners' sugar

Preheat oven to 375° F. Grease a 8-in. deep cake pan. Place eggs and sugar in a large bowl and whisk until thick, pale, and creamy. Sift flour over mixture and fold in gently, using a metal spoon.

Pour mixture into prepared cake pan, tilting pan to level surface. Bake for 25–30 minutes until well risen and firm to touch. Turn out and cool on a wire rack. In a bowl, whisk cream until stiff. In a bowl, gently mix grapes, melon, and kiwi fruit together. To assemble gâteau, cut the sponge cake across into 3 layers. Place one slice on a serving plate, cut-side up. Spread one third of the cream over base, then arrange some fruit on top.

Place a sponge cake on top and spread this with another third of cream. Arrange fruit on top. Place remaining sponge cake slice on top, cut-side down. Spread or pipe remaining cream over top, and arrange remaining fruit decoratively over cream. Dust fruit with sifted confectioners' sugar and serve immediately.

Serves 10.

LEMON MOUSSE GÂTEAU

CAKE:
3 eggs
½ cup plus 3 teaspoons superfine sugar
few drops vanilla extract
¾ cup all-purpose flour
FILLING:
grated rind and juice 2 lemons
2 teaspoons powdered gelatin
3 eggs, separated
½ cup superfine sugar
⅔ cup heavy cream
TO DECORATE:
confectioners' sugar
raspberries
lemon geranium or raspberry leaves, if available

Preheat oven to 350° F. Grease a 9-in. spring-release pan and line with nonstick paper. To make cake, whisk eggs and superfine sugar together in a bowl until very thick and light. Stir in vanilla extract, then sift flour over mixture and fold in gently. Spoon into prepared pan and bake for 25 minutes until golden and cake springs back when pressed. Turn on to a wire rack covered with sugared greaseproof paper. Peel off lining paper and leave to cool.

Slice cake horizontally in 2 layers. Wash and dry cake pan and line base and sides with greaseproof paper. Place one half of cake in base of pan.

To make mousse filling, put juice of 1 lemon and 3 teaspoons water in a bowl. Sprinkle gelatin over, ensuring it is completely covered with liquid. Leave to stand for 10 minutes until spongy. In a bowl, whisk together egg yolks, sugar, and lemon rind until thick and mousse-like. Gradually whisk in remaining lemon juice, keeping mixture as thick as possible.

Place bowl of gelatin over a pan of simmering water until gelatin has dissolved. Immediately whisk it into egg yolk mixture. In a bowl, whip cream until it just holds its shape. Fold cream into egg mixture. Whisk egg whites until stiff but not dry. Gently fold into mousse. Poor mixture into prepared pan. Level surface. Cover and chill for 45–60 minutes until lightly set. Place second layer of cake on top. Cover and chill overnight.

To serve, remove sides of pan and carefully peel away paper. Place a flat plate on top of cake and quickly invert cake. Ease off bottom of pan. Dust gâteau with sifted confectioners' sugar and decorate with raspberries, and geranium or raspberry leaves, if using.

Serves 8–10.

INDIVIDUAL PEAR PUFFS

8 oz. fresh or frozen puff pastry, thawed if frozen
2 large ripe pears
1 egg yolk
1 tablespoon milk
superfine sugar
fresh herbs, to decorate (optional)
Poire William liqueur (optional)

Preheat oven to 425° F. Roll out pastry to about ¼ in. thick. Using half a pear as a guide, cut out pastry pear shapes ½ in. larger than pears.

Cut around pear leaving a pear-shaped 'frame'. Cut out solid pear shape to same size as frame, dampen edges with water, and fit frame on top. Press edges together lightly. Prepare 3 more pastry pear shapes in same way. Peel and halve pears. Core pears and cut crosswise in thin slices.

Place sliced pears in pastry shapes and place on a baking tray. In a small bowl, beat egg yolk and milk, and brush edges of pastry. Bake 15–20 minutes, until pears are tender and pastry edges are puffed up and golden. Remove from oven, sprinkle with sugar, and broil 1 minute. Transfer to serving plates. Decorate with fresh herbs, if desired. If desired, heat liqueur in a small saucepan, light, and pour flaming over puffs. Serve at once.

Serves 4.

CHARLOTTE RUSSE

16 ladyfingers
1 tablespoon unflavored gelatin
4 egg yolks
⅓ cup superfine sugar
2½ cups heavy cream
1 vanilla pod, split open
1¼ cups sour cream
additional whipped cream and 1¼ cups fresh
   raspberries, to decorate

Line bottom of a 4¼ cup charlotte mold with waxed paper. Stand ladyfingers, pressing against each other, around sides of mold and trim to fit.

In a small bowl, sprinkle gelatin over 3 tablespoons water and let stand 2–3 minutes, until softened. In a bowl, whisk egg yolks and sugar until thick and mousse-like. In a saucepan, place 1½ cups of heavy cream and vanilla bean and bring almost to a boil. Strain over egg mixture, stirring well. Return mixture to saucepan and stir over low heat until mixture has thickened slightly: do not boil.

Strain into a clean bowl and add gelatin. Stir until dissolved. Cool, then set bowl in a larger bowl of iced water and stir until mixture thickens. Whip remaining cream with sour cream and fold into mixture. Pour into prepared mold, cover with plastic wrap, and chill overnight. To serve, turn out on to a serving plate. Remove waxed paper and decorate with additional whipped cream and raspberries. Tie ribbon around pudding.

Serves 6–8.

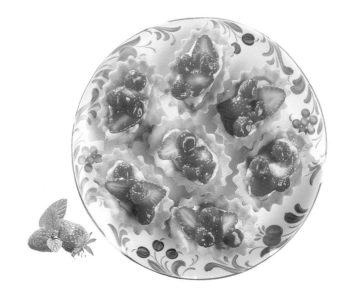

LIME & COCONUT MERINGUE PIE

¼ cup cornstarch
1¼ cups coconut milk
grated rind and juice 2 limes
2 extra large eggs, separated
¾ cup superfine sugar
PASTRY:
1½ cups all-purpose flour
salt
⅓ cup butter
1 teaspoon superfine sugar
1 egg yolk

SUMMER FRUIT TARTLETS

PASTRY:
1¾ cups all-purpose flour, sifted
½ cup ground almonds
½ cup confectioners' sugar, sifted
½ cup butter
1 egg yolk
3 teaspoon milk
FILLING:
1 cup cream cheese
superfine sugar, to taste
2½ cups fresh summer fruits, such as red currants,
  black currants, raspberries, and wild strawberries
red currant jelly, heated, to glaze

To make pastry, sift flour and salt into a bowl. Rub in butter to resemble bread crumbs. Add sugar. Mix in egg yolk, adding enough cold water to make a firm dough. On a floured surface, roll out pastry and use to line a 8-in. loose-based quiche pan. Chill for 30 minutes. Preheat oven to 375°F. Line pie shell with baking parchment and baking beans. Bake for 15 minutes. Remove paper and beans and return pie shell to oven for 5–10 minutes until cooked. Reduce oven temperature to 375°F.

In a bowl, mix together flour, ground almonds, and confectioners' sugar. Rub in butter until mixture resembles bread crumbs. Add egg yolk and milk; work in with a palette knife, then with fingers, until dough binds together. Wrap dough in plastic wrap and chill for 30 minutes. Preheat the oven to 400°F. On a floured surface, roll out pastry thinly and use to line 12 deep tartlet or individual brioche pans; prick bases.

In a saucepan, gradually combine cornstarch with coconut milk. Bring to a boil slowly, stirring constantly. Cook, stirring, for 3 minutes until thickened. Remove from heat and add lime rind and juice, egg yolks, and ¼ cup of the sugar. Pour into pie shell. Whisk egg whites until very stiff then gradually whisk in remaining sugar. Spread egg whites over filling and swirl with a palette knife. Bake for 10–15 minutes until lightly browned. Serve hot or cold.

Press a piece of foil into each tartlet, covering the edges. Bake for 10–15 minutes until light golden brown. Remove foil and bake for an additional 2–3 minutes. Transfer to a wire rack to cool. To make filling, mix cream cheese and superfine sugar together in a bowl. Put a spoonful of filling in each pastry case. Arrange fruit on top, brush with glaze and serve at once.

Serves 12.

Serves 6.

RED FRUIT TART

9½-in. loose-bottomed fluted quiche pan lined with
  pâte sucrée (see page 234)
about 26 each raspberries, halved strawberries, and
  pitted cherries
3 tablespoons red fruit jam
1 tablespoon lemon juice
raspberries and raspberry leaves, to decorate
CRÈME PÂTISSIÈRE:
⅔ cup milk
⅔ cup light cream
1 vanilla pod
3 egg yolks
¼ cup sugar
1 tablespoon all-purpose flour
1½ tablespoons cornstarch
1 tablespoon unsalted butter

To make crème pâtissière, put milk, cream
and vanilla pod in a saucepan, and heat
gently to simmering point. Remove from
heat, cover, and leave for 30 minutes. Whisk
egg yolks and sugar until pale and very thick.
Stir in flour and cornstarch. Remove vanilla
pod from milk and return to a boil. Slowly
pour into egg mixture, whisking constantly.
Return to pan and bring to a boil, whisking.
Simmer for 2–3 minutes. Remove from heat,
stir in butter, and pour into a bowl. Leave to
cool, stirring occasionally. Cover and chill.
Preheat oven to 400°F.

Prick pastry case with a fork, line with
greaseproof paper or foil, and fill with baking
beans. Bake for 10–12 minutes. Reduce oven
temperature to 375° F. Remove paper and
beans and bake for 8–10 minutes. Cool on a
wire rack. Fill pastry case with crème
pâtissière and arrange fruit on top. Put jam
and lemon juice in a pan and heat gently, to
soften. Pass through a sieve and brush over
fruit. Leave to cool, decorate, and serve.

Serves 6.

GLAZED BLUEBERRY TARTLETS

5 oz. low-fat oatmeal cookies
¼ cup ground almonds
⅓ cup soft brown sugar
¼ cup low-fat spread, melted
3 cups blueberries
9 tablespoons red currant jelly
1 tablespoon confectioners' sugar (optional)
mint leaves, to decorate

In a bowl, crush cookies to crumbs and mix
together with almonds, sugar, and melted
low-fat spread.

Press mixture into12 greased deep patty pans
and chill in the refrigerator until firm.
Carefully remove tartlet cases from pans and
pile blueberries into the cases.

In a saucepan, warm red currant jelly with
2 tablespoons water. Brush over blueberries
to glaze. Serve blueberry tartlets dusted with
sifted confectioners' sugar, if desired.
Decorate with mint leaves.

Makes 12.

TARTE AU CITRON

3 eggs
1 egg yolk
¾ cup superfine sugar
grated rind and juice 3 lemons
grated rind and juice 1 orange
½ cup confectioners' sugar
thinly pared rind 1 lemon
confectioners' sugar, for dusting
lemon twists and chervil sprigs, to decorate
cream, to serve (optional)
PÂTE SUCRÉE:
¾ cup all-purpose flour
pinch salt
4 tablespoons superfine sugar
½ cup unsalted butter, softened
2 egg yolks

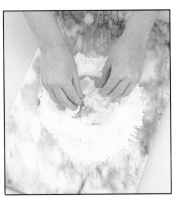

To make pâte sucrée, sift flour and salt on to a marble slab or a counter and make a well in center. Put sugar, butter, and egg yolks into well and pinch them together to form a paste, then lightly draw in the flour, adding about 1 tablespoon cold water to make a soft but firm dough. Cover and chill for 2 hours.

Roll out pastry on a lightly floured surface and line a 9½-in. loose-bottomed fluted quiche pan, pressing pastry well into sides and base. Run rolling pin over top of pan to cut off excess pastry. Chill for 20 minutes. Preheat oven to 400°F.

Prick base of pastry case with a fork, line with greaseproof paper or foil, and fill with baking beans. Put quiche pan on a baking tray and bake for 10–12 minutes. Reduce oven temperature to 375°F. Remove paper and beans and bake for 5 minutes, until golden. Transfer pan to a wire rack and leave to cool. Leave oven on.

Mix together eggs, egg yolk, superfine sugar, and lemon and orange rind and juice. Return quiche pan to baking tray and ladle in filling. Bake for 25–30 minutes, until set. Transfer pan to a wire rack, cool slightly, then remove outer ring of quiche pan. Leave tart to cool completely.

Put confectioners' sugar and ⅓ cup water in a small pan and heat gently, stirring, until dissolved. Boil for 2 minutes then add pared lemon rind and simmer until glassy. Remove with a slotted spoon and leave to cool on greaseproof paper. Just before serving, dust tart thickly with sifted confectioners' sugar, and sprinkle with candied lemon rind. Decorate with lemon twists and chervil sprigs, and serve with cream, if desired.

Serves 6–8.

BANANA & GINGER ICE CREAM

16 fl oz. canned evaporated milk, chilled
½ cup soft light brown sugar
3 ripe bananas, mashed
2 tablespoons syrup from ginger jar
⅔ cup preserved stem ginger, chopped
ginger syrup, to serve

Turn freezer to its coldest setting. Pour evaporated milk into a bowl and, using an electric beater, whisk until thick and mousse-like. Whisk in sugar.

Whisk bananas and ginger syrup into evaporated milk. Stir in chopped ginger. Cover and freeze for 3 hours until just frozen. Spoon into a bowl and mash with a fork or whisk to break down ice crystals.

Return mixture to container and freeze again for 2 hours. Mash once more then freeze for 2–3 hours until firm. Remove from freezer and leave at room temperature for 20–30 minutes before serving. Scoop into chilled glasses, and serve with a little ginger syrup drizzled over.

Serves 6–8.

CANDIED FRUIT TARTS

1 cup ricotta cheese
3 egg yolks
¼ cup superfine sugar
1 tablespoon brandy
grated rind 1 lemon
1 tablespoon lemon juice
⅔ cup crystallized fruit, finely chopped
confectioners' sugar, for dusting
mint sprigs, to decorate
PASTRY:
1½ cups all-purpose flour
⅓ cup butter
⅓ cup white vegetable fat

To make the pastry, sift the flour into a bowl. Add the butter and vegetable fat.

Rub in the butter and vegetable fat until the mixture resembles fine bread crumbs. Stir in 2 tablespoons of cold water and use a knife to mix to a smooth dough. Knead lightly, wrap in plastic wrap, and chill for 30 minutes. Preheat oven to 350° F. On a lightly floured surface, roll out the pastry until ⅛ in. thick. Cut out 4 circles to fit four 4-in. quiche pans.

Put ricotta cheese, egg yolks, superfine sugar, brandy, and lemon rind and juice in a bowl. Beat together until smooth then stir in the crystallized fruit. Divide the mixture among the pastry cases. Bake for 30–40 minutes or until the filling is set and golden. Leave to cool. Dust with confectioners' sugar, decorate with mint sprigs, and serve cold.

Serves 4.

TARTE TATIN

½ cup unsalted butter, softened
½ cup superfine sugar
about 3 lb. firm, well-flavored apples, such as Cox's,
    peeled, cored, and cut into wedges
juice 1 lemon
strips lemon rind and mint sprigs, to decorate
cream, to serve
PASTRY:
2 cups all-purpose flour
1 tablespoon superfine sugar
½ cup butter, diced
2–3 tablespoons crème fraîche

Sprinkle with lemon juice and cook over a moderately high heat, shaking pan or skillet occasionally, for 20–30 minutes, until apples are lightly caramelized. If a lot of juice is produced, pour it off into a saucepan, boil to a thick syrup and pour back over apples.

To make pastry, combine flour and sugar in a bowl. Add butter and rub in until mixture resembles fine bread crumbs. Add enough crème fraîche to bind to a dough. Form into a ball, cover and chill for at least 30 minutes.

Preheat oven to 425°F. Roll out pastry on a lightly floured surface until slightly larger than pan or skillet. Lay pastry on top of apples, tucking edge of pastry down side of pan or skillet.

Spread butter over base of a heavy 9½-in. cake pan or ovenproof skillet. Sprinkle sugar over and arrange apples on top, rounded-side down.

Prick pastry lightly with a fork and put pan or skillet on a baking tray. Bake for 20 minutes, until pastry is golden. Turn tart on to a warmed serving plate, decorate with lemon rind and mint sprigs, and serve with cream.

Serves 6–8.

Note: Be careful when turning out the tart as the syrup will be very hot and can burn.

CRÈME CARAMEL

2½ cups milk
1 vanilla pod
2 eggs
2 egg yolks
⅓ cup sugar
mint sprigs, to decorate
CARAMEL:
½ cup superfine sugar

To make caramel, put superfine sugar in a small heavy saucepan with 5 tablespoons water and heat gently until sugar has dissolved. Increase heat and boil until golden brown.

Remove from heat and pour into six ⅔ cup ramekins, turning dishes to coat sides with caramel. Put in a roasting pan and leave to cool. Preheat oven to 325°F. Put milk and vanilla pod into a small saucepan and bring to a boil. Cover, remove from heat, and leave to infuse for 20 minutes. Put eggs, egg yolks, and sugar in a large bowl and whisk together. Remove vanilla pod from milk and return milk to a boil. Stir into egg mixture.

Strain into ramekins. Pour boiling water into roasting pan to come halfway up sides of ramekins and bake for 40–50 minutes, until lightly set. Remove from pan and leave to cool. One hour before serving, run knife around the edge or caramels and turn out on to serving plate. Decorate with mint, and serve.

Serves 6.

FIG & ORANGE TART

1½ cups ready-to-eat dried figs, chopped
juice 2 oranges
⅓ cup butter, diced
2 eggs, beaten
2 tablespoons pine nuts
confectioners' sugar, for dusting
orange slices, to decorate
PASTRY:
1¼ cups all-purpose flour
⅓ cup butter
2 tablespoons confectioners' sugar
1 egg yolk

To make pastry, sift flour into a bowl. Rub in the butter until the mixture resembles fine bread crumbs.

Stir in confectioners' sugar. Add egg yolk and 1 teaspoon of water. Stir with a knife to form a smooth dough. Knead lightly, wrap in plastic wrap, and chill for 30 minutes. On a lightly floured surface, roll out dough to fit a 8-in. loose-bottomed quiche pan. Line quiche pan with pastry and chill again for 20–30 minutes. Preheat the oven to 375°F. Prick pastry all over with a fork, then line with foil and fill with baking beans. Bake blind for 10–15 minutes until the pastry has set.

Remove baking beans and foil, and bake for an additional 10–15 minutes until firm and golden brown. Put figs and orange juice in a saucepan. Cook for 5–10 minutes, stirring, until thickened. Remove from the heat, add butter, and stir until melted. Beat in eggs. Pour mixture into tart case and sprinkle with pine nuts. Bake for 15 minutes until just set. Dust with confectioners' sugar, decorate with orange slices, and serve warm or cold.

Serves 6.

FROZEN LOGANBERRY SOUFFLÉ

3 cups loganberries or raspberries
lemon juice
⅔ cup superfine sugar
3 egg whites
1¼ cups heavy cream
fresh raspberries and mint leaves, to decorate
  (optional)

In a blender or food processor fitted with a metal blade, process berries to a purée, then sieve to remove seeds. Flavor with lemon juice.

In a small saucepan, combine sugar and ½ cup water. Cook over low heat. When sugar dissolves, bring syrup to a boil and boil to 240°F. In a large bowl, whisk egg whites until stiff. Gradually pour in sugar syrup, whisking constantly. Continue whisking until meringue is firm and cool. In a bowl, whip cream lightly and fold into meringue mixture with fruit purée.

Divide mixture among 6 ramekin dishes and freeze 2–3 hours. Transfer to refrigerator 30 minutes before serving. Decorate with fresh raspberries and mint leaves, if desired.

Serves 6.

Note: For a special occasion, wrap foil around tops of small ramekin dishes so that foil extends 2 in. above rim. Keep in place with freezer tape. Fill dishes to come over the top, so when foil is removed, they look like risen soufflés.

COCONUT ICE CREAM

2 oz. creamed coconut
2 eggs, separated
½ cup superfine sugar
1¼ cups light cream
3 tablespoons coconut liqueur
⅔ cup heavy cream, whipped
pulp of 6 passion fruit, to serve

Set freezer to maximum. In a bowl, blend creamed coconut with 2 tablespoons hot water. Add egg yolks and half the sugar, and beat well.

In a saucepan, heat light cream. Bring to a boil then pour on to egg yolk mixture, stirring vigorously. Return to pan and cook gently until slightly thickened. Leave to cool. Stir in coconut liqueur. In another bowl, whisk egg whites until stiff, then whisk in remaining sugar. Fold into whipped cream, then fold in coconut custard.

Pour mixture into a shallow freezerproof container. Cover and freeze for 3 hours until just frozen. Spoon into a bowl and mash with a fork or whisk to break down ice crystals. Return mixture to container and freeze again for 2 hours, mash once more, then freeze for 2–3 hours until firm. Remove from freezer and leave at room temperature for 20–30 minutes before serving. Serve with passion fruit pulp.

Serves 6.

FROZEN KIWI-FRUIT TERRINE

1 recipe Passion-Fruit Mousse (see page 222)
6 kiwi fruit
¾ cup heavy cream

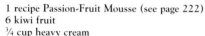

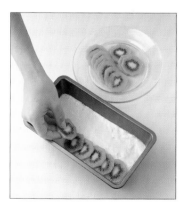

Lightly oil a 8 x 4-in. loaf pan. Prepare mousse as directed and spoon one third of mousse into oiled pan. Freeze until set.

Peel kiwi fruit and cut across fruit in thin slices. Arrange 2 sliced kiwi fruit over top of mousse in rows, then carefully spoon half of remaining mousse on top. Freeze again until set. Repeat process with 2 more sliced kiwi fruit and top with remaining mousse. Return to freezer.

About 2 hours before serving, remove terrine from freezer and turn out on to a serving dish. In a bowl, whip cream until stiff. Using a pastry bag fitted with a star tube, pipe a ruff down each side of terrine. Decorate with remaining 2 sliced kiwi fruit.

Serves 6.

Note: Select kiwi fruit that give slightly when squeezed, but are not too soft.

MOCHA ESPRESSO ICE CREAM

2 cups milk
⅔ cup heavy cream
⅓ cup medium ground espresso coffee
3 oz. dark chocolate, chopped
6 egg yolks
¾ cups superfine sugar
chocolate shavings, to decorate

Place the milk, cream, coffee grains, and 2 oz. of the chocolate in a small saucepan and heat slowly until almost boiling. Remove from the heat and set aside for 30 minutes for the flavors to infuse.

Beat the egg yolks and sugar together in a large bowl until thick and pale. Gradually beat in the mocha mixture and transfer to a clean saucepan. Heat gently, stirring, until the mixture thickens, but do not allow to boil. Leave to cool.

Transfer the mixture to a plastic container and freeze. Beat to mix and break up ice crystals after about 1 hour, and again at hourly intervals until almost firm. Stir in the remaining chocolate, cover, and allow to freeze completely. Remove from the freezer for 20 minutes before serving to allow ice cream to soften. Decorate with chocolate shavings, if desired.

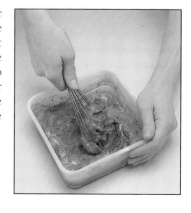

Serves 4.

PISTACHIO ICE CREAM

2 cups roasted pistachio nuts
1 cup superfine sugar
4 egg yolks
2 cups whole milk
1¼ cups heavy cream
½ cup Greek-style yogurt
roughly chopped pistachio nuts, to decorate
quartered fresh figs, to serve

Turn the freezer to its coldest setting. In a food processor, finely grind pistachio nuts with 1 tablespoon of the sugar.

Whisk egg yolks and remaining sugar in a large bowl until thick and foamy. Put pistachio nuts, milk, and cream in a small saucepan and bring to a boil. Pour on to egg yolk mixture, whisking constantly. Put the bowl over a pan of simmering water. Heat, stirring, for about 8 minutes, until the mixture is thick enough to coat the back of the spoon. Cover and leave to cool. Stir in the Greek-style yogurt.

Pour the mixture into a freezerproof container. Put in the freezer. When the sides are beginning to set, transfer to a bowl and beat thoroughly or process in a food processor or blender. Return to the container and freeze for 30–40 minutes. When the ice cream is just beginning to solidify, transfer to a bowl and beat again. Return to the freezer until firm. Transfer to the refrigerator 20 minutes before serving. Decorate with pistachios and serve with figs.

Serves 4–6.

LAVENDER HONEY ICE CREAM

5 lavender flower sprigs
2½ cups milk
½ cup lavender honey
4 egg yolks
⅔ cup heavy cream
⅔ cup crème fraîche
lavender flowers, to decorate

Turn the freezer to its coldest setting. Put lavender sprigs and milk in a saucepan and heat to almost boiling. Remove from the heat and discard lavender sprigs.

Heat honey in a small saucepan until just melted. Whisk egg yolks in a large bowl until thick and foamy. Gradually whisk melted honey into egg yolks. Bring milk back to a boil. Pour boiling milk on to egg yolks, whisking constantly. Put the bowl over a pan of simmering water. Heat, stirring, for about 8 minutes until the mixture is thick enough to coat the back of the spoon. Strain into a bowl, cover, and leave to cool. Stir in heavy cream and crème fraîche.

Pour the mixture into a freezerproof container. Put in the freezer. When the sides are beginning to set, transfer to a bowl and beat thoroughly or process in a food processor or blender. Return to the container and freeze for 30–40 minutes. When the ice cream is just beginning to solidify, transfer to a bowl and beat again. Return to the freezer until firm. Transfer to the refrigerator 20 minutes before serving. Decorate with lavender flowers and serve.

Serves 4–6.

LEMON & LIME YOGURT ICE

2½ cups low-fat plain yogurt
⅓ cup superfine sugar
grated rind and juice 1 lemon
grated rind and juice 1 lime
lime slices and strips lemon and lime rind, to
decorate

In a bowl, beat yogurt and sugar together until sugar has dissolved.

Add grated fruit rinds and juices and mix well. Pour into a chilled, shallow plastic container. Cover and freeze for 1½–2 hours or until mushy in consistency. Transfer to a chilled bowl and beat with a fork or whisk until smooth. Return mixture to container, cover, and freeze until firm.

Transfer to the refrigerator for 30 minutes before serving to soften. Serve in scoops, decorated with lime slices and strips of lime and lemon rind.

Serves 4.

COFFEE BOMBE

1½ cups reduced-fat light cream
⅔ cup reduced-fat heavy cream
4 tablespoons Greek-style yogurt
2 teaspoons instant coffee powder
⅓ cup confectioners' sugar, sifted

In a large bowl, mix cream and yogurt together.

Dissolve coffee powder in 1 tablespoon warm water. Fold into cream mixture with the confectioners' sugar and mix gently but thoroughly. Pour mixture into a lightly greased 3¾-cup bombe mold or pudding basin. Freeze until firm.

Transfer bombe to the refrigerator 45 minutes before serving to soften slightly. Turn out on to a serving dish.

Serves 8.

MIXED BERRY SHERBET

¼ cup raspberries
1 cup black currants
¼ cup strawberries
½ cup superfine sugar
2½ cups skimmed milk
⅔ cup reduced-fat heavy cream
⅔ cup reduced-fat cream
fresh berries, to decorate

PLUM ICE

10 oz. plums or damsons
¼ cup superfine sugar
1¼ cups reduced-fat evaporated milk
1¼ cups reduced-fat light cream
mint sprigs, to decorate

Place fruit and sugar in a saucepan with 2 tablespoons water. Cover and cook gently until soft. Allow to cool completely.

Place plums or damsons in a saucepan with sugar and 2 tablespoons water. Cover and cook gently until just soft. Allow to cool, then remove pits. Place plums or damsons in a blender or food processor and blend until smooth. Allow to cool completely.

Place cooked fruit, milk, and creams into a blender or food processor and blend until smooth. Pour mixture into a chilled, shallow plastic container. Cover and freeze for 1½–2 hours or until the mixture is mushy in consistency.

In a large bowl, whisk evaporated milk until thick. Fold in cream and plum or damson purée, mixing gently but thoroughly. Pour mixture into a chilled, shallow plastic container. Cover and freeze for 1½–2 hours or until the mixture is mushy in consistency. Transfer to a chilled bowl and beat with a fork or whisk until smooth.

Transfer to a chilled bowl and beat with a fork or whisk until smooth. Return mixture to container, cover, and freeze until firm. Transfer to the refrigerator for 30 minutes before serving to soften. Serve in scoops, decorated with mixed berries.

Serves 6.

Return mixture of container, cover, and freeze for 1 hour. Beat mixture as before and return to container. Cover and freeze until firm. Transfer to the refrigerator for 30 minutes before serving to soften. Serve in scoops, decorated with mint sprigs.

Serves 6.

KIWI WATER ICE

6 kiwi fruit
1 tablespoon lemon juice
½ cup superfine sugar
4 ripe passion fruit

Peel kiwi fruit and place in a blender or food processor with lemon juice. Blend until smooth and then set aside.

Place superfine sugar in a saucepan with 1¼ cups water. Bring slowly to a boil and boil gently for 10 minutes. Add kiwi purée, mix well, and allow to cool. Put cooled mixture into a chilled, shallow plastic container. Cover and freeze for 1½–2 hours or until the mixture is mushy in consistency. Transfer to a chilled bowl.

Cut each passion fruit in half and scoop out flesh. Add to kiwi water ice. Beat with a fork or whisk until smooth. Return mixture to container, cover, and freeze until firm. Transfer to the refrigerator for about 15 minutes before serving to soften. Serve in individual dishes, accompanied by cookies.

Serves 6.

LIGHT VANILLA ICE CREAM

1 vanilla pod
5 cups lactose-reduced milk or low-fat milk
4 tablespoons cornstarch
1½ cups superfine sugar
few drops vanilla extract

Split vanilla pod in half and place in a saucepan with 4 cups milk. Heat to boiling point, remove from heat, and leave to infuse for 20 minutes. Remove vanilla pod, scrape out seeds, and whisk seeds back into milk. Wash and dry the pod and store in your sugar jar.

Dissolve cornstarch in remaining milk and stir in sugar. Pour this into the hot milk. Set over the heat again and bring to a boil, stirring constantly until thickened.

Cover the surfaces with plastic wrap and allow to cool to room temperature. Stir in vanilla extract, chill, then freeze in an ice cream maker for best results. Alternatively, pour into a shallow freezer tray and freeze until ice cream is frozen around the edges. Mash well with a fork, beat, and refreeze until almost solid. Repeat this twice more.

Serves 6.

ORANGE SORBET

10 juicy oranges
1 cup superfine sugar
2 tablespoons orange flower water

Pare rind from oranges with a potato peeler or sharp knife avoiding any white pith. Chop rind roughly. Squeeze juice from oranges and strain through a sieve.

Pour ¾ cup water into a saucepan, add sugar, and heat gently to dissolve. Stir in pared orange rind, juice, and orange flower water. Boil rapidly for 1 minute. Cool, then chill in refrigerator. Strain the syrup.

Freeze in an ice cream maker for best results. Alternatively, pour into a shallow freezer tray and freeze until sorbet is frozen around the edges. Mash well with a fork, beat, and refreeze until almost solid. Repeat this twice more. Serve in chilled glass dishes.

Serves 4.

STRAWBERRY SORBET

1¼ cups superfine sugar
3 cups fresh sweet strawberries
1 tablespoon balsamic vinegar

Pour 1 cup water into a saucepan and add sugar. Heat gently to dissolve sugar, then bring to a boil and boil for 1 minute. Cool then chill in refrigerator. Meanwhile, wash and hull strawberries. Purée in a blender or food processor until smooth, and pass through a sieve, if desired. Chilled the purée.

Stir the syrup into the chilled strawberry purée and add balsamic vinegar. Freeze in an ice cream maker for best results.

Alternatively, pour mixture into a shallow freezer tray and freeze until sorbet is frozen around the edges. Mash well with a fork, beat, and refreeze until almost solid. Repeat this twice more. Serve in chilled glass dishes.

Serves 6.

WATERMELON GRANITA

1½ cups superfine sugar
2 cinnamon sticks
1¾ lb. peeled watermelon, cut up
juice 1 lemon
mint sprigs, to decorate

Put sugar and cinnamon sticks into a pan with 1¼ cups water. Stir over gentle heat until sugar has dissolved, bring to a boil, and boil for 1 minute. Allow to cool completely, then remove, wash, and dry cinnamon sticks.

Mash watermelon flesh in a large bowl then press through a sieve to remove seeds. Mix watermelon pulp with cold syrup, adding lemon juice to taste, then chill in refrigerator. Pour into a shallow container to a depth of ¾ in. Cover and freeze for 1 hour until the liquid has formed an ice rim around the edge and is starting to freeze on the base.

Scrape this away with a fork and mash evenly with remaining liquid. Repeat every 30 minutes until mixture forms a smooth consistency of ice crystals. Serve mounded high in chilled glasses (frosted in freezer, if suitable), decorated with mint.

Serves 6.

POMEGRANATE SORBET

1 cup granulated sugar
4–6 large pomegranates
grated rind and juice ½ orange
grated rind and juice ½ lemon
1 egg white
pomegranate seeds and mint sprigs, to decorate

Turn the freezer to its coldest setting. Put sugar and 1¼ cups water in a saucepan. Heat gently until sugar has dissolved then bring to a boil and simmer for 5 minutes. Leave to cool. Cut the pomegranates in half.

Squeeze pomegranates on a lemon squeezer to give 1¾ cups juice. Strain pomegranate juice into the cooled syrup. Stir in orange and lemon rind and juice. Pour into a freezerproof container. Put in the freezer. When the sides are beginning to set, transfer to a bowl and beat thoroughly or process in a food processor or blender. Return to the container and freeze for 30–40 minutes.

When sorbet is just beginning to solidify, whisk egg white until stiff. Beat sorbet again until smooth. Fold in egg white. Return to the freezer until firm. Transfer sorbet to the refrigerator 20 minutes before serving. Decorate with pomegranate seeds and mint sprigs, and serve.

Serves 4–6.

COFFEE GRANITA

½ cup finely ground espresso coffee
finely grated rind 1 lemon
⅔ cups superfine sugar
1 tablespoon lemon juice
whipped cream, to decorate (optional)

Put espresso coffee into a pan with 2¼ cups water. Bring to a boil and remove from the heat. Add lemon rind and leave to infuse for 5 minutes. Strain through a coffee filter.

Mix ⅔ cup water with superfine sugar until dissolved. Stir in infused coffee and lemon juice, leave to cool, then chill in the refrigerator. Pour into a shallow container to a depth of ¾ in. Cover and freeze for 1 hour until the liquid has formed an ice rim around the edge and is starting to freeze on the base.

Scrape away ice rim with a fork and mash evenly with the remaining liquid. Repeat every 30 minutes until the mixture forms a smooth consistency of ice crystals. Serve in chilled glasses (frosted in freezer, if suitable) with a dollop of whipped heavy cream, if desired.

Serves 8.

LYCHEE SORBET

2 16-oz. cans lychees in syrup
grated rind and juice 1 lemon
2 egg whites
mint leaves, to decorate (optional)

Drain lychees, reserving 1¼ cups of syrup. In a blender or food processor fitted with a metal blade, process lychees, syrup, and lemon juice to a purée.

Stir in lemon rind, pour into a plastic container, and freeze about 1 hour, until mixture is slushy.

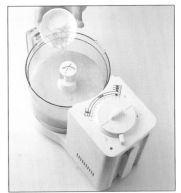

In a large bowl, whisk egg whites until stiff. Fold in semifrozen lychee purée and combine thoroughly. Freeze until firm. To serve, scoop sorbet in balls and decorate with mint leaves, if desired.

Serves 4–6.

Note: For a smoother texture, whisk sorbet about 1 hour after adding egg whites. Serve sorbet as soon as possible for the best flavor.

THAI SWEETMEATS

⅓ cup split mung beans, rinsed
½ cup dried coconut
1 egg, separated
½ cup palm sugar, crushed
few drops jasmine extract

Put mung beans into a saucepan, add sufficient water to cover by 1½ in. Bring to a boil, then simmer for about 30–45 minutes until tender. Drain through a strainer, then mash thoroughly.

Using your fingers, mix in coconut and egg yolk to make a firm paste. Divide into pieces about the size of a walnut and shape into egg-shaped balls using a spoon. Put sugar into a saucepan, add ¾ cup water and heat gently, stirring until sugar has dissolved. Bring to a boil. Add jasmine extract to taste, and keep hot.

Using a fork, thoroughly beat egg white in a bowl. Using 2 forks, dip each ball into egg white, then lower into syrup. Cook for 2–3 minutes. Using a slotted spoon, transfer to a plate. When all sweetmeats have been cooked, spoon a little syrup over. Leave until cold.

Makes about 16.

CHOCOLATE MINI MUFFINS

1¼ cups self rising flour
2½ tablespoons cocoa powder
1 teaspoon baking powder
pinch salt
¼ cup soft light brown sugar
1 small egg, lightly beaten
⅔ cup milk
¼ cup butter, melted and cooled slightly
½ teaspoon vanilla extract
chocolate and hazelnut spread or chocolate spread,
  for filling

Preheat oven to 400°F. Grease 20 mini muffin cups, about 1¾ x ¼ in., or put small paper cases in cups.

Sift flour, cocoa powder, baking powder, and salt into a shallow bowl. Stir in sugar. Stir egg into milk, butter, and vanilla extract. Pour on to dry ingredients and mix briefly, using a large metal spoon and a lifting figure-of-eight movement; there should not be any free flour but mixture should still be lumpy.

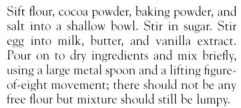

One third- to half-fill paper cases or muffin pans with mixture. Put ½–1 teaspoon of spread on each portion of mixture and cover with more mixture so that cases or cups are almost filled. Bake for 20 minutes until risen and tops spring back when lightly touched. Paper cases can be removed immediately, alternatively place cups on a wire rack and leave to cool for 5 minutes, then remove muffins from cups. Serve warm.

Makes about 20.

PINEAPPLE & MANGO PUNCH

1 ripe pineapple
½ large, ripe mango, peeled and chopped
⅔ cup traditional ginger ale
sparkling mineral water, for topping up
lemon or lime juice

Using a large, sharp knife, slice top off pineapple. Scoop fruit from center without piercing shell. Set aside shell. Discard tough core. About ½ lb. of the flesh and juice should remain.

Put pineapple flesh and juice, mango, and ginger ale into a blender. Mix until smooth. Dilute to drinking consistency with sparkling mineral water. Flavor drink with lemon or lime juice to taste. Pour into reserved pineapple shell. Serve with straws.

Serves 2.

PASSION-FRUIT COOLER

thinly pared rind 1 lemon
2 teaspoons sugar
6 ripe passion fruit
1 large, very ripe mango, peeled and chopped
juice 1 lemon
juice 1 lime
ice cubes, to serve
soda water, chilled, for topping up
lemon and lime slices, for decoration

Put lemon rind in a stainless steel saucepan with ⅔ cup water. Bring to a boil, stirring to dissolve sugar. Boil for 1 minute. Remove from heat, cover, and cool.

Refrigerate until very cold. Scoop seeds from passion fruit into a nylon sieve and rub firmly with the back of a spoon to remove all the flesh. Discard seeds. Purée mango flesh, and mix with passion-fruit flesh. Strain in lemon and lime juices. Put ice cubes into 4 tall glasses. Add passion-fruit mixture and top up with soda water. Decorate with lemon and lime slices. Serve at once with straws.

Serves 4.

MELON SPRITZER

1 ripe Galia melon, about 4 lb.
grated rind and juice 1 lemon
grated rind and juice 2 limes
superfine sugar
mint sprigs, to decorate

Cut melon in half and scoop out and discard seeds. Put melon flesh in a blender with lemon and lime rinds, and juice. Blend until smooth. Pour through a sieve, if desired. Sweeten to taste. Chill.

To serve, half-fill cold glasses with melon purée. Top up with sparkling wine. Decorate with mint sprigs.

Serves 6–8.

ORANGE & PINEAPPLE CRUSH

1 pineapple, about 2 lb.
1¼ cups fresh orange juice
2 tablespoons fresh lemon juice
12 ice cubes
soda water or sparkling mineral water, for topping up
orange slices and pineapple chunks, to decorate

Slice across pineapple. Cut off skin. Remove core and 'eyes' and chop flesh. Put into blender or food processor. Add half orange juice and blend for 1–2 minutes. Strain through nylon sieve into a jug and press firmly with the back of a spoon to extract all the juice. Strain in lemon juice and stir.

Put 3 ice cubes into each of 4 tall glasses. Divide fruit juices among glasses. Top up with soda water or sparkling mineral water. Decorate glasses with orange slices and pineapple chunks. Serve with straws.

Serves 4.

ICED ROSE TEA

1½ oz. Ceylon breakfast tea
sugar
few drops rose water
12 ice cubes
6 mint sprigs
fresh rose petals

Put tea in a bowl, pour 4½ cups lukewarm water over, and leave to stand overnight.

Strain tea into a large jug. Stir in sugar and rose water to taste, and add ice cubes. Place a sprig of mint and a few rose petals in each of 6 glasses, and pour the tea on top.

Serves 6.

Variations: For Vanilla Iced Tea, omit rose water. Put a vanilla pod in the bowl with tea to soak overnight. Remove it before serving.

For Mint Tea, omit the and rose petals. Put a sprig of mint in the bowl with tea to soak overnight. Remove it before serving. Place a small sprig of mint in each glass.

GRAPEFRUIT BARLEY WATER

¼ cup pearl barley
¼ cup sugar
2 pink grapefruit
mint leaves, to decorate

Put barley into a saucepan. Just cover with cold water and bring to a boil. Tip barley into a colander and rinse thoroughly under cold running water.

Return barley to the saucepan, add 2½ cups cold water and bring to a boil again. Cover and simmer for 1 hour. Strain liquid into a jug, stir in the sugar, and leave until completely cold.

Squeeze juice from grapefruit and add to cooled barley water. Chill well. Serve decorated with mint leaves.

Makes about 2½ cups.

Variation: To make Lemon Barley Water, use 2 lemons instead of grapefruit.

OLD-FASHIONED LEMONADE

LIMEADE

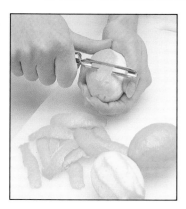

3 lemons
½ cup superfine sugar
ice cubes
mint sprigs and lemon slices, to decorate

Using a potato peeler or sharp knife, thinly pare rind from lemons and put in a bowl or large jug with sugar. Squeeze juice from lemons into a bowl and set aside.

Pour 3¼ cups boiling water over lemon rind and sugar. Stir to dissolve sugar and leave until completely cool. Add lemon juice, and strain into a jug. Chill well. Serve in ice-filled tumblers, decorated with mint and lemon slices.

Serves 6.

Variations: To make Pink Lemonade, add just enough pink grenadine syrup to each glass to give lemonade a pale pink color. Omit the mint and lemon slices, and decorate each glass with a cherry.

To make Orangeade, use 3 oranges and 1 lemon instead of 3 lemons. Omit mint and lemon slices, and decorate the glasses with orange slices.

6 limes
½ cup superfine sugar
pinch salt
lime slices, to serve

Cut each lime in half and squeeze juice.

Place skins in a jug, then stir in sugar and pour in 3 cups boiling water. Cover and leave for 15 minutes.

Stir in salt. Strain into another jug and add lime juice. Leave to cool, then cover and chill. Serve over ice with lime slices.

Makes about 4¼ cups.

TENNIS CUP

SANGRIA

1 cup granulated sugar
1 lemon
2 oranges
2 bottles red or white wine
2½ cups soda water
TO DECORATE:
thin slices of cucumber and orange
borage flowers or violets, if available

ice cubes
1 bottle red wine, chilled
2 strips orange rind
2 strips lemon rind
2 tablespoons sugar
juice 4 oranges
juice 2 lemons
3 cups soda water, chilled
mint sprigs and orange and lemon slices, to decorate

Put sugar in a saucepan with ⅔ cup cold water. Heat gently until sugar has dissolved. Bring to a boil until syrup reaches 220°F.

With a potato peeler or sharp knife, thinly pare rind from lemon and oranges. Add to syrup, and simmer gently for 10 minutes. Set aside until completely cold.

Into a large cold bowl, put 6 to 8 ice cubes, pour in the wine, and add orange and lemon rind.

Squeeze juice from lemon and oranges, and strain into syrup, then pour in the wine and chill. Just before serving, add soda water. Pour into glasses. Decorate with slices of cucumber and orange, and sprigs of borage or violets.

Makes about 9 cups.

Into a small bowl, put orange juice. Add sugar, and stir until sugar dissolves. Stir into wine with lemon juice. Pour into a large, cold serving jug. Add soda water. Decorate with mint sprigs, and orange and lemon slices.

Serves 4.

INDEX

INDEX

INDEX